BRITISH AND AMERICAN PLAYWRIGHTS

1750-1920

General editors: Martin Banham and Peter Thomson

H. J. Byron

OTHER VOLUMES IN THIS SERIES

TOM ROBERTSON edited by William Tydeman
HENRY ARTHUR JONES edited by Russell Jackson
DAVID GARRICK and GEORGE COLMAN THE ELDER
   edited by E. R. Wood
W. S. GILBERT edited by George Rowell
THOMAS MORTON and GEORGE COLMAN THE YOUNGER
   edited by Barry Sutcliffe
ARTHUR MURPHY and SAMUEL FOOTE edited by George
   Taylor
WILLIAM GILLETTE edited by Rosemary Cullen and Don Wilmeth

Further volumes will include:

J. R. PLANCHÉ edited by Don Roy
A. W. PINERO edited by Martin Banham
DION BOUCICAULT edited by Peter Thomson
CHARLES READE edited by M. Hammet
TOM TAYLOR edited by Martin Banham
AUGUSTIN DALY edited by Don Wilmeth and Rosemary Cullen

Plays by
H.J. Byron

THE BABES IN THE WOOD
THE LANCASHIRE LASS
OUR BOYS
THE GAIETY GULLIVER

Edited with an introduction and notes by
Jim Davis

The right of the
University of Cambridge
to print and sell
all manner of books
was granted by
Henry VIII in 1534.
The University has printed
and published continuously
since 1584.

CAMBRIDGE UNIVERSITY PRESS

Cambridge

London   New York   New Rochelle

Melbourne   Sydney

Published by the Press Syndicate of the University of Cambridge
The Pitt Building, Trumpington Street, Cambridge CB2 1RP
32 East 57th Street, New York, NY 10022, USA
296 Beaconsfield Parade, Middle Park, Melbourne 3206, Australia

First Published 1984

Printed in Great Britain at
the University Press, Cambridge

Library of Congress catalogue card number: 83-7852

British Library cataloguing in publication data
Byron, H. J.
Plays. – (British and American playwrights,
1750–1920)
I. Title   II. Davis, Jim
III. Series
822′.912   PR4399.B3
ISBN 0 521 24175 8 hard covers
ISBN 0 521 28495 3 paperback

B.B.

GENERAL EDITORS' PREFACE

It is the primary aim of this series to make available to the British and American theatre plays which were effective in their own time, and which are good enough to be effective still.

Each volume assembles a number of plays, normally by a single author, scrupulously edited but sparingly annotated. Textual variations are recorded where individual editors have found them either essential or interesting. Introductions give an account of the theatrical context, and locate playwrights and plays within it. Biographical and chronological tables, brief bibliographies, and the complete listing of known plays provide information useful in itself, and which also offers guidance and incentive to further exploration.

Many of the plays published in this series have appeared in modern anthologies. Such representation is scarcely distinguishable from anonymity. We have relished the tendency of individual editors to make claims for the dramatists of whom they write. These are not plays best forgotten. They are plays best remembered. If the series is a contribution to theatre history, that is well and good. If it is a contribution to the continuing life of the theatre, that is well and better.

We have been lucky. The Cambridge University Press has supported the venture beyond our legitimate expectations. Acknowledgement is not, in this case, perfunctory. Sarah Stanton's contribution to the series has been substantial, and it has enhanced our work.

Martin Banham
Peter Thomson

CONTENTS

ILLUSTRATIONS

ACKNOWLEDGEMENTS

I should like to thank the editors of the British and American Playwrights series for their support and help; the staffs of the British Library, the Theatre Museum, the Harvard Theatre Collection and the New York Public Library Theatre Collection at the Lincoln Center, for their help and co-operation; the librarians of the Garrick Club, the Hoblitzelle Theatre Collection in the University of Texas and the City of Manchester Central Library for answering queries; and Pat Chetwyn, Victoria Coke-Smythe and Sally Surin for help with typing. I am also indebted to the Roehampton Institute of Higher Education for support whilst I was working on this volume.

London, 1983   Jim Davis

I H. J. Byron as Sir Simon Simple in *Not Such a Fool as He Looks*

INTRODUCTION

The most prolific playwright of the mid-Victorian period was H. J. Byron. He gave us much that we take for granted in modern pantomime, including the characters of Buttons and Widow Twankay. He wrote burlesques, comedies and dramas which enhanced the careers of Marie Wilton, J. L. Toole and the young Henry Irving, among others. He was instrumental in introducing the work of Tom Robertson to the Bancroft management at the Prince of Wales's Theatre and he abetted W. S. Gilbert's career by commissioning the *Bab Ballads* for *Fun*. Actor and editor, manager and playwright, he contributed greatly to the theatre of his time, breaking all known records when his play *Our Boys* ran from 1875 to 1879 at the Vaudeville Theatre. An adept craftsman, bolstered by a facility for punning, he composed little of literary value – his plays tell us a lot about middle-class Victorian theatrical taste and social attitudes, but are written with an eye for the stage rather than for the study.

In order to consider the work of H. J. Byron in context, it is necessary to review developments that had occurred earlier in the century. When the Theatre Regulations Act of 1843 ended the monopoly of the patent theatres, changes already apparent in London theatrical life were further accentuated. The steady growth of population in London and its suburbs had led to an increase in the demand for entertainment, which was already being met by a number of minor theatres. Now that any theatre could present legitimate drama, the function of the old theatres altered. Drury Lane and Covent Garden accelerated their move towards new forms of entertainment, whilst Phelps at Sadler's Wells and Charles Kean at the Princess's provided more traditional and classic fare for the London playgoer. By the mid 1850s there existed a wide variety of theatres, playing everything from Shakespeare and melodrama to comedy and burlesque, from which to select an evening's entertainment.

Melodrama was still the predominant form popular with mid-Victorian audiences. Interest had shifted away from the Gothic, the Oriental and the remote: playgoers now preferred melodramas located closer to home, often with a strong domestic emphasis, but also supported by sensational and spectacular climaxes. Dion Boucicault, in particular, provided these factors in such melodramas as *The Colleen Bawn*, *The Streets of London* and *The Corsican Brothers*, all of which proved very popular. Although playwrights like Byron continually burlesqued the plot and acting conventions of melodrama, especially those associated with the working-class theatres south of the Thames, they were not averse to producing the real thing when it was required of them.

The interest in domestic situations, so central in melodrama, was also reflected in the comedy and farce of the period. Money, marriage and class still figured as the prominent themes in such plays, but the more aristocratic framework of eighteenth-century sentimental comedy was replaced by a concentration on middle-class domesticity. Whenever possible Victorian comedy firmly reinforced the ethic of marital fidelity and the inevitability of living happily ever after with one's partner. Even Tom Robertson, for all his surface realism, did as much as anyone to emphasise this ethic.

Apart from melodrama and domestic comedy burlesque proved to be a very popular form. Ever since Planché had presented his series of extravaganzas under the Vestris management at the Olympic, a taste for travestie and burlesque had been whetted, although no other exponents of this form possessed the sophistication and refinement of Planché. Victorian audiences particularly enjoyed such entertainments if they were top-heavy with puns, many of which called upon extreme verbal ingenuity in the actor or actress delivering them. At theatres such as the Strand and Adelphi audiences could watch their favourite melodramas, Shakespearian scenes and operas burlesqued ludicrously in the doggerel verse of Talfourd, Byron, Burnand and many others.

H. J. Byron began to write burlesques almost by accident. After a series of abortive attempts at careers in medicine and acting, he had entered Temple Bar with a view to becoming a barrister. Spurred on by a visit to one of Talfourd's burlesques, he decided to try his hand at the genre. The first offering, *Richard of the Lionheart*, was performed at the Strand Theatre without great success, but his third attempt, *Fra Diavolo*, proved an enormous hit and contributed greatly to the early success of the Strand as a centre for burlesque. Before he knew where he was, he had relinquished his legal studies and was writing for two or three theatres simultaneously. His treatment of melodrama and opera often gave new twists to old tales, usually expressed in a continual outpouring of puns. According to H. Barton Baker it was H. J. Byron who filled the gap left by Planché:

> He took the transpontine drama – of the ludicrous exaggerations of which the north side of the Thames was far from being free – as the butt at which to shoot his shafts of ridicule; the brigand in six-tab tunic and buckled belt stuck all round with pistols and daggers, and basket kilted swords, with combats to music, the heavy father always invoking his grey hairs, and given alternately to cursing and blessing, the village maiden, walking through frost and snow in silk stockings and sandalled shoes, of which playgoers were beginning to tire, here were splendid materials for burlesque.

The evenings at the Strand, where such plays were regularly burlesqued, proved very vigorous, for the company cultivated a very exuberant style of performance:

> And there certainly was a 'go', an excitement, about burlesque at the Strand in those days that was never approached by any other house. The enjoyment of the performers was really, or apparently, so intense that the wild ecstatic breakdown into which they broke at the end of almost every scene seemed perfectly spontaneous: it was a frantic outburst of

irrepressible animal spirits, and they seemed to have no more control over
their legs than the audience had over their applause. You might call it
rubbish, buffoonery, vulgarity, anything you liked, but your temperament
must have been abnormally phlegmatic if you could resist the influence of
that riotous mirth and not be carried away by it.[1]

The breakdown referred to above was the practice of introducing a lively dance,
usually in the style of negro minstrels, at the end of a song or duet. Byron is credited by Marie Wilton as the first author to introduce this feature into burlesque in
The Maid and the Magpie (1858).

A useful background to the circumstances of burlesque performance at the
Strand is provided by Harley Granville-Barker, in his essay 'Exit Planché – Enter
Gilbert':

One thing, by the way, must always be remembered about these burlesques; they were no lengthy affairs . . . the typical burlesque was the affair
of an hour, no more, split into five or six scenes for variety's sake (front
cloths alternating with full sets, and nothing very elaborate about these)
played through without an interval – this was most important – for reflec-
tion. At the Strand there would be at least two, but more probably three
plays in the programme, which began at seven; this meant a comedy and
a farce besides. The burlesque would come at the end or in the middle. If
you booked your seat you could dine comfortably and take it as a diges-
tive; and such was the manly habit of the day. It was a romp, a riot of
absurdity, and it pretended to be nothing else.[2]

The 'sacred lamp' of burlesque may have burned most brightly at the Strand
Theatre, but Byron also contributed burlesques to other theatres. One of his earliest
burlesques for the Adelphi was *The Babes in the Wood* (1859), a reworking of the
familiar tale made popular in Thomas Morton's melodrama *The Children in the
Wood.* Byron hadn't taken many liberties with the original tale, but he did include
a number of Shakespearian parodies within the text. There are numerous verbal
echoes of *Macbeth* and a sleep-walking scene for Lady Macassar, complete with
lamp. A dream sequence is derived to a limited extent from *Richard III*, whilst
King John is parodied directly when Tommy, one of the babes, solicits Smith, a
'good' ruffian, for mercy, just as Arthur solicits Hubert. A final combat is fought to
the tune of a polka and one of the grotesquely adult babes, played by the comic
actor J. L. Toole in the original, kills one of the robbers. Paul Bedford, often paired
with Toole in farce and burlesque during this period, was the good ruffian, Smith,
whilst, C. J. Smith as Brown, the bad ruffian, was praised by *Entr'acte* (19 July
1859) for his make-up 'in the style of the Victorian murderer of the old dramatic
school'. The audience not only responded to the parody in the writing and the
acting of the play, but also loudly applauded the picturesque scene of 'The Home
of the Fairy-Birds' at the play's conclusion.

During these early years Byron burlesqued many familiar subjects, including the
well-known tales of *Aladdin* and *Cinderella.* He built the entire action of *Aladdin*

around puns on China tea and he invented Widow Twankay as a pun on one of the ports central to the tea trade. For the first time Aladdin's mother was a recognisable English housewife, equally at home in China at the court of the Emperor as anywhere else. The comedian Jimmy Rogers created the part and with his skimpy form, grief-stricken face and outlandish make-up turned it into the trump card of the piece. Pekoe was another Byronic invention in this lively burlesque, from which most modern versions of *Aladdin* derive. In *Cinderella* (1860) Byron extensively developed the characters of Clorinda and Dorinda, the ugly sisters, as well as Dandini, the Prince's valet. Jimmy Rogers played Clorinda as a waspish old maid:

> Nothing can be conceived more completely illustrative of a jealous, domineering damsel than the manner which Mr Rogers assumed in his relationship to the neglected sister. The glaring, glowering eyes, the cat-like propensities of spitting and scratching, the thin and sparse ringlets, first of all ludicrously enfolded in curl papers, and then, when the figure emerged from the chintz morning wrapper, coquettishly arranged about the head for the captivation of the Prince, were little touches of the artist that should not pass unnoticed.[3]

Buttoni (our modern Buttons) was a Byron interpolation, as were the rhyming couplets of the Fairy Godmother. The now traditional scene which follows – Cinderella's scene with Buttons before going to the Ball – is very much Byron's handiwork:

> BUTT: She sleeps; I wonder very much if she,
> In peaceful slumber dreaming is of me. (CINDERELLA
>   *murmurs.*)
> She speaks! Is it of me? (*rhapsodically*) Befriend me, Cupid!
> Hush!
> CIND: (*asleep*) You unmitigated little stupid!
> BUTT: He-*hem*! that wasn't me - yet dreams, it's said,
> Should be con*rary*wise interpreted.
> 'Unmitigated little stupid', p'raps,
> In that case means the pleasantest of chaps.
> CIND: Where am I? Oh at home! Buttoni!
> BUTT: Yes!
> CIND: I dreamt that I was decked in gorgeous dress;
> With gems and jewels - oh! in such rich profusion!
> And 'midst a scene of glittering confusion,
> A youth in whose toilet there were no faults,
> Whirl'd me round wildly in the giddy *valse.*
> I wake, alas!, to life's far different round,
> In these the dullest *vaults* that could be found.
> BUTT: (*aside*) Alas! with all her *vaults*, I love her still!
> (*rapturously*) Oh, make me happy, Miss, do say you will.
> Love in a 'Buttons' may appear a riddle;
> I know I'm *but an* 'umble indiwiddle,

But still my heart's in the right place – I mean
That you have got it, as you must have seen. (CINDERELLA
turns aside.)
Oh, don't be deaf as *post*, Miss, I beseech you;
Let this memorial of a sad page reach you;
Don't stop its course by letting pride prevail,
Or *wrong de-livery* of this *mourning male.*

CIND: Impossible!

BUTT: (*severely*) Some rival has your heart! (CINDERELLA *starts.*)
My sweet – my very *sweet* one – why this s-*tart*?
Come, come – confess – who is it, I entreat?
Sweet girl, come t't at once in fact, *tout de suite*!

DUET – '*Toll The Bell*' (*Christy's*)

BUTT: My wages here are trifling,
And I've to find my tea;
They give me only once a year
A suit of livery.
The table beer's atrocious,
And don't make me agree,
And what makes me endure it,
But the love I bear for thee?
Oh! Cinder *rel* – la, say that you'll be mine!

CIND: Sorry, but I really must decline.
In truth, my troth is plighted.

BUTT: Then if that's the case –

CIND: It's true!

BUTT: I go away
A month today. Adoo! Adoo! Adoo! (*Rushes off.*)

CIND: What could he see to like in *me*, I wonder?
(*light music in distance*)
What's that? the music at the palace yonder!
Look chandaliers light up the Prince's *salle*!
What would I give to be there!
(*Enter* FAIRY QUEEN.)

F. QUEEN: So you shall.

CIND: Some peeress! What a strange way to appear!

F. QUEEN: I am your fairy godmamma, my dear.

The actors and actresses who owed something of their popularity to their performances in Byron burlesques included Ada Swanborough, Marie Wilton, J. L. Toole, Jimmy Clarke, Fanny Josephs and, later, the Gaiety Quartette – Nellie Farren, Kate Vaughan, Edward Terry and Edward Royce. Marie Wilton made a particular hit at the Strand as Pippo in Byron's *The Maid and the Magpie*, as she recounts in her memoirs, although at first she was reluctant to play the part:

When I first received the part of Pippo in the *Maid and the Magpie*, I was disappointed at its being another boy and wrote to ask if any change could be made in the cast. Miss Swanborough kindly agreed for me to meet her as well as Mr Byron, whose acquaintance I thus made for the first time. ... He said he had written the part of Pippo expressly for me, and that he was distressed I did not like it. I explained that I did not wish to play burlesque boys, and that I objected to the part on that account. Miss Swanborough seemed to be perplexed and anxious, and Mr Byron remarked that he was a young author, and my not acting Pippo would mean a serious loss to him, that there was no-one else in the theatre to whom he could entrust it, and that he could 'see me in every line of it'. He added, 'I am only a beginner, you know, and this burlesque may make or mar me'. This appeal decided me; I could hold out no longer, so promised to play Pippo.[4]

As Pippo, the 'saucy and amusing' boy, Marie Wilton was a great favourite and people flocked to see her night after night. Among the audience one evening was Charles Dickens, who wrote to John Forster:

There is the strangest thing in it that I have ever seen on the stage – the boy Pippo, by Miss Wilton. While it is so astonishingly impudent (must be, or it couldn't be done at all), it is so stupendously like a boy, and unlike a woman, that it is perfectly free from offence. I have never seen such a thing. She does an imitation of the dancing of the Christy minstrels – wonderfully clever – which, in the audacity of its thorough-going, is surprising. A thing that you *cannot* imagine a woman's doing at all; and yet the manner, the appearance, the levity, impulse and spirits of it, are so exactly like a boy, that you cannot think of anything like her sex in association with it. It begins at eight, and is over by quarter past nine. I never have seen such a curious thing, and the girl's talent is unchallengeable. I call her the cleverest girl I have ever seen on the stage in my time, and the most singularly original.[5]

Male impersonation had been a highlight of burlesque for many years and Marie Wilton was not the only actress to distinguish herself in this field. In 1863 Ada Swanborough, at the Strand Theatre, achieved a particular hit as Abdalla, 'the polished leader of the brassiest band imaginable', in *Ali Baba and the Thirty-Nine Thieves*, another of Byron's burlesques:

Miss Ada Swanborough evinced a decided improvement on her previous impersonations. Her vocal powers have also been considerably developed, and both her singing and acting were characterised by great spirit and freshness. The elegant dresses in which she appeared were also well calculated to set forth the additional attractions of a face and figure to be included among this lady's prepossessing attributes. (*The Era* 12 April 1863)

The same account also lavished praise on the supporting cast, especially George Honey, Charlotte Saunders and Polly Marshall.

The splendour of the presentation of this burlesque further enhanced its impact –

a difficult feat, when one bears in mind that the Strand was a relatively small theatre with little scope for extraordinary or spectacular effects. Indeed, some of Byron's burlesques actually contain apologies for the limitations imposed by the small size of the theatre. During his version of *The Lady of Lyons* one of his characters addresses the audience, amidst a scene change, with the following words:

> Ladies and gentlemen our stage is small,
> In fact we've hardly any room at all;
> We can't afford effects, we couldn't do 'em,
> As for transparencies you'd soon see through 'em . . . .

Puss in a New Pair of Boots concludes with a similar apology for lack of space, since this renders it impossible to conclude with a transformation scene. Byron particularly regrets that there is insufficient room either side of the stage to hang iron bars:

> Suspending in mid-air, in costume airy,
> A smiling but uncomfortable Fairy.

Byron's *Ali Baba*, however, seems to have transcended these difficulties. The play, also known as *The Forty Thieves*, had long been popular on the nineteenth-century stage, ever since George Colman the younger's melodrama had first been performed at Drury Lane in 1806. There had been many subsequent versions, including one by Gilbert A'Beckett, which had been performed by the Keeleys at the Lyceum in 1844. In 1860, when members of the Savage Club staged a burlesque version, Byron had played Ali Baba. Although Byron's version was, perhaps, eclipsed by the great success of Reece's *Forty Thieves* at the Gaiety in 1880, it has been revived in this century at the Player's Theatre. Of this production, staged in 1950, *The Times*, formerly one of Byron's sternest critics, wrote in praise of 'the rollicking knockabout fun, the brisk burlesque of grand opera, the cascades of excruciating rhymes, fetched from the end of the earth and the dictionary'.[6]

It was in 1863, the year in which Byron's *Ali Baba* was first performed, that Byron provided a justification for the sort of burlesques he was writing in *1863, or Sensations of the Past Season*. Despite the fact that it concludes with a rather indifferent burlesque of *Lady Audley's Secret*, the play contains an interesting dialogue between Fancy and the Author. The Author justifies his use of burlesque by claiming:

> Though some may doubt it, it's as oft been seen,
> Burlesque is like the winnowing machine:
> It simply blows away the husks, you know –
> The goodly corn is not moved by the blow.
> What arrant rubbish of the clap-trap school
> Has vanished – thanks to pungent ridicule;
> What stock stage customs, nigh to bursting goaded,
> With so much blowing up have now exploded.
> Had our light writers done no good save this,
> Their doggerel efforts scarce had been amiss.

Fancy accepts his justification, but warns him:

> Don't vulgarise; be droll, but don't deride;
> Most serious subjects have their funny side.[7]

Paradoxically, of course, the effectiveness of Byron's burlesques depended strongly on the continued accessibility of 'arrant rubbish of the clap-trap school'. It is interesting to note that, as the more outrageous tendencies of melodrama died out, burlesque practically disappeared. In so regularly attacking the form on which it fed, it had, perhaps, sounded its own death-knell.

Throughout the 1860s burlesque continued to be popular. Byron's facility in dashing off burlesques eventually led to an invitation to join Marie Wilton as joint manager of the Prince of Wales's Theatre, which she opened in 1865. He provided one of its opening productions, a new burlesque, *La! Somnambula!*, and a few weeks later a new comedy, *War to the Knife*. Although *La! Somnambula!* proved successful on its first performance, it is a little disappointing to read today. Like Thomas Dibdin's *Bonifacio and Bridgetina* and *Morning, Noon and Night* it parodies Gothic and Germanic melodrama: it contains some good lines, but the joke is over-extended. Marie Wilton persuaded Byron to give his 'exclusive services' as author to the new venture, feeling that his involvement would greatly strengthen her position, 'knowing Mr Byron's popularity, and his expressed willingness to write comedies'. It was Byron who recommended Tom Robertson's play *Society* to Marie Wilton and thus helped to forge the strong link between Robertson and the Prince of Wales's Theatre, which was to become the foundation of its success.[8] This was to be Byron's most lasting service to the Prince of Wales's, for his managerial partnership with Marie Wilton was soon dissolved. He was incensed by Marie Wilton's refusal to play in burlesque, whilst Marie Wilton felt that Byron was neglecting the Prince of Wales's and providing mediocre plays for the theatre, on account of his newly acquired managerial commitments in Liverpool. In 1866 he had undertaken the management of the Theatre Royal, Liverpool, to which he soon added the management of the Alexandra and Ampitheatre. The Liverpool venture didn't last for long, however, for in March 1868 Byron declared himself bankrupt. Although his management had been perfectly competent, the external economic pressures of running three theatres simultaneously had proved insuperable.

Despite the assumption of managerial duties Byron continued to write a prolific number of plays and burlesques. His early phase as a burlesque writer had been strongly linked with the Strand and the Adelphi; in the 1870s, however, he formed a close association with the Gaiety Theatre. The manager of the Gaiety, John Hollingshead, paid Byron a fixed sum to devote his energies as a burlesque writer solely to the Gaiety. In August 1876 Byron provided the entire programme for the opening of the new Gaiety season: a play, *Bull by the Horns*, and a burlesque, *Little Don Caesar de Bazan*, founded on Wallace's opera, *Maritana*. Nellie Farren, the Gaiety's principal burlesque performer, was joined by Edward Terry, Edward Royce and Kate Vaughan in Byron's burlesque, which launched them into a long and fruitful association, during which they became known as the Gaiety Quartette. Not everyone was pleased to see the re-emergence of burlesque, especially in a form that included the introduction of songs from the music-hall, but Byron's Gaiety burlesques were to prove very popular: 'The announcement of a new burlesque by Mr Byron', noted the *Illustrated Sporting and Dramatic News* (5 April 1879), 'attracts people to the Gaiety . . . . Gaiety audiences do not care for plot; all they demand is pretty faces and bright dresses, dialogue sprinkled with puns, and songs to the airs popular in the music-halls'. The very popular *Little Doctor Faust* (1877), *Young Fra Diavolo* (1878) and *Pretty Esmeralda* were among the other Byron burlesques brought to life by the Gaiety Quartette in the 1870s.

In 1879 Byron provided a Christmas burlesque for the Gaiety based on *Gulliver's Travels*. The *Gaiety Gulliver*, as it was called, was innovative in form and helped to point the way towards a new type of burlesque at the Gaiety. It was a mixture of pantomime (without the conventional clown or harlequinade) and spectacular burlesque. It was five acts in length and included several tableaux, not to mention a spectacular shipwreck scene and some magnificent scenery. An allegorical tableau of the *Golden Age*, at the very end of the play, reminded *Punch* (10 January 1880) of the time when Madame Vestris used to play in such Planché extravaganzas as *The Island of Jewels* and *The King of the Peacocks*, when all London crowded to see *the* Christmas extravaganza and the *last* scene became the talk of the town. Another memorable moment was the *Flying Dance* of Mlle. Aenea during the *Grand Ballet* sequence. *Gulliver* was the largest piece produced at the Gaiety up to this time and it helped to pave the way for a succession of longer burlesques, mainly in a three-act form. The first of these was Reece's *The Forty Thieves*, which proved such a success at the Gaiety the following year.

Gulliver involved the services of nearly 400 people, including 100 children playing Lilliputians. This was not the first time that children had been used to represent Lilliputians in a stage version of *Gulliver*. In 1876 the *Illustrated London News* (30 December 1876) reported that 200 children played Lilliputians in *Gulliver's Travels; or Harlequin Prince Rover and the Good Fairy Tricksy Wicksy* at the Pavilion, Whitechapel. There were mixed reactions to the use of children in Byron's Gaiety version: although the child who played the Lilliputian Queen was generally praised, *The Times* (27 December 1879) noticed that 'there were some poor little mites, scarce a thumb nail high, to employ the Lilliputian standard, who looked woefully scared'. The large cast included not only the children and the regular Gaiety company, but also recruits from the music-halls. As men, women and children entered the stage door every night, the place was crammed, according to the manager Hollingshead, with *half-boiled humanity*. Hollingshead eventually withdrew the piece, even though it was very successful: 'A few foggy evenings had something to do with the decision . . . . I could not forget that the hundred children dressing in a big room under the pit, which looked, for the time being, like a Sunday School, lived in nearly every distant district of London.'[9]

Byron's adaptation would have made Swift turn in his grave, for it had very little bearing on the original. This was not the first time Byron had drawn on *Gulliver's Travels* as a source for a Christmas burlesque. In 1867 he had been the major contributor to *The Wonderful Travels of Gulliver*, which was staged at the Theatre Royal, Manchester. This version, which involves a lot of comic business with a giant donkey and the eventual transformation into the Harlequinade, bears scarcely any resemblance to *The Gaiety Gulliver*. At the Theatre Royal, Liverpool, a version of *Gulliver's Travels* by Byron was also presented in December 1867 – like the Manchester version it also developed into a Harlequinade, but it anticipated the Gaiety version in that it incorporated a review of the Lilliputian army. Although the *Athenaeum* (10 January 1880) complained that there was 'no novelty of idea or treatment' about the Gaiety version and that Byron had dealt with the subject matter 'gingerly', there was plenty in it to satisfy the tastes of Gaiety audiences:

> *Gulliver's Travels* constitute the theme and supply the story of the eccentric drama, that of sea-voyages and shipwrecks, leading to the discovery of Lilliput and the Brobdignagian kingdom, together with a curious island called The Island of Comic Song. Here we may expect most of the comic business, including the military evolutions of an infant army, the antics of a giant baby and nurse, the eccentricities of comic singers and dancers, a flying ballet, and many other entertainments.[10]

The general consensus was that *Gulliver* provided a very successful Christmas entertainment.

The Gaiety Quartette brought *Gulliver* to life with their customary skill. Edward Terry, renowned for his performance of melancholy characters and for his comic singing in burlesque, was Scowlygrowls, whilst Edward Royce, an accomplished dancer as well as actor, played Smuggins, an unpleasant apprentice. Kate Vaughan, 'dancing her best', was Gulliver's sweetheart Polly. Nellie Farren, 'livelier than ever' and continually encored, played Gulliver in travestie. *The Times* noted that she wore two remarkably pretty dresses, 'of which the latter would be more becoming were there more of it'. The continual assumption of male roles by actresses in the burlesques of H. J. Byron was to draw the fire of at least one critic. Augustin Filon disputed Byron's boast that he had never given offence to delicate ears. Byron had helped, said Filon, 'to depreciate the moral tone of the theatre by lowering the standard of decency in regard to the female costume upon the stage'.[11] He meant, of course, the way in which actresses dressed in tights and breeches for travestie roles.

The burlesques that Byron wrote during his career were not always written especially for Christmas and were aimed, largely, at an adult audience. This was certainly the case, for instance, with *The Babes in the Wood, Aladdin* and *Ali Baba*. Although they often contributed to the form and content of modern pantomime, they would not have been considered as pantomimes or as necessarily appropriate to Christmas in Byron's lifetime. Christmas entertainment at the major theatres still tended to pay lip-service to the old tradition of the Harlequinade and Byron provided a number of entertainments of this sort. *Robinson Crusoe, Whittington and His Cat, Beauty and the Beast* and *Bluebeard* were among the pantomimes that he provided for Covent Garden and the Princess's, usually with a transformation into the

Harlequinade at the conclusion. The usual Byron vitality is apparent in these pieces, but the burlesques have the edge over them. His sources for such pieces were not, however, limited to the *Arabian Nights* or the fairy tales of Perrault, already transmuted through many previous stage adaptations. The fairy tales of the Countess D'Anois provided the basis for such adaptations as *Lady Belle-Belle*, performed at the Adelphi in 1863, whilst Washington Irving's *Legends of the Alhambra* was the source for *The Pilgrim of Love* (Haymarket Theatre, 1864).

Byron's burlesques effectively bridged the gap between the extravaganzas of Planché and the comic operas of W. S. Gilbert. He was, however, too slapdash to emulate Planché's elegance or to anticipate Gilbert's wit. His major weakness, perhaps, was that he could never resist a pun, however obvious or obscure. In *La! Somnambula!*, for instance, occurs the line:

That chamber's *haunted, harn't it, haunty* dear.

whilst in *Esmeralda* Quasimodo concludes a grotesque description of his appearance by stating:

While, to this picture so extremely frightful,
This round back forms a back-round most delightful.

Such lines led Granville-Barker to comment:

It was the pun, probably, which did most to sap the vitality of burlesque in the 'sixties – though, indeed, by the end of them, and before, the thing had had its day and was fit for death. Byron came at last to punning as a stammerer stammers, 'till the very sense of his nonsense would be obscured – and nothing, of course, needs to be made clearer. They punned and punned, he and the rest, 'till there were no puns left to make. Then they began to repeat them; and, really, the pun served up cold for the seventh time is pretty poor fare . . . .[12]

Barker is a little unfair on Byron, for the pun was a central and expected ingredient of a Byron burlesque. Byron's object was to build a cumulative series of puns which depended on the ingenuity of the actor to convey them clearly to the audience. The Strand company, in fact, became:

a sort of stage rifle corps for firing off puns; every verbal bullet has not at all times its billet, but of the multiplicity of missiles hurled at the heads of people during a Byronic burlesque, many fall above below or beyond the immediate comprehension, and the victory of the evening is generally achieved by the comparative few that go straight to the mark.[13]

The secret of the long runs enjoyed by Byron's burlesques, suggested the author of this review, was that people kept coming back to catch the jokes they'd missed on previous occasions. This was due to the quantity of puns with which Byron's burlesques were laden rather than to any failing of the performers, most of whom were very skilled at bringing out the ambiguities of the words they uttered. Indeed, *Ali Baba* provides a good example of how much these puns were enjoyed:

The couplets [commented *The Era*] have all the smartness of the Byronic pen, crammed with verbal distortions of every degree of atrocity, and exhibiting the writer's riotous enjoyment of puns in all their phases. Each speaker seems to be bent on dragging each word in the 'Dictionary' desperately down and ripping it open to pluck out the heart of a joke. In extenuation of this it must be acknowledged as usual that the very worst specimens of syllabic dislocation were those that aroused the most uproarious merriment.

Apart from puns topical allusions were regular features of the Byronic burlesque. Although the burlesques contain no evident social or political satire, they are full of references to current affairs and to figures in the news. Such references are usually included to raise a quick laugh and because they can be appropriately introduced at a particular point in the dialogue. They are subordinate to, not the object of, the burlesques in which they appear. Consequently, topical allusions in Byron's burlesques tend to be of rather a general nature. A good example occurs at the opening of *Little Doctor Faust*, one of the Gaiety burlesques. H. M. Walbrook recalls how old Faust was revealed pottering around in his study, while far off a chorus of villagers could be heard singing, 'For He's a Jolly Good Fellow'. As the strains died away, Faust quavered, with his hands to his ears: 'They sing in praises of the great Gladstone.' All the liberals in the audience cheered, while the conservatives hissed and booed. When the uproar died down, Faust remarked: 'Oh, what a noise! Enough to make one dizzy!' and pandemonium raged again.[14]

The fundamental object of Byron's burlesques would seem to have been the parody of current dramatic forms, especially romantic opera and melodrama. Among the operas burlesqued by Byron were *Il Trovatore* (1863), *Lucia di Lammermoor* (1865), *Der Freischutz* (1866) and *William Tell* (1867). The operas were rendered incongruous, even ludicrous, by the introduction of songs sung to the accompaniment of popular airs of the day. *Going Home to Dixie, Cork Leg, Nix My Dolly* and *Stood it like a Lamb* are among the airs introduced into *Ill-Treated Il Trovatore*. Although the absurdities of the opera are largely parodied through popular tunes, opportunity is also provided for a more direct parody of Verdi's music. The following sequence occurs just after the Count has ordered that Manrico and Leonora should be seized and dragged off to prison:

MANRI: Ruffian! (*aside*) If I could only get my knife!

    (*aloud*) Let me have one hand loose.

COUNT: *Hand lose* my life?

    Not if I know it – in a dungeon fetter her.

LEON: Agony!

MANRI: Rage!

COUNT: Revenge!

LEON: Despair!

MANRI: Et cetera.

            CONCERTED PIECE – '*Vivra Contende*'. (*Trovatore*)

LEON: Away, vile Count, you, below contempt, as well as hate and scorn, indeed, are truly. All pity, mercy, you refuse, vile coward!

COUNT: My rage, despair and hatred, too, combine to make a friend your
foe. Dog, dearly you'll pay for this insult unto me!

MANRI: Fright to keep parleying with thee, with thee, low wretch; let go
Leonora, and my pardon deliver you, p'raps then may I - me beware!
(*Repeat.*)

(MANRICO *and* LEONORA *are dragged off.*)

The verbal and musical conventions of opera are parodied by Byron in such an
excerpt, but the musical satisfaction of the evening lay, for the audience, in the
singing and dancing of spritely popular airs rather than in a direct musical parody
of the opera itself.

It is the parody of melodrama, of course, that is so central to many of Byron's
burlesques. Not only did he provide burlesques of such popular hits as *The Corsican
Brothers* (1869), *The Lady of Lyons* (1858 and 59) or *The Colleen Bawn* (*Miss Eily
O'Connor*, 1861), but the conventions of melodrama seem to creep into most of
his burlesques whenever the opportunity arises. Byron particularly parodied the
style of melodrama current at theatres such as the Surrey, the offerings of which
are vividly described by *Pan at the Play* in *Fun* (21 September 1861), a magazine
which Byron edited:

Urrah! The Surrey is returning to first principles. *PAN* rejoices to find that
there is still a theatre where an interesting damsel in white muslin walks
about through three acts, armed with nothing but her native modesty and
a horse-pistol; where the heavy ruffian does not attempt by an assumed
calmness of demeanour, to cheat you into a belief that he is *not* a heavy
ruffian, but goes in boldly for right hand corners, back falls and black eye-
brows; where the comic man and the pert chambermaid trip on as naturally
as possible in the first scene after the duel, and make love in a medley
duet, swearing never to part, and going off immediately afterwards on
opposite sides; where, in short, for two hours and a half, a closely-packed
and full-flavoured British audience is kept in a state of the liveliest excitement, only to be alloyed by the highly elaborate death of the villain, the
rapturous embrace of the hero and heroine, the unselfish shouts of delight
of the clean-looking tenantry (who are all to have fifty per cent taken off
their rents by the rightful heir), the soothing smell of the gunpowder, the
timely descent of the green curtain, and the opportune arrival of the lady
with the ginger beer.

The over-simplification of character, the sententiousness of the dialogue and the
over-reliance on coincidence characteristic of such melodramas are all continually
burlesqued by Byron.

In satirising the excesses of melodrama Byron incidentally sheds light on the
nature of performance as well. The traditional speech patterns used by the actors
are often incorporated into his burlesques.[15] In *The Gaiety Gulliver* Scowlygrowls
and the Mutinous Mate establish their villainy through the way they speak:

MATE: Do you defy me?

SCOW: To the death -a-

MATE: Ha! I have met my match. Now if I had only got my gunpowder.

SCOW: You would blow up the ship.

MATE: I would, ah.

SCOW: Ha! Good, ah! So would I.

MATE: You hate everybody.

SCOW: Like p-ison.

In *The Rosebud of Stinging-Nettle Farm* the pronunciation of the local squire immediately marks him out as the villain:

SQUIRE: And so they ge*roan* when my name is *per*-anounced. Varlets!
and *she* – SHE turns pale and *tere*mbles when perchance her eye meets mine. And *I* – *I*, Sir Narcissus Slapdash *tere*mble a-too. She must be mine-a. *Ter*ue, I am married to another; but, no matter. (*music*) What mean these *ster*ains? . . .

Not only is the dialogue larger than life in this particular piece; so are the stage directions. When Bill Hugly, an awful-looking tramp, agrees to help the Squire in *ke-rushing* his foes, the following takes place:

SQUIRE: . . . Have you weapons handy?

HUGLY: Be-old. (*Produces a large horse-pistol, then a life-preserver, then an enormous claspknife – a chord on the production of each.*)

The death of Squire Slapdash is similarly excessive:

SQUIRE: Ha! Then there is nothing but this. (*Drinks poison.*) And to make that certain – *this*. (*Stabs himself, falls.*) And this. (*Goes to well and tumbles in.*)

Few of Byron's burlesques resist such digs at the genre and, in a way, Byron must be credited amongst those who highlighted the absurdities of the form and paved the way for new developments. Yet, for all the mockery, there is a residual affection for, even enjoyment of, this object of parody, which gives the burlesques a certain charm.

Paradoxically, Byron didn't just burlesque melodrama; he sometimes wrote the real thing. He almost equalled Boucicault in his ability to fashion the sort of melodramatic fare then popular. His compositions were fairly conventional: 'only better than the run of melodramas in that they are as a rule grammatical, brisk and business-like'.[16] *Blow for Blow* (1868) and *Haunted Houses* (1872) are among his most melodramatic works, whilst *Lost at Sea* (1869) he actually wrote with Boucicault, but his most outstanding melodrama was perhaps *The Lancashire Lass*, which was first performed during his management of the Ampitheatre, Liverpool, in 1867. In structure the play is rather like Boucicault's *Streets of London*, with a Prologue that provides the historic background to the remainder of the play, a practice originated by Douglas Jerrold, and a sensational climax dependent on the most outlandish coincidences. The action ranges from Liverpool to the Australian outback (Italy in the original version), involves a sensational death by drowning at Egremont pier, and provides the usual concoction of dissembling, black-mailing villains, virtuous heroines and unjustly accused heroes. When the play was first staged, 'a real ferry steamer which was a marvel of mechanical ingenuity'[17] created quite a stir. It actually sailed on, disgorged its passengers at the pier, then sailed off again. The quest for sensational and realistic effects could sometimes leave casualties in its wake. At Liverpool Miss Denvil, who played Fanny Danville, screamed so loudly and convincingly during a performance of the play that she ruptured a blood vessel and died from the consequences of this eight days later.[18]

Not surprisingly, a year after its première in Liverpool the play re-emerged at the Queen's Theatre in London, where it enjoyed a reasonable run. Some critics were scathing, especially with regard to Byron's development of plot and character:

> At the Queen's – commented the *Athenaeum* – a melodrama of almost unexampled extravagance and absurdity is being performed. . . . In the opening of the piece some signs of an attempt at characterisation are traceable; but after the preliminary amble Mr Byron falls into the jog-trot of melodrama. One after another the familiar characters shuffle on the scene. First comes the village maiden; a fashionable seducer and a rustic lover follow; and a little in the background stand the heroine's rival and her broken-hearted father. When to these characters are added a rich and honoured merchant, who is a returned convict; a second convict, poor and unscrupulous, drawing from his former associate large sums of money as the price of secrecy; – the materials for the melodrama are complete. Throw into this brewage a sprinkling of detectives, bush-rangers and the like, to make the gruel thick and slab, and one may predict how the whole will work.[19]

This sounds like a description of the type of composition usually burlesqued rather than emulated by Byron. *The Daily Telegraph* (27 July 1868) was kinder in suggesting that Byron's sense of the ludicrous had occasionally led him into endangering the serious interest of the piece. Generally Byron was praised by the critics for fashioning a skilfully constructed melodrama, crowded with startling incidents and sensational effects; a perfect example of its genre, in fact. So popular did the play become that George Leybourne produced a song bearing the play's title, the refrain of which ran:

> My Lancashire Lass!
> Sure none can surpass
> My Lancashire Lass for style and beauty!
> To my Lancashire Lass
> Then fill up your glass,
> And drink to the health of my Lancashire Lass!

One of the major interests that the play holds retrospectively is that the gentlemanly villain, Robert Redburn, was played by the young Henry Irving, then on the threshold of his career. Its run of six months helped to keep Irving before the London public at a time when such exposure was very useful to him. Austin Brereton,

one of Irving's biographers, described Redburn as 'an adventurer of the most conventional pattern – a cigar-smoking scamp, whose rascality is associated with the
utmost degree of cool audacity, and whose heartlessness is displayed by simulta-
neous knitting of the brows and caress of the moustache'. Brereton also refers to a
review in the *Morning Star*, which strongly praised Irving's performance:

> He dressed with great care and modest variety – made-up as to the head, in
> dealing with which most of our actors are exceedingly clumsy, with most
> suggestive, yet most natural significance. . . . ingenious in those little
> actions which, while intrinsically unmeaning, reveal character and relieve
> the stress on an audience's attention, this admirable actor of polished vil-
> lains is a most unbounded success. Neither he nor his audience were for a
> moment ill-at-ease. His repose was perfect without langour, his strong pas-
> sages emphatic without effort; that he was capable of real feeling was
> proved by the volumes of emotion revealed in the voice with which, during
> Clayton's imprisonment, Redburn urged his mad suit to Ruth: that he was
> incapable of weakness or soft-heartedness was evident from the aspect of
> the man as he listened to the description of his own character by his would-
> be accomplice 'the party of the name of Johnson'.[20]

Dickens was also impressed by Irving's performance in the play, predicting that one
day Irving would become a great actor. The conviction with which Irving played
Redburn was the strongest point of the production, although Irving's son is a little
unfair when he suggests that his father's performance saved the play from total con-
demnation. The proprietors of the Queen's – he says – had dedicated themselves to
a higher class of drama, but with Byron's play threw in the sponge and devoted
themselves to 'catch-penny commercial melodramas'. As a result Irving 'had to
jump through every hoop in the melodramatic routine'.[21]

The early career of Irving is also associated with appearances in other plays by
Byron. With J. L. Toole he played in *Dearer than Life* (1868), a comedy which
added to the reputation of both actors. (It was also staged at the Queen's.) Toole
showed wonderful pathos as Michael Garner, an honest tradesman and loving
father, playing the part with great earnestness and attention to detail. During the
play his only son is lured into evil paths by Bob Gassett, 'a vulgar, dissipated scoundrel, – a flash, uneducated loafer'.[22] Toole recalled how Irving, of whom Byron had
a very high opinion, made a big mark as Bob Gassett. 'I had many a Bob Gassett to
play with me', he recounted, 'but never one that played it with the reality and truth
that Irving put into the part.'[23]

In 1869, when Toole joined the Gaiety Theatre, he appeared in another comedy
especially written for him by Byron, *Uncle Dick's Darling*. The play owed something
to Dickens's characters of Dr Marigold and Dombey, but was technically interesting
for the transformation scene central to it. The core of the play is a dream – a rather
contrived means of resolving the action – and the final change of scene occurs as
Uncle Dick awakes from his reverie:

> The final change from the blacksmith's shop – a very elaborate and pic-

turesque scene – to the village green, and the dreaming hawker still asleep on the cart shafts, is perhaps one of the most marvellous performances of stage mechanism yet achieved. Time was, when inexperienced authors were warned against expecting one heavy set scene to follow another; and even now the most experienced are not able to escape the clumsy contrivances known as 'carpenters' scenes – that is, scenes painted on a mere curtain, brought near the footlights, for the purpose of giving time for the building of more elaborate scenery behind. But if the changes such as those effected in the last act of *Uncle Dick* are possible, it is certainly difficult to understand why these rude devices should continue to flourish.[24]

Uncle Dick's Darling, which deals with the familiar themes of money and class, concerns a foundling, Mary Belton, who is looked after by Uncle Dick and placed, by him, at a fashionable boarding school. She receives a formal proposal of marriage from Dick's friend, Joe, a humble blacksmith, but seems more interested in Chevenix, a gentleman, who also seeks her hand in marriage. In the second act of the play she is married to Chevenix, who proves so cold and austere that she begins to encourage the attentions of another man. In the third act Mary has become an outcast: Chevenix has divorced her and the man for whom she left him has died in a shipwreck; she dies penitent in the presence of Uncle Dick and Joe. At this point occurs the transformation, described above: Uncle Dick wakes up, the marriage between Chevenix and Mary proves to have been a dream, and the play ends happily since Mary decides to marry Joe. Toole played the half-pathetic, half-amusing tinker, Uncle Dick, and Irving was Chevenix, the character closely modelled on Dombey. 'It was with his performance of Chevenix', says Irving's biographer Hiatt, 'that he emerged from comparative obscurity to the full light of day':

> He was no longer merely a useful player, who could be trusted to do whatever he undertook with his might; he was an actor who had separated himself from the crowd of more-or-less capable mediocrities to which the majority of the practitioners of any art belong . . . . Irving's Chevenix possessed the breadth, so difficult to define, and yet so easy to appreciate, which comes of imaginative and intellectual force. And it had the exquisite finish born of infinite carefulness. The actor had seen the character and seen it whole, and had realised it richly and fully. In this relation it is far more accurate to say that he had created it.[25]

In his performance of the 'conceited, cold, pompous methodical man of the world' Irving proved that he could do more than just play villains. In 1870 Yates wrote to Irving that Dickens had seen him as Chevenix and that: 'he spoke in very high terms of your performance in *Uncle Dick's Darling.* He seemed specially struck with your earnestness and your never forgetting to elaborate, even by small detail, your conception and study of the character . . .'[26]

Although Irving moved on to higher things, Byron was one of the first playwrights to provide him with original parts to play on the London stage. Toole, on the other hand, relied on Byron for new material throughout his life. When Toole undertook the management of the Folly Theatre, soon to be renamed Toole's Theatre, in 1879, he immediately revived *A Fool and His Money*, a farci-comedy that Byron had written for him two years previously. Other plays by Byron followed, including *The Upper Crust* (1880), in which Toole played Barnaby Doublechick, *The Light Fantastic* (1880), in which Toole scored a success as Professor Slithey, a dancing master, and *Auntie* (1882). Toole paid tribute to Byron when he said: 'The principal works I played up to this time were written by H. J. Byron. Poor fellow, he had the most endearing qualities, and a wonderful sense of humour; his fun was always genial, never coarse, never cruel; he was more than a wit, he was a true humorist.'[27]

The type of play in which Toole appeared revealed Byron not only as a writer of burlesques and melodramas, but as an author of comedies as well. Back at the Strand Marie Wilton had urged him to write comedies and, by the mid-sixties, he had begun to follow her advice. The praise accorded Byron by Toole was not, however, reflected by the more serious critics of the day. William Archer described him as 'as nearly as possible destitute of talent':

> He was the author of 30 or 40 so-called comedies or dramas, but he never invented a story that was not trivial, and he generally contrived to combine triviality with extravagance. His characters are the absurdest of rag dolls, conventionally masked and costumed, and with no backbone of consistency.[28]

Not only had Byron fostered a taste for puerile and trivial work, according to Archer, but he had also encouraged an attitude of cynicism towards love and marriage:

> After a course of Mr Byron one begins to doubt whether fine sensibility, serious thought and worthy emotion exist anywhere in the world. In so far as his comedies are full of marrying, and giving in marriage, they are conventionally moral; but in so far as they represent a little punning flirtation intermingled with 'chaff' as the only necessary prelude to putting up the banns, they seem to me little short of immoral . . . . In Mr Byron's eyes love is synonymous with flirtation and flirtation with more or less impertinent banter. Passion, chivalry, even the commonest sober respect are all foreign to his conception of love.

Archer summed up his criticism of Byron on the grounds that:

> a humorist does not of necessity constitute a dramatist and that of Mr Byron's three dozen comedies and dramas there is not one whose construction is skilful, whose characters are possible, or whose dialogue natural. His plays are a carnival of cockneyism. They do not contain a thought worth thinking, a lesson worth learning, a scene worth remembering or a character worth loving or hating. Their pathos savours of the theatre, their humour of the minor comic papers, their wit and wisdom of the theatrical clubs.[29]

Other critics also felt uneasy about Byron's comedies. According to Joseph Knight:

> Mr Byron's comedies are like fruit trees growing on espaliers. The slightest possible amount of fabric serves to support the utmost obtainable quantity of product. Not very valuable is the crop, concerning which Mr Byron is anxious; its abundance is, however, beyond question. A thick foliage of speech hides the branches and their frail support, and red-cheeked apples of wit gleam through the leafy screen . . . .[30]

He cites *Married in Haste* (1875), in which a young girl defies her socially pretentious parents in order to marry the man she loves, a match that degenerates into poverty and jealous suspicions, as a play in which the story is artificial and improbable, as well as flimsy, the dialogue forced and the characters inconsistent and insufficient. He saw Byron's plays as 'burlesques in modern dress', weakened in particular by poor characterisation. Whatever his profession, complained Knight, a Byron hero always remained the same from play to play.[31] Even Pinero, who was later to champion Byron against some of his more hostile critics, was dismayed by his lax stagecraft. In particular he was aghast at Byron's use of soliloquy or of letters read aloud, invariably overheard by another character, as a means of communicating information and furthering the plot.[32]

Byron himself seems to have been relatively immune to criticism, although his preface to *Cyril's Success* (1868), reputedly his favourite play, attempts to refute some of the prejudice against him:

> I have endeavoured in *Cyril's Success* to write a play that would be effective in performance, and not altogether unworthy perusal . . . . And now you naturally ask - why write and print this? Simply because I am somewhat tired of being termed a 'droll', a 'punster' and so on; and, as a mere piece of self-justification - self-assertion it may be termed - beg to remind anyone who may care to recollect the fact, that *Cyril's Success* is original, and a comedy - and, even in these vicious dramatic days - in five acts! There!

Original is, perhaps, the key word in this passage. For Byron, like Gilbert and like Robertson at his best, did not rely on translation or adaptation as a means of inspiration. However repetitive the themes and characters in his plays might seem, they were nevertheless his own creations. In 1878 he wrote to *The Times* (17 January 1878) in support of W. S. Gilbert's assertion that dramatic authors were writing successful original plays and that these pieces often eclipsed translated plays in popularity. In a highly derivative age, dramatically, Byron was one of a small number of dramatists who relied on their own initiative for the creation of subject matter and plot.

To a modern audience Byron's dramas and comedies certainly seem dated and over-contrived. Most of them deal with marriage, class and money, but whenever a fraught domestic relationship is treated with conviction, the effect is usually destroyed in the last act, when reconciliation triumphs, however improbable. *Cyril's Success*, which is about a successful playwright who neglects his wife, with the result that she leaves him, convinced that he has been unfaithful to her, is ruined by its sentimental and moralising conclusion. Cyril Cuthbert, the playwright, and his wife are finally reconciled and the play concludes with Mrs Cuthbert's expectation that she and her husband will achieve a new zenith of domestic happiness:

> We will make it a home of happiness again. We will stay there, and make our dear old friends come to *us*. I will have more time then to love you even more than I did in our early loving days. And when the past floats away before us, we will look into one another's eyes and seeing the love light glowing there, say that we have a gladness in our hearts beyond the best we ever knew, in what the world called *Cyril's Success*. (*Hides her face on* CUTHBERT*'s breast*.)

Married in Haste and *Partners for Life* (1871) reflect, as their titles imply, this concentration on domestic themes and on the philosophy of unlikely reconciliation. In the latter play Tom and Fanny have been separated for five years because Tom thought he had married a penniless girl and then discovered she was an heiress. So determined is he to be independent that he has accused her of deceiving him and they have separated after a quarrel; paradoxically, although he is determined not to depend on his wife's money, he has kept the marriage secret, since he has married without the consent of a rich uncle, from whom he expects to inherit a fortune. In the second act of the play he meets his wife again for the first time in five years, since both unwittingly find themselves as guests in the same house. The act concludes with the following confrontation between the couple:

> TOM: . . . After a quarrel one day you said –
>
> FANNY: I said what I didn't mean. I said words which if tears could have washed them from one's recollections would have been obliterated long since.
>
> TOM: You told me of my dependant position. You flung your money in my face.
>
> FANNY: Having previously flung it at your feet.
>
> TOM: I didn't choose to stoop and pick it up, Fanny, and I left you, as any man of spirit would have done.
>
> FANNY: And I never asked you to come back, as any woman of spirit would have applauded me for –
>
> TOM: (*with a burst of affection*) Make me once more a slave, Fanny; I have suffered more than you can *ever* have done.
>
> FANNY: No, no, my days of making slaves are past. My heart is softer now.
>
> TOM: (*bitterly*) Harder you mean, or you would not let your husband plead for your forgiveness vainly.
>
> FANNY: (*up to him quickly*) And you *do* plead for forgiveness, then. You do regret the past – you –
>
> TOM: (*with half-comic tearfulness*) I want my wife once more . . . I want to make up for lost years of what might have been a happy companionship, but which has been a bitter lonely life for *me*. (*seizing*

her hand, and speaking with great rapidity and great fervour) You don't know what it is – after the day's work, worry and excitement – to find yourself in your dull, dusty chambers without a living soul to speak to – with no sound audible but the distant roar of the busy streets, and the ticking of the clock upon your mantelpiece, that seems to mock you with its ceaseless 'I go on for ever' kind of monotony. (*Draws her closer to him*.) Ah, Fanny, if you could only be a bachelor for a little bit, you'd *pity* me; pity's akin to love, and you'd forgive me.

     FANNY: (*turning to him with great affection*) I do, Tom . . .

Inevitably the couple embrace, to be interrupted by the sudden entry of a number of other characters, none of whom are aware of Tom and Fanny's marital status. This provides an effective tableau with which to close the scene and a complication to resolve in the following act, since the expectations aroused by Tom's flirtation with a cousin earlier in the play are now thwarted.

    Consequently, it is not only the introduction of puns and witty retorts at every opportunity that devalues the impact of these plays, but also their failure to provide endings that are unsentimental or even psychologically appropriate to their characters. It was not even as if Byron was unaware of the existence of extra-marital entanglements and the problems they could lead to. In his novel *Paid in Full* (1865) he accepts the possibility of his hero, Horace, falling in love with someone other than his wife:

> Horace . . . was a selfish, rash, impulsive and somewhat shallow-principled young man; and he was over head and ears in love with a lady who was not his wife; all very reprehensible and shocking: but such things have happened, do happen, will happen, despite the improved 'moral tone' of society one hears about, and the public teachings of that beautiful institution, the Divorce-Court. Horace was no hero of romance; he was a human being, and and a very ill-conditioned one into the bargain.

Horace is chastened when his wife eventually falls ill and dies; Byron again evades the exploration of marital infidelity on anything other than a superficial level. His plays, indeed, ultimately tell us more about Victorian social morality and attitudes to marriage than about human nature. Perhaps it was this feature that led T. E. Pemberton to lament the passing of Byron when he wrote in 1904 that he greatly preferred the domestic dramas of Byron to the 'probing' plays of Ibsen.[33]

    One must remember that Byron's dramas and comedies were middle-class plays for a predominantly middle-class audience. Just as his burlesques provided the middle-class audiences of the West End with an opportunity to mock the sort of fare enjoyed by working-class audiences south of the Thames, so his comedies reinforced a sense of social worth among his audiences. Although some derided the motto of *The Girls* (1879), 'always marry a poor man', Byron's plays generally set worth before wealth. *Uncle Dick's Darling* and *The Lancashire Lass* are both true to this precept, whereby 'the quality of a man is in an inverse ratio to that of his coat' and virtue is associated with 'corduroy rather than with clothing of finer texture'. The record-breaking success of *Our Boys* owed something to its emphasis on class-consciousness and to its acknowledgement that a man's worth did not depend solely on his pedigree.

The celebration of middle-class domesticity, abetted by snatches of extraneous wit and touches of sentimentality, is at the heart of Byron's work, especially *Our Boys*. Nothing had ever run so long up until the continuous presentation of this play at the Vaudeville Theatre from 1875 to 1879. Its popularity created something of a sensation, but it is interesting to look at the antecedents of this rather traditional play, before dwelling on the circumstances of its performance. Among the comedies already frequently revived during the nineteenth century were Holcroft's *Road to Ruin*, Poole's *Paul Pry* and Boucicault's *London Assurance*. All had a slightly dated feel, even for the time for which they were written, and all dealt with marriage, money and class, concluding with some sort of reconciliation between estranged father and son or uncle and nephew. All three plays, strongly dependent on a mixture of comedy and pathos, contained a central core of sentimentality. Their initial success had been helped by their provision of good acting parts: Joseph Munden had made a hit as Old Dornton, the key role in *Road to Ruin*; John Liston had created a craze for *Paul Pry*, when he played the name-part in Poole's play; and *London Assurance* had owed a lot to the brilliant staging and acting provided by the Vestris–Mathews management at Covent Garden. A close examination of *Our Boys* reveals that its success was dependent on almost identical factors.

Our Boys was originally written for Henry Montague, manager of the Globe Theatre, where the popular comedian Sam Emery was to play Perkyn Middlewick. However, Byron eventually took the play to the Vaudeville Theatre, then under the joint management of the actors David James and Thomas Thorne. Normally Byron would have sold the manuscript of a new play outright, for a few hundred pounds, but fortuitously, he didn't on this occasion. Although an early response, when the play was read at rehearsal, was 'this cursed nonsense will not run a week',[34] a view which Byron endorsed, the reverse was proved to be true. Its worth was noted by Charles Mathews, who was in the billiard room of the Garrick Club after the first night. Several of those present expressed the view that the comedy would only have a limited run, to which Mathews replied: 'I don't agree with you fellows. I was there and haven't laughed so heartily for a long time. Byron this time – he doesn't always – has taken his goods to exactly the right shop. The play is sure to run.'[35]

Mathews was right. Even the press assented. The *Illustrated London News* (23 January 1875) felt that Byron had 'surpassed' himself and for once Joseph Knight responded favourably, although he felt the play still contained some of the usual Byronic weaknesses:

> Byron has risen nearer excellence than in any previous piece. Evidence of careful workmanship, or workmanship, that is, that in his case may be considered careful, is abundant; his worst faults are kept in check; and one or

two of the blemishes that disfigured his style have almost, if not entirely, disappeared. An attempt is visible to give the dialogue the appropriateness without which wit is dramatically ineffective, and the rudeness of speech which, doing duty for repartee, communicated to previous compositions an indescribable artificiality, less frequently shocks the audience. Add to this that the motive is more tender than in any previous work, and sufficient proof of amendment is afforded.[36]

In *Our Boys* Charles Middlewick and the foppish Talbot Champneys return from their travels abroad. Both sons defy the wishes of their fathers, the vulgar Perkyn Middlewick and the arrogant Sir Geoffry Champneys, when Charles falls in love with Violet Melrose, an heiress designed by Sir Geoffry for Talbot, and Talbot falls for the impoverished Mary, Violet's cousin. The two sons depart, to make their own living in London, but the fathers pursue them and eventual reconciliation occurs, as well as the marriages the sons desire. The principal theme of the play is class-consciousness and much of the humour derives from Sir Geoffry's disapproval of the wealthy, good-hearted Middlewick. According to the *Bath Herald* (8 February 1879):

> An evening with *Our Boys* teaches as much as many years' experience of men and things touching the real meaning of the words of Burns –
> The rank is but a guinea's stamp,
> A man's a man for a'that.

In demonstrating that a successful middle-class tradesman was as good as any haughty aristocrat Byron appealed directly to the complacency of the middle-class theatre-going public. When the play was revived at the Strand Theatre in 1881 *The Daily Telegraph* (3 June 1881) commented:

> Mr Byron has deliberately appealed to the great bulk of the Middle Classes, from whom the staunchest playgoers are drawn. He depicted with infinite truth in the character of Mr Perkyn Middlewick their virtues and their failings, their sense of humour and their kind-hearted generosity, their occasional vulgarity and their depth of heart. The bulk of the people who went to see *Our Boys* saw there the life or something like the life, that was familiar to them. They were not taken out of themselves. They chuckled over their imperfections. Best of all the play was so kind-hearted and pleasant . . .'

Whether the audience identified quite so closely with Perkyn Middlewick as this account suggests, they certainly accepted the social ethos of the play unstintingly.

The success of *Our Boys* was doubly assured by its cast: Charles Warner and Thomas Thorne were excellent as the 'boys', William Farren 'gave a good study of aristocratic pride', but the triumph of the evening belonged to David James as the retired butterman, Perkyn Middlewick:

> The *Perkyn Middlewick* of Mr David James . . . would be unworthily treated by merely a passing word of conventional praise . . . In spite of the fact that the character of the old butterman is often awkwardly portrayed

– though his pathetic utterances are not naturally introduced . . . the artist
is determined to fix the man vividly on the mind, and to show how
thoroughly humour is appreciated. In walk, manner, gesture, intonation
and dress we perceive *Perkyn Middlewick*, the butterman. Clever lines were
never more admirably spoken, and caricature seldom conveyed with less
exaggeration. Well might the audience appreciate the twinkle of delight
with which the old fellow questions his boy on the details of his foreign
trip with an honest sense of pride in the possession of his hard-earned
capital; the fussy vulgarity of the ex-tradesman when he finds himself on
the same platform as his friend the baronet; his irritation under correction;
his natural and tender love for his boy, which will come welling up,
swamping all the obstinacy and determination for which he considers himself famous; his horror to find that the eggs his lad has been taking in his
poverty are merely 'shop 'uns', and that the bread has been buttered with
'Dosset'. These are but few of the points of a thoroughly characteristic and
intelligent specimen of acting.[37]

Even if the 'palm of the evening' was awarded to David James, the entire cast, down
to Cicely Richards as the lodging-house 'slavy', were praised for their contributions.

The play was such a 'hit' that people frequently returned to see it again and
again. Londoners went almost as a matter of duty, provincial visitors as a matter of
course. Added to this was the influx of foreign visitors, who also found it necessary
to sample *Our Boys*. It was a favourite with the Prince of Wales and even the bus
stop outside the Vaudeville became known as 'Our Boys' for the duration of the
play's run. On the 1,000th night of *Our Boys* the proceeds were given to charity
and a special commemorative supper was held at the Westminster Club. So phenomenal was the play's popularity that some critics began to carp: 'I wonder how
many people are sick of perpetual *Old Boys*?' commented the *Illustrated London
News* (9 October 1878) 'A good many I'll be bound!' Postcards and newspapers
celebrated the play's success: one postcard, showing a very ancient cast, was entitled *Our Boys Grown Old*.

Our Boys was just as successful in the provinces as it was in London. A special
company was formed by William Duck and set out from Bath to take the play the
length and breadth of the British Isles:

Since then Mr Duck's Company has wandered far and wide over the three
kingdoms; it has played in Edinburgh, Dublin and all the other great towns;
we have heard of it as far south as Jersey, as far north as Aberdeen, as far
west as Limerick – everywhere its journey has been like a monarch's pro-
gress, and thousands have flocked to see it.[38]

On the thousandth night of its tour the company returned to Bath for a series of
celebratory performances. At the end of the thousandth provincial performance an
address, especially composed for the occasion by H. J. Byron, was spoken to the
audience:

When Mr Duck asked of our author, where

He thought we'd better start the play, with fair
And honest hope of kind appreciation,
And thus commence a tour throughout the nation;
He answered with almost unseemly haste –
'I think the *Bath chaps* have a deal of taste,
As for your management I cannot doubt you,
(A Duck with nothing of the *quack* about you)
With care and judgement, failure will defy'.

And this, our thousandth night is the reply.

Wheresoever,
We wander through the kingdom we shall never,
Never forget *you*, and that fact to poise,
On *your* part, pray thee don't forget 'Our Boys'.[39]

The evening concluded with a small gathering at the Grand Hotel, when Byron's
health was drunk and commemorative gold lockets were presented to the entire
cast. William Duck eventually bought the provincial rights to the play for £1,000
and made a large fortune out of leasing them. Even in 1920 Byron's surviving
daughter was still benefiting financially from revivals of the play.

When Pascoe's *Dramatic List* was published in 1880, it commented on the continuing popularity of *Our Boys*:

> It has been played by a travelling company of comedians for over 1200
> nights and is still [June 1879] being played by the same company in the
> provinces. It has been successfully produced in the principal American and
> colonial cities and towns, and has been adapted or translated and played in
> Norway, Denmark, Switzerland, Holland, Bavaria and France. Such a
> career is unparalleled in the history of drama.

In Rome and Milan it proved very popular under the title of *I nostri bimbi*, although
Byron made no money from these translations due to the inadequate nature of
international copyright arrangements. The first American production of *Our Boys*
was at the Chestnut Street Theatre, Philadelphia, in September 1875. A year later
the Philadelphia production was attended by the President of the United States,
President Grant. Other American venues included New York and Boston, where it
proved to be very popular. Indeed, prior to *Charley's Aunt, Our Boys* held the
record for unbroken performance on either side of the Atlantic.

Not everyone felt the play an outstanding success. Archer considered that the
plot's 'minus qualities' made it one of Byron's least objectionable works, but felt it
was no wonder that the stage fell into disrepute with sensible men if the sort of
lines spoken in *Our Boys* could draw the public for 12,000 or 13,000 nights.[40]
Modern commentators have been even less favourable: George Rowell has called it
'a wholly commonplace piece'[41] and, more recently, the *Revels History* described
act III of the play, in which the heroines think that the two heroes have women concealed in their rooms, as 'a masterpiece of squirming Victorian nastiness'.[42] Pinero

was among its few champions in this century. He acknowledged that it contained many of the weaknesses prevalent in Byron's work, but felt that it contained good construction and characterisation and human interest. The public, said Pinero, doesn't analyse, it feels – and, to account for the success of *Our Boys*, one ultimately has to trust in the feelings of the public.[43]

Byron's contemporary success did not outlast him. Although he helped to create the sort of climate in which the more searching dramas of Pinero and Henry Arthur Jones might be accepted and the wit of Gilbert and even of Wilde and Shaw might be enjoyed, he wrote nothing to equal the work of any of these later playwrights. He was, however, original in his selection of material, relying on his own native wit rather than on translations and adaptations of foreign, particularly French, sources. His achievement is very much in his provision of the fare required by Victorian audiences, rather than in stretching their tastes or horizons. If the prolific range of his works demonstrated a somewhat slapdash approach to their composition, he nevertheless provides us with a sure guide to the taste of Victorian audiences.

Byron's reputation as a playwright was helped, in his own time, by the quality of the actors and actresses who appeared in his plays. His success was partly due to his provision of good 'acting' parts and their effectiveness on stage. Because he possessed a facility for delivering the sort of lines that he wrote, he even began to act in his own plays himself. He had, of course, attempted a career as an actor earlier in his life and had subsequently participated in amateur productions, as well as performing in a revival of his own *The Maid and the Magpie* after the death of 'Papa' Bland, who was playing Fernando Villabella. His official professional debut on the London stage, however, was as Sir Simon Simple in *Not Such a Fool as He Looks* at the Globe Theatre on 23 October 1869. Although he had already played the part in Liverpool and Manchester, the occasion of a well-known playwright appearing in one of his own plays in a London theatre constituted quite an event. As the languid, monocled, drawling Sir Simon, who turns out to be generous and good-hearted rather than the mindless fop he initially appears to be, Byron was sufficiently successful to repeat the experiment with other of his plays. On 23 March 1870, at the Adelphi, he played Fitzaltamont, a provincial tragedian, in *The Prompter's Box*. His role was that of a gloomy, but kindly, tragedian, who talked only in blank verse. He created the part of Lionel Leveret in a comic drama *Old Soldiers* at the Strand, in 1873, and, in *An American Lady*, played Harold Triviass, when it opened the Criterion Theatre, under Byron's joint management, on 21 March 1874. In the role of Gibson Greene, who contrives to bring about the happy ending to *Married in Haste*, he was similarly successful. The *Daily News* reviewer considered that the character, who was very loosely connected with the plot, was merely an excuse for Byron to indulge 'in his irresistible passion for saying good things'; however, whilst praising Byron's delivery of his own lines, the review was less complimentary about his talents as an actor: 'Mr Byron has never acquired perfect ease on the stage, nor that variety of tone, movement and expression which are the triumph of the finished artist.'[44] Wisely, perhaps, Byron restricted himself to appearances in a specific line of parts in his own plays. Only once did he appear in a role which he hadn't written for himself: in 1881, at the Court Theatre, he played Cheviot Hill in a revival of W. S. Gilbert's *Engaged*. The part was so similar to the roles that he had been writing for himself that it provided little challenge. The one respect in which Gilbert had derived an advantage from this new interpreter of Cheviot Hill, considered *The Daily Telegraph* (2 December 1881), was through Byron's ability to bring out the full meaning of a line through an emphasis, a glance or a pause.

Not everyone could see why H. J. Byron chose to appear in his own plays as well as write them:

> Why a man who was so busy at his desk that he could not keep pace with his commissions should also choose to act, no-one knew. His best friends, foremost among whom was Tom Robertson, were opposed to the step, but he would have his own will. Though he fired off his own witticisms in a way that was irresistable, he never was a particularly good actor, but there was a certain charm in the gentlemanly ease with which he strolled through his parts . . .[45]

Some felt that the footlights took all the sparkle out of him; that he simply acted himself, pulled at his moustache and stared into space. J. H. Barnes also had doubts about Byron's abilities as an actor, but praised the delightful way in which he delivered his own lines.[46] Indeed, Byron's delivery of the witty lines he had written for himself and the fact that he always wore a moustache, whatever part he was playing, were his trademarks as an actor, although he could achieve effects by other means as well. In *The Prompter's Box* he was praised for one scene in which he stood with his back to the audience, leaning against a chimney-piece, and expressed his sentiments merely by a change of attitude.[47] A letter to John Clarke, playing Lattimer in Byron's play *Minnie*, reveals a sharp eye for detail: 'you will find Lattimer a capital part. I should make him genial – the gruffness of his character he's evidently assumed. Don't leave him for a moment 'til you can *play* with the words.'[48] Generally, within its limited range, Byron's acting was competent. His special style of acting:

> originated a variety of the listless swell, whose chief peculiarity is a marvellous gift of saying (it is assumed, accidentally) the sharpest possible things in the most innocent manner. With a style founded on that of Mr Sothern – modified perhaps by the slightest suggestion of Mr Bancroft – the author-actor delighted by his coolness and sharpness the audience of an age which objects to any display of emotion only less than to a moment's dullness . . .[49]

His acting was 'marked by his ease and keen perception' and his performances were considered 'pleasant and light, always the essence of good breeding'. A comment on Byron's performance in *An English Gentleman* at the Globe in 1879 succinctly summed up his attributes as an actor:

> Mr Byron has no rival in the art of delivering caustic speeches and dry witticisms neatly and incisively. His acting is occasionally too quiet and

self-contained . . . but there is a distinct flavour of originality about the author–actor's histrionic method, which is very welcome in an age when such a characteristic is by no means common.[50]

Still, it is as a writer rather than as an actor that Byron became well known to his contemporaries. He himself attempts to define what it is that drives anyone to write for the stage in his novel *Paid in Full*:

There must surely be some unaccountable charm about writing for the stage, or the young beginner would inevitably break down and rush from the scene of bitter recrimination and general discontent and devote himself to other pursuits, rather than suffer so much mortal agony as he who would win dramatic fame must invariably go through . . . When the dramatist's literary labours are accomplished, his real work begins. He must alter this, expunge that, crowd the incidents of three scenes into one, and introduce ten minutes talk in front of a hastily-painted 'interior' to allow the carpenters time to arrange a grand closing scene . . .

What can equal the first night, what approach the concentrated agony of those feverish two hours, which frequently leave the patient prostrate? The hurried nervous meal devoured after a long wearying day's rehearsing, with nothing ready, and everybody anxious and snappish; the rush down to the theatre in a cab, flushed and dyspeptic; the sickly feeling as the music commences; and the despairing misery when the curtain does not rise at the conclusion of the overture, but there is a fearful pause, and a sharp hiss pierces the painful silence . . . Then the delicious reaction which comes with the first laugh, and the long sigh of real relief when the curtain descends upon the first act amidst some enthusiasm. What is it, then, which induces the dramatist to go on piling up the list of his pieces and working away for his fickle friends, the playgoers? Why, it is a nameless charm, an unaccountable attraction, which is felt but cannot be described, that lends to his labour an excitement no other style of composition possesses, and which renders him impervious to annoyances, which in any other calling, would make his life a burden and a misery.

Byron is writing here of his early experiences as a playwright. Later, he seems to have become very sure of his abilities: in *Paid in Full* he states that an experienced dramatist is often the first to suggest the elimination of those portions of a play which seem vague or unnecessary; in 1880 he refused to adapt a new play along the lines suggested by David James and Thomas Thorne, on the grounds that his own notions were more likely to be successful, since he had spent several months thinking them out. He apparently liked to work on several plays simultaneously: on Monday, for instance, he might turn his hand to a comedy; on Tuesday a new drama might occupy him; and on Wednesday he might have a go at a burlesque. He said that this was the only way he could relieve the fatigue of writing; consequently he often had two or three plays ready for performance simultaneously.[51] Edward

Sothern, the comedian, who was very fond of Byron, recalled Byron's working habits:

> It is a prevailing impression that Byron writes too rapidly, but, to my certain knowledge, he frequently does not take a pen in his hands for weeks at a time. I have often seen him after a chatty dinner-party, go to his desk and make a half-dozen memoranda. During that time he probably evolved the skeleton of a play. He never commences a drama wondering how he is going to finish it; the framework is all clear before he puts pen to paper. The beginning and the end of every act are definitely settled; as to the dialogue, that comes to him more naturally than he can scribble. I once asked him why he did not use a short-hand reporter. He replied that the scratching of his quill upon paper was like music to him! Another thing; he scarcely ever is guilty of an erasure, and once he has once written a piece he has the strongest possible objections to alterations. He rarely goes to see a first night's performance of his own work, and a play once produced seems to lose all interest in his mind, doubtless because it is so quickly succeeded by the plot of the next, which you may be sure he will speedily write.[52]

Another account of Byron's working habits slightly contradicts Sothern's:

> He rises with or soon after the sun, and from that time until his dinner hour is usually at work. Unlike the majority of authors, he affects no room in particular, but writes wherever his fancy happens to dictate . . . Those who speak of Mr Byron's contributions to the stage as dashed off without much or perhaps any previous consideration are sadly in error. He spends a good deal of time in devising his plots and the mode in which they are developed, in fixing the motives and the distinctive peculiarities of his particular characters and even in marking the entrances and exits. Not until this part of his task is accomplished does he proceed with the dialogue, which to him is a comparatively easy matter . . .[53]

Byron used to collect witticisms in notebooks and, if some comic notion occurred to him as he was walking along the street, he would 'jot it down on an envelope or on his sleeve, or on the margin of a newspaper, using his hat as a writing-desk or else making shift with a wall'.[54]

Byron's attitude to rehearsals was as idiosyncratic as his attitude to writing. Even though he was unwilling to alter his plays once they were written, he seems to have been more adaptable with burlesque. He wrote anything into the piece that was wanted, reminisced John Hollingshead, on the spur of the moment, then left the task of putting everything together to the actors, the stage manager, the musical director and the manager. He used to arrive late at rehearsals, slope off into little corners and tell jokes and, at the first opportunity, creep out of the theatre unobserved. He detested rehearsals and would often spend the afternoon wandering around Covent Garden or drinking in a nearby bar. Once, in an emergency, Byron was discovered in the Wellington Bar. Asked his advice on a particular scene, Byron replied:

> End your dance by disappearing through a vampire trap, return through a 'star' trap – don't tell me you can't do it, for I saw you in a Dublin panto-mime – and say these lines:
>
> I've cut sly passages and secret doors,
> Panels that slide, and traps let in the floors
> So that my movements are eccentric – very:
> One moment deep below myself I bury,
> But 'ere you say I'm there with words emphatic,
> I'm that erratic,
> I'm in that there attic.[55]

Byron was very popular with his contemporaries. A bon viveur, clubman and notable wit, he bore no rancour and was generous in the help he proffered to his fellow dramatists. Towards the end of his life he had to withdraw from society on account of his ill-health and a growing restlessness manifested itself in the way he kept changing houses. Yet, even at the end of his life his sense of humour did not desert him. When a groom asked advice about the treatment of a sick horse, Byron replied, 'Give him a ball, but be sure you don't ask too many.' He was, said Robert Reece, 'the most lovable, most unselfish, the wittiest, brightest man of his time'.[56]

Byron's contribution to the history of the British theatre may seem small, if judged in terms of literary achievement or continuous influence. On the other hand, it would be wrong to dismiss the man of whom Dutton Cooke wrote: 'The performance, say, of one of Mr Byron's plays is an occasion of some excitement. Expectation is astir, there assembles a crowded and interested house . . . His comedies are more frequently performed than are the comedies of any other author.'[57] Although he suffered a critical reaction against his work towards the end of the nineteenth century, when the 'Wild Ducks' and 'Belgian Shakespeares' so abhorred by Clement Scott were in the ascendant, in his own day Byron was frequently referred to as the Dickens of the stage.[58] Like Dickens's novels his plays appealed strongly to the Victorian middle classes, who reacted well to his emphasis on domesticity and moral propriety. If his plays lack the depth of Dickens's novels, he nevertheless succeeded in reflecting perfectly the requirements, and embodying the attitudes, of his audiences. The purpose of this edition is to demonstrate the range and achievement of the man who, for a time, dominated mid-Victorian theatre.

NOTES

1   *A History of the London Stage* (London, 1904), p. 446.
2   Harley Granville-Barker, 'Exit Planché – Enter Gilbert' in *The Eighteen-Sixties: Essays by Fellows of the Royal Society of Literature*, ed. John Drinkwater (Cambridge, 1932).
3   Unidentified clipping, undated, British Library Theatre Cuttings.
4   *Mr and Mrs Bancroft On and Off the Stage* (London, 1888), p. 37.

5   *Ibid.*, p. 38.
6   Quoted in Paul Sheridan, *Late and Early Joys of the Players Theatre* (London, 1952), p. 75.
7   *George de Barnwell* (1862) opens with a similar dialogue, praising the way in which burlesque wreathed:

> a garland of jest, prank and pun,
> Pointing a moral too amidst our fun.

8   For a fuller account of Robertson, *Society* and the Prince of Wales's Theatre see William Tydeman (ed.), *Plays by Tom Robertson* (Cambridge, 1982), pp. 8–15.
9   John Hollingshead, *Gaiety Chronicles* (London, 1898), p. 418.
10 Unidentified clipping, dated 27 December 1879, Theatre Museum.
11 Augustin Filon, *The English Stage*, trans. F. Whyte (London, 1897).
12 'Exit Planché – Enter Gilbert'.
13 Unidentified clipping, undated, British Library Theatre Cuttings.
14 *A Playgoer's Wanderings* (London, 1926), p. 106.
15 Dickens also refers to some of these vocal oddities in his essays on the theatre. See Frank Rahill, *The World of Melodrama* (Pennsylvania, 1967), p. 152.
16 *Illustrated Sporting and Dramatic News*, 14 August 1875.
17 R. J. Broadbent, *Annals of the Liverpool Stage* (Liverpool, 1908), p. 241. According to the *Star*, 27 July 1868: 'To the credit of the scene painter and machinist must be especially placed the complete success of the striking scene at Egremont Ferry, with the wonderful boat which steams up and turns round, and disembarks her passengers just before the attempted murder of Johnson. The representation of Liverpool in the distance must delight all who have ever gazed across the Mersey from the Cheshire side at night.'
18 *Liverpool Journal*, 23 November 1867.
19 Quoted in Charles Hiatt, *Henry Irving* (London, 1899), pp. 72–3.
20 *Life of Henry Irving* (London, 1908), pp. 93–4.
21 Laurence Irving, *Henry Irving* (London, 1951), p. 151.
22 Brereton, *Life of Henry Irving*, p. 89.
23 Joseph Hatton, *Reminiscences of J. L. Toole* (London, 1889), p. 131.
24 Hollingshead, *Gaiety Chronicles*, p. 106, quoting *Daily News*.
25 Hiatt, *Henry Irving*, p. 78.
26 Irving, *Henry Irving*, p. 160.
27 Hatton, *Reminiscences of J. L. Toole*, p. 425.
28 *The Old Drama and the New* (London, 1923), p. 273.
29 *English Dramatists of Today* (London, 1882), pp. 137–46.
30 *Theatrical Notes* (London, 1893), p. 71.
31 *Ibid.*, p. 202.
32 A. W. Pinero, 'The Theatre in the Seventies' in *The Eighteen-Seventies: Essays by Fellows of the Royal Society of Literature*, ed. Harley Granville-Barker (Cambridge, 1929), pp. 153–4.
33 *Sir Charles Wyndham* (London, 1904), p. 56.
34 H. G. Hibbert, *A Playgoer's Memories* (London, 1920), p. 17.
35 Squire Bancroft, *Empty Chairs* (London, 1925), p. 153.
36 *Theatrical Notes*, p. 13.
37 *The Daily Telegraph*, 18 January 1875, quoted in C. E. Pascoe, *Our Actors and Actresses: The Dramatic List* (London, 1880), p. 210.

38   *Bath Herald*, 8 February 1879.
39   *Ibid.*
40   *The Old Drama and the New*, p. 273.
41   *The Victorian Theatre* (Oxford, 1967), p. 89.
42   T. W. Craik and C. Leech (eds.), *The Revels History of Drama in English: Vol VI 1750–1880* (London, 1975), p. 262.
43   'The Theatre in the Seventies', p. 156.
44   *Daily News*, 4 October 1875, quoted Pascoe, *Our Actors and Actresses*, p. 78.
45   Pemberton, *Sir Charles Wyndham*, p. 97.
46   *Forty Years on the Stage* (London, 1914), p. 21.
47   *Illustrated Sporting and Dramatic News*, 19 April 1884.
48   Letter, undated, to John Clarke, Theatre Museum.
49   *Illustrated Sporting and Dramatic News*, 14 August 1875.
50   Unidentified clipping, dated 11 November 1879, Theatre Museum.
51   Howard Paul, *Anecdotes of H. J. Byron, Wit*, from unidentified clipping, undated, Harvard Theatre Collection.
52   T. E. Pemberton, *Edward Askew Sothern: A Memoir* (London, 1889), pp. 128–9.
53   Unidentified clipping, undated, Theatre Museum.
54   Filon, *The English Stage*, p. 97.
55   Hibbert, *A Playgoer's Memories*, p. 58.
56   *The Theatre*, III New Series (1 May 1884), 272.
57   *Ibid.*, I New Series (1 March 1880), 143.
58   Ernest Reynolds, in *Early Victorian Drama 1830–1870* (Cambridge, 1936), p. 142, suggests that dramatisations of Dickens's novels had called forth a new type of character acting which in turn influenced the depiction of character in the works of such playwrights as H. J. Byron.

BIOGRAPHICAL RECORD

8 January 1835	Henry James Byron born in Manchester, elder son of Mr Henry Byron (1804–84), British consul at Hayti, and Elizabeth Josephine née Bradley. Paternal great-grandfather Rev. Henry Byron of Leicestershire, cousin of Lord Byron, the poet. Maternal great-grandfather Dr Solomon of Liverpool of 'Balm of Gilead' fame.
1835–49	Educated at school in Essex, then at St Peter's College, Eaton Square. Subsequently sent to a private tutor in the country.
1849	The Hon. Mrs Leigh uses influence to obtain HJB a cadetship in Navy, but parents refuse consent for him to go.
1849–53	Becomes an articled clerk to Mr Miles Morley, a surgeon resident in Cork Street, Burlington Gardens. Continues studies with maternal grandfather, Dr Bradley of Buxton.
1853–8	Goes on stage. Acts at Theatre Royal, Colchester; then at Oldham, Rochester, etc. Meets Tom Robertson. London performances include *A Bottle of Champagne Uncorked by Horace Plastic*, a monologue performed at Marionette Theatre.
4 January 1856	Marries Martha Foulkes, daughter of Mr John Foulkes of Ashfield, near Wrexham, at St Marylebone Parish Church.
23 November 1857	*Richard of the Lion Heart* performed at Strand Theatre, London.
1858	William Swanborough takes Strand Theatre with his daughter, Ada, as nominal manager.
14 January 1858	Enters Middle Temple with a view to becoming a barrister.
5 April 1858	*Fra Diavolo Travestie* performed at Strand Theatre. Proves very popular.
11 October 1858	*The Maid and the Magpie* helps to establish reputation of Marie Wilton when she plays Pippo at Strand Theatre.
18 July 1859	First burlesque for Adelphi Theatre, London. *The Babes in the Wood and the Good Little Fairy-Birds.* Cast includes J. L. Toole and Paul Bedford.
7 March 1860	Plays Ali Baba in an amateur production of *Ali Baba* at the Lyceum Theatre, London, with fellow members of the Savage Club, in aid of the widows and children of two literary gentlemen, recently deceased.

26 December 1860	*Cinderella; or the Lover, the Lackey and the Little Glass Slipper* at Strand Theatre introduces character of Buttoni.
1 April 1861	*Aladdin; or the Wonderful Scamp* at Strand Theatre introduces character of Widow Twankay.
21 September 1861	Edits *Fun* from first number.
7 November 1861	E. A. Sothern plays Lord Dundreary in Tom Taylor's *Our American Cousin* at Haymarket Theatre, London.
2 September 1862	HJB appears with members of the Savage Club in *Retained for the Defence* and *Valentine and Orson* at the Free Trade Hall, Manchester.
1863	Founder member of Arundel Club.
6 April 1863	*Ali Baba, or the Thirty-Nine Thieves . . .* staged at Strand Theatre.
July 1863–May 1864	Edits *Comic News*.
1864	Resident in Doughty Street.
1865	Novel in three vols, *Paid in Full*, published.
10 April 1865	HJB joins Marie Wilton in management of Prince of Wales's Theatre, Tottenham Street, London. Agrees to write exclusively for P of W.
15 April 1865	*La! Somnambula!* opens Prince of Wales's Theatre.
10 June 1865	*War to the Knife*, drama by HJB, staged at P of W.
11 November 1865	Tom Robertson's *Society* staged at P of W as a result of HJB's recommendation.
September 1866	HJB undertakes the management of the Theatre Royal, Liverpool, and becomes sole lessee of the Royal Ampitheatre, Liverpool.
1867	Adds Royal Alexandra Theatre to Liverpool commitments. Resigns connection with P of W Theatre after dispute with Marie Wilton.
6 April 1867	Tom Robertson's *Caste* staged at P of W.
28 October 1867	*The Lancashire Lass* staged at Ampitheatre, Liverpool.
26 November 1867	*Dearer than Life* staged at Alexandra, Liverpool.
8 January 1868	J. L. Toole a great hit as Michael Garner in *Dearer than Life* at Queen's Theatre. Irving a successful Bob Gassett.
4 March 1868	HJB files a petition for bankruptcy. Debts equal £10,000–£15,000. Relinquishes management and undertakes to repay every penny owed.
22 March 1868	Testimonial held for Byron in Liverpool.
30 March 1868	Appears in bankruptcy court in London.
3 April 1868	Benefit for Byron held in Liverpool.
24 July 1868	*The Lancashire Lass* staged at Queen's Theatre, London. Irving plays Robert Redburn.
28 November 1868	*Cyril's Success*, reputedly Byron's favourite play, staged at Globe Theatre, London.

2 October 1869	*Lost at Sea*, collaboration with Dion Boucicault, staged at Adelphi.
23 October 1869	Makes professional debut on the London stage as Sir Simon Simple in one of his own plays, *Not Such a Fool as He Looks* (Globe Theatre).
13 December 1869	Toole and Irving a great success in *Uncle Dick's Darling* at Gaiety Theatre.
23 March 1870	Byron plays Fitzaltamont in *The Prompter's Box* at the Adelphi.
3 February 1871	Death of Tom Robertson.
7 October 1871	*Partners for Life* staged at the Globe.
21 March 1874	Becomes joint manager of the Criterion Theatre with E. P. Hingston. Theatre opens with HJB's *An American Lady*, in which he also acts.
1875-9	Record-breaking run of *Our Boys*.
16 January 1875	First night of *Our Boys* at Vaudeville Theatre. Joint managers of Vaudeville, David James and Thomas Thorne, play principal parts.
25 March 1875	*Trial by Jury* staged at Royalty Theatre: association of Gilbert and Sullivan with D'Oyly Carte commences.
26 August 1876	HJB provides entire opening programme for Gaiety Theatre: *The Bull by the Horns* and *Little Don Caesar de Bazan*. The latter helps to establish famous Gaiety Quartette.
25 September 1876	Death of HJB's wife, Martha, at Brighton in her 45th year.
October–December 1876	Before end of year HJB remarries in Lambeth. His second wife is Eleanor Mary Joy, daughter of Edward Joy.
1876-9	Writes burlesques regularly for Gaiety.
3 October 1877	W. S. Gilbert's *Engaged* staged at Haymarket Theatre.
13 October 1877	*Little Doctor Faust* staged at Gaiety.
29 October 1877– October 1878	Edits *Mirth*.
13 February 1878	Collaborates with W. S. Gilbert, F. C. Burnand and R. Reece to write *Ali Baba and the Forty Thieves* for charity performance at the Gaiety.
19 February 1878	1,000th night of *Our Boys*.
18 April 1879	*Our Boys* closes after 1,362 performances.
19 April 1879	*The Girls* replaces *Our Boys* at the Vaudeville, but proves less successful.
26 December 1879	*The Gaiety Gulliver* is first spectacular burlesque to be presented at Gaiety. Helps pave way for three-act Gaiety burlesques of future years.
31 March 1880	J. L. Toole appears at his own theatre, the Folly, in HJB's *The Upper Crust*.
1881-4	HJB's health begins to decline.

1881	HJB chosen at Literary Congress in Vienna, without usual preliminary formalities, as member of Executive Council.
13 November 1881	HJB plays Cheviot Hill in W. S. Gilbert's *Engaged* at Court Theatre.
1882	Moves from Ecclestone Square to 5 Bedford Square.
4 February 1882	Relinquishes part of Cheviot Hill on account of severe bronchial attack.
13 March 1882	*Auntie* staged at Toole's Theatre.
1883-4	Wintering at Hastings.
12 April 1884	Dies, aged 49, of lingering consumption at Rocklemont, Queen's Rd, his residence in Clapham Park.
18 April 1884	Buried in Brompton Cemetary.
16 May 1885	*The Shuttlecock*, completed by J. A. Sterry, first performed at Toole's Theatre for benefit of HJB's widow.

NOTE ON THE TEXTS

There is no collected edition of H. J. Byron's work. Many of his plays were published as Lacy's, later French's, acting editions; a few were published under other
imprints; some were never published at all. Nearly all his plays were submitted in
manuscript to the Lord Chamberlain for licensing purposes. The present volume is
based on the most authentic acting edition of each play, collated with the manuscript submitted to the Lord Chamberlain (henceforth referred to as LC) and with
surviving prompt copies, when available.

The text of *The Babes in the Wood* is taken from Lacy's acting edition of the
play, collated with LC. Prompt copies in the Harvard Theater Collection and in the
New York Public Library (Performing Arts Library at the Lincoln Center) have
been examined. These are both Lacy editions and the cuts in both remove topical
allusions and Shakespearian parodies in particular. None of these cuts has been
incorporated in the present edition. Nor, at the risk of cluttering the text with
excessive footnotes, have notes on the Shakespearian allusions in this particular
play been included. As noted in the introduction the major sources of parody are
Macbeth and *King John*. (When literary allusions and quotations occur in the subsequent texts, a footnote has usually been provided.)

The Lancashire Lass was first performed in Liverpool in 1867 and the LC copy
is the Liverpool version. The play was subsequently altered for its London production in 1868 and French's acting edition, published in London and New York,
incorporates the changes. A prompt copy in the Becks Bequest (hereafter referred
to as BB) in the New York Public Library (Performing Arts Library at the Lincoln
Center) contains a manuscript version of the play that retains some of the features
of LC, but includes all the major changes found in French's edition. The property
of J. W. Couldock, this was probably the prompt copy for the first New York
production of the play, at Wallack's Theatre on 26 October 1868. The text in this
volume is based primarily on French's edition. When it has seemed appropriate to
add dialogue or stage directions from LC, these interpolations are enclosed in
square brackets.

The major difference between French's edition (hereafter referred to as FAE)
and the LC copy is the fourth act of the play. In LC it consists of three scenes,
takes place in Italy and is much longer than FAE. Unlike FAE it contains a sentimental reconciliation between Ruth and Ned, further pursues the fortunes of
Danville and Fanny and provides Redburn with a less bloody fate. FAE shifts the
conclusion to Australia, omits much of the action in LC and moves rapidly to its
powerful climax. Since the LC version of act IV is so different, it has been included
as an appendix, so that the reader can compare the two endings provided to the
play. The other changes in the Prologue and first three acts of the play consist

mainly of cuts. In the Prologue in LC the character of Jellick as a comically des-
pondent lover is considerably more developed. In act I, scene 1 dialogue between
Milder and Spotty and between Redburn and Johnson has been cut in FAE. Dialogue superfluous to the development of the action or merely designed for comic
effect has been ruthlessly pruned. Some of the more conventionally melodramatic
dialogue, such as Ruth's long remorseful speech in act I, scene 2, has been cut.
Whereas in LC the flirtation between Redburn and Fanny in the same scene is quite
extensive, in FAE it is considerably shortened. There are some differences in the
directions provided in LC and BB for the setting and effects in act II, scene 2, and
these are referred to in a separate appendix. Act II, scene 2 in LC differs also in
that Ned fetches policemen, who subsequently arrest him, at the end of that scene;
Kitely is not introduced until FAE. In act III, scene 2, LC contains considerably
more dialogue between Jellick and Sergeant Donovan. A comic drunken scene
develops between them, culminating in a number of long drunken speeches and a
comic drinking song sung by Donovan. Ruth's dialogue persuading Jellick to
release Ned is also more extensive in LC. Generally, the alterations in FAE stream-
line the play considerably by cutting much superfluous and repetitive dialogue,
reducing some rather tediously comic episodes and removing unnecessary exposi-
tion and explanation.

The text used for *Our Boys* is French's acting edition, no. 1728, published in
1879, collated with French's acting edition published in 1923 and with the LC
copy. Reference has also been made to the edition published as no. 2 in the Library
of English Literature, Gouda, edited by J. H. Van Der Doort. This is more or less
identical to FAE, but contains more abbreviated stage directions. It was published
in 1885. A prompt copy in Harvard Theater Collection, based on French's American edition, has also been consulted, but no material from this version has been
incorporated.

The text used for *The Gaiety Gulliver* is that published and printed by Aubert's
Steam Press in 1879–80, collated with an almost identical edition (although arranged in a different order), of which the publisher is unknown, and the LC copy. The
Aubert text is in five acts whereas the unidentified text is extended to seven acts.
It is clear, from an examination of programmes and reviews, that the Aubert version
follows the original staging of the play, whereas the unidentified text represents a
revised order of staging, which had been adopted by 10 January, when *Punch* refers
to the play as being in 'seven acts and twelve tableaux'. *The Athenaeum* (10
January 1880) complains that the Lilliput scenes, now relegated to the sixth act,
are in no way connected with the rest of the play. The new arrangement of scenes,
in fact, renders the development of the plot illogical and unclear. It seems that
Spectacle rather than a logically developing sequence was the primary consideration in the revised presentation of *Gulliver*. For the sake of clarity I have therefore
retained the earlier sequence. However, I have incorporated one cut from the
unidentified edition and transferred the relevant lines to an appendix. I have also
included as an appendix the revised order of scenes in the unidentified edition.

In accordance with the general editorial policy of the British and American Playwrights series, stage directions have been adapted when they serve no clear or useful purpose for a modern reader. When an archaic stage direction has remained, because it contributes very definitely to the feel of the play in performance, a footnote has usually been provided.

THE BABES IN THE WOOD AND THE GOOD LITTLE FAIRY-BIRDS

A burlesque drama in one act

First produced at the Theatre Royal, New Adelphi, on 18 July 1859, with the following cast:

SIR ROWLAND MACASSAR, *the remorseless 'Uncle', in whose care his elder brother has left his Pledges*	Miss Woolgar
SIR RODERICK ⎱ *Youths of good presence, but inferior parts*	Mrs A. Mellon
SIR RUPERT ⎰	Miss Hayman
TOMMY ⎱ *Sir Rowland's nephew and niece, very dreadful*	Mr J. L. Toole
SALLY ⎰ *children indeed*	Miss Kate Kelly
SMITH, *the First Ruffian – a mysterious creature who eventually proves by no means so black as he is painted*	Mr Paul Bedford
BROWN, *the Second Ruffian – a villain of deeper dye*	Mr C. J. Smith
THE FAMILY PHYSICIAN	Mr W. H. Eburne
LADY MACASSAR, *Sir Rowland's aider and a-better half, who, although she allows him no will of his own, assists him in appropriating his brother's*	Mrs Billington
MISS JONES, *Nursery Governess*	Miss Arden
THE QUEEN OF THE FAIRY-BIRDS	Miss Laidlaw

A numerous flock of Fairy-Birds, by an efficient Corps de Ballet and Egg-stras

---

Sir Rowland Macassar: Rowland's Macassar Oil first appeared about 1793. It was the invention of Alexander Rowland, who created a hair oil out of vegetable ingredients, as opposed to the bear's grease normally used for the commodity. It was patronised by several European sovereigns, including the English Royal Family.

SCENE 1.   *Courtyard of Macassar Hall. A walk runs across back of stage; and there is an entrance to the Hall right; door (practicable) in wall left. Melodramatic music as the curtain rises, during which a large* COCK *flies on the wall centre and crows lustily through the music.* RETAINERS *in hunting dress enter from the house – they all have drinking horns.*

> (*Enter* SIR RUPERT *and* SIR RODERICK.)
> OPENING CHORUS –'*Bright Chanticleer*'
> Bright Chanticleer proclaims the morn:
> We've spangled dress forsworn,
> And luxuries and velvet ease,
> > At sound of hunting horn.
> > Away, away! a jolly day!
> > > Be every sportsman's cry.
> > > Arise, the time is getting on,
> > > > Away we soon must hie!
> > > > With a hey-ho! chevy, etc.

SIR RUPERT: I'll give you, gentlemen, a worthy toast:
Here is Sir Rowland – our most noble host;
You'll please to honour it with three times three,
Be good enough to take the time from *me*. (*cheers*)
> (SIR ROWLAND MACASSAR, *a blasé semi-Sir Charles Coldstream, semi-Macbeth individual, enters from the house, in hunting costume and bearing a whip.*)

SIR ROWL: Silence that dreadful bel-lowing; keep steady!
RETAINER: (*excited*) Hip! Hip! Hip! Hip!
SIR ROWL: I'm *hipp'd* enough already:
I'm sick of life, and –
SIR RODERICK: Why I say, old fella',
What sick of life! – a fella' with your cella'?
SIR RUPERT: Why, you are snugly laid on luxury's pillow,
House in Belgravia –
SIR RODERICK: Furniture by Gillow;
This place in Norfolk, shooting boxes, carriages –
SIR RUPERT: Ya-as, there've been fella's who have made worse marriages.
SIR RODERICK: You've not done badly.
SIR ROWL: (*musingly*)   Haven't I; so – so –
SIR RUPERT: You were a younger brother, don't you know?
SIR ROWL: Oh, bitter, bitter phrase – a younger brother!

Sir Charles Coldstream: a bored, languid character played by Charles Mathews in *Used Up*, a comedy by Mathews and Dion Boucicault, first performed on 6 February 1844 at the Theatre Royal, Haymarket.
hipp'd: depressed, low spirited.
Gillow: Lancaster furniture firm founded in early 1700s, initially providing furniture for very wealthy families and the nobility; by the mid-nineteenth century it was providing solid domestic furniture for the prosperous middle classes.
shooting boxes: small country houses in or adjacent to shooting localities, used as residences on shooting trips.

Obliged within his heart of hearts to smother,
That gnawing passion for some peerless belle,
Which, though it madden him, he may not tell;
To have commissions troublesome by dozens,
To dance with none but snub-nosed country cousins;
To aye be ready at the beck and call
Of fifty flirts at picnic – party – ball!
And if his love he breathes, the cruel mother,
Exclaims, 'Good gracious! had it been your brother!'
I'd rather be a dog and bay the moon,
Than such a slow man.

SIR RUPERT: (*aside to* SIR RODERICK) The inflated spoon.
　　(*aloud*) But you *are* married.

SIR ROWL:　　　　　　　　　　　Yes, the more's the pity;
　　Tied to a wife by no means young or pretty,
　　One who's strong-minded, friends, and seldom smiles,
　　Sings, plays, or dances, or her time beguiles
　　As other ladies do –

SIR RODERICK:　　　　　　Ya – as, I expect,
　　She's all – all – all, – confound it! –

SIR ROWL:　　　　　　　　　　　Intellect.
　　Ha, I don't wonder at your sticking so;
　　It's not a word you're used to, is it?

SIR RODERICK:　　　　　　　　　No!

SIR ROWL: When ladies find their youthfulness is gone,
　　They don't *get off*, and that they're *getting on*;
　　When partners soon give in, and slyly slink
　　Off to some 'common little thing in pink';
　　When watering places have been 'done' in vain,
　　From Baden to Herne Bay; when they e'en deign
　　To visit Margate, so saline and breezy,
　　Proving that poor ma-*ma gets* quite uneasy;
　　About this time I say, my friends, you'll find,
　　A wondrous change come o'er the female mind –
　　No longer picnics, parties, flower shows
　　Amuse her – scientific now she grows;
　　Minerva-like, upon her chair she sits,
　　Calls laughing girls of twenty 'thoughtless chits'.
　　My wife was such a one, strong-minded, clever,
　　When I was taken in and done for ever.
　　Political economy she's glib on;
　　My rib on no account would wear a rib-bon;
　　She'd walk down Regent street and wouldn't stop,
　　To look into a single bonnet shop;

---

spoon: foolishly over-demonstrative lover.
Minerva: Roman Goddess of handicrafts and war.

I'm sure she'd perish rather than be seen,
In the most unpretending crinoline. –
Would I were single as in days of yore,
In chambers, studying a *batch-o'-law*,
At number fifty, Fig-tree Court, third floor.

      SONG – '*The Muleteer*'
I shed a single pearly tear,
    When my thoughts turn to my two rooms
On the third floor – by no means dear,
    At three feet off your window looms,
Through your bird's-eye fumes –
        Where I attempt to read the laws,
        The weary dreary laws;
        And signally I fail because,
        Always fail because,
Ma'mas' won't let me stay a-night,
    From balls and dances drear;
But now indeed it's different quite,
    All day, alas, I hear,
        Clack, clack, that is all I hear.

    (CHORUS – HUNTSMEN *join in with their whips.*)

SIR RUPERT: Bravo!

SIR RODERICK: *Pwae-Waphaelite*, upon my life!

LADY MACASSAR: (*without*)   Sir Rowland.

    (SIR ROWLAND *starts violently.*)

SIR RUPERT: Hi, old fella', there's your wife.

    (SIR RODERICK *hastily shaking hands to be off* – RETAINERS
    exhibit symptoms of fear and anxiety to go.)

SIR RODERICK: We'll not detain you – so, goodbye.

SIR RUPERT: (*in same manner*)   Goodbye.

SIR ROWL: Go and enjoy yourselves, my friends, while I –
    (*Stands in a desponding attitude* – *the* FRIENDS *hurry off through
    door – melodramatic music.*)

SIR ROWL: (*through music*) If it were done when 'tis done, it were well
    It were done quickly, so that none can tell; –
    For like unto th'Australian boomerang,
    Which when returning hits us with a bang,
    This even-handed justice, who is not
    By any means connected with a lot
    Of justices of various professions,
    Who punish poachers at the quarter sessions,
    Commends the ingredients of our poisoned chalice
    To our own lips in instances of malice.

    (LADY MACASSAR, *a Lady Macbeth-looking lady, with her hair in
    curl papers, enters from house and comes down behind* SIR
    ROWLAND, *unseen by him, with tragedy queen strides.*)

> The boy's my nephew, and the girl's my niece –
> I cannot, *will* not kill them.

LADY M: (*suddenly striking his shoulder*) Ha!

SIR ROWL: (*with a wild shriek*)   Police!
> Thou can'st not say *I* did it.

LADY M: (*laughs scornfully*)   Silent be!

SIR ROWL: Nay, never shake your curl papers at me.
> Why – why – it's only you, my – my – (*with difficulty*) – my dear!

LADY M: What were those words that broke upon mine ear?
> Poor puny milksop? Are you not aware
> That to these broad possessions Tom is heir?
> Their father's lost –

SIR ROWL: No proof has yet been found
> That the ship foundered, or that he was drowned.

LADY M: The girl disposed of, Rowland, and the boy dead –

SIR ROWL: But might not danger, dear one, be avoided,
> By waiting, and allowing the small pair to
> Fall victims to some ills which flesh is heir to?
> They have not had the whooping cough you know.

LADY M: That's too uncertain, man, and much too slow.

SIR ROWL: A mild attack of measles might –

LADY M: Oh, stuff!
> It would not kill *'em easily* enough,
> Coward!

SIR ROWL: Indeed! You seem to quite forget,
> That I've just joined a rifle corps, my pet,
> Though I must own although I like the corps,
> A heavy rifle's a tremendous *bore*.

LADY M: '*A soldier and afeard!*'

SIR ROWL: Ah! There you make
> A very prevalent absurd mistake,
> A truly brave man's not obliged to be
> A bear or tiger, of necessity,
> Although he parts his hair a down the middle,
> And in his hand an eye glass he may twiddle,
> And seeks his looking glass each morning where
> He spends two hours parting his back hair,
> Though his dress neck-tie is a little wisp,
> His conversation marr'd by drawl and lisp,
> Take him and put a sword into his hand,
> And then to guard from foes his native land,
> You'll find that he's as truly brave and bold,
> As were the doughty warriors of old,
> Now *I* for one have proved I know not fear.

LADY M: Indeed! How so?

SIR ROWL: By marrying *you*, my dear.

LADY M: Their governess costs fifty pounds a-year,
    Including board and washing.
SIR ROWL: I'm afraid.
    That's *almost* what you give your *lady's maid.*
LADY M: Last night she had the insolence to sneer
    At our nice wholesome sparkling table beer,
    At sevenpence the gallon.
SIR ROWL: Oh, my jewel,
    To feed a *gal on* that, by Jove! it's cruel.
LADY M: If it were heady she'd forget her station,
    And quite neglect the children's *hedi*-cation.
        (*clutching* SIR ROWLAND, *bringing him down centre, and speaking with great energy)*
    What think ye! Promise that ye do not start,
    At dinner Thomas asked three times for tart,
    And simulated symptoms of a fit
    So well I was obliged to give him it;
    When his nurse came for him last night he hit her,
    And when she slapp'd him, flew at her and bit her.
    A *bitter* punishment he shall receive;
    Too long we've *h-ad'em* – they shall go this *eve!*
    This very night they shall be off, the twain,
    Never to darken our front door again.
    You know my purposes are fixed as rocks.
SIR ROWL: Oh, no!
LADY M: I've said *tonight.* (*postman's knock heard*)
                Two knocks. (*nox*)
SIR ROWL: (*dropping in chair*) What can that sudden summons be – oh – lor!
LADY M: It merely means that *some un's* at the door.
SIR ROWL: 'Tis like a postman's – fears my bosom fill.
LADY M: Why should the *postman* make my *Rowland h-ill?*
    There are two gentlemen – I bade them call.
    They have no qualms, and anything at all
    Will do for *lucre.* – *Look a* little pleasant,
    At all events whilst visitors are present.
        (*Music. Enter the two* RUFFIANS. *The first* RUFFIAN *is a good-tempered looking fellow; the second one, a regular Coburg villain, with a particularly sulky savage appearance.*)
        DUET – '*Farewell my old Pals and Tories*'
1ST RUF:
    We've just dropp'd in, my noble commander,

Rowland Hill: inventor of the adhesive postage stamp and a leading campaigner for administrative reforms within the Post Office.
Coburg villain: the Royal Coburg Theatre opened in Waterloo Road in 1818. Renamed the Royal Victoria Theatre in 1833, it is now known as the Old Vic. It specialised in the performance of lurid and sensational melodramas in the nineteenth century.

As we were passing your gate;
We were told by that old lady yonder
You had something to com-mu-ni-cate.
(*to sulky friend*) Now sing – Tooral I – tooral I – tooral I –

2ND RUF: (*sulkily*) Shan't!

1ST RUF: Tooral I – tooral I, day.
We heed not policeman or 'Charley',
For locks, bolts, and bars little care,
And all the more par-tic-u-*lar*-ly,
When a gent *is* a gent – which you *air*.
(*Chorus repeated.*)

SIR ROWL: Your names and business – quick, reply with pith.

1ST RUF: *My* name is Norval – that is, *Novel* – Smith.
The sentiments that I profess to foller
Are, that all folks should have what they could collar.
There should be no such thing as taxes – rent;
And we should all have seats in parliament,
For which we should receive a salary good.

SIR ROWL: To sit out *some* debates I think you *should*.

2ND RUF: In all he does, I back him to the letter:
And the more violence there is the better;
For when well paid, compunction's fears I stifles,
And don't mind knives, or guns, or stick at t'*rifles*.

1ST RUF: If to assist you, sir, in aught you wish us,
You'll find us very cheap and expeditious. (*producing card*)
There is our scale of charges for our crimes,
'*In accordance with the spirit of the times.*'

SIR ROWL: (*Snatching it eagerly – reads.*)
'Easy and simple thrashings, *half-a-crown.*
Incendiarism, seven shillings down.
Garrotting, if the patient's strong and hearty,
Ten shillings – but according to the party.
Clearing for next-but-one of kin the way,
Our full expenses and a pound a day.'

2ND RUF: That is the sort of job in which we glory.
It's what we term our new 'depilatory'.

1ST RUF: (*explaining*) Depilatory's stuff, as you're aware,
(*significantly*) *For getting rid of an annoying heir!*

SIR ROWL: (*aside*) Ha! Ha! A dreadful hint! It is my cue! – But
I fear – and yet I don't (*in imitation of King John and in allusion to* 1ST
RUFFIAN*'s size*) Come hither, 'you but'. – (*Hubert*)
(LADY MACASSAR *and* 2ND RUFFIAN *at back*)

'*Charley*': a night watchman.
My name is Norval: a well-known speech, much favoured for recitation, from Home's *Douglas*.
'*In accordance . . . times*': the phrase 'spirit of the times' was first used in Shakespeare's *King John*.

SIR ROWL: I had a thing to say – but let it go –
    And yet, of course – that is –
1ST RUF: (*doggedly*)   Precisely so.
SIR ROWL: Within this wall of flesh there is a soul,
    Counts thee her creditor, and will not dole
    A scant reward. I like much your demeanour;
    Give me they hand! Why don't you keep 'em cleaner?
    (*Points left.*) Pray have the kindness just to throw thine eye
    On yon young boy – (RUFFIAN *appears suddenly ill at the sight.*)
               – at marbles playing? – Why,
    What is the matter?
1ST RUF: Merely a slight spasm;
    A temporary thing – I often has'em.
SIR ROWL: He must be – pah! The word sticks in my throat – a
1ST RUF: Consider him defunct as potted bloata.
        CONCERTED PIECE – '*Poetry of Motion*'
SIR ROWL: Harkye, fellow, though *I can* sing,
        Now with little kind of ease,
    For my blood like mad is dancing
        Through my veins and arter*ies.*
    Ne'er more let me see thy features,
        Henceforth must we strangers be,
    When you kill those little creatures,
        Do it, do it tenderly.
             Leave't to me,
             One, two three,
    And it is over, then in clover,
    You will be – don't you see?
    Or what folks term up a tree.

LADY M:
SIR ROWL:
2ND RUF:
1ST RUF:
} Tra, la lal, lal, etc. (*with different expressions*)

(1ST *and* 2ND RUFFIANS *exeunt melodramatically.* SIR
ROWLAND *and* LADY M *waltz off.*)

SCENE 2.   *The school room in Macassar Hall. Window to open; door; a desk; a*
form.

    (*Enter* MISS JONES, *the governess.*)
    SONG – '*The Monks of Old*'
        I'm governess here
        At just ten pounds a-year,
    And I find my own sugar and tea;
        The small table beer
        Is excessively queer,
    And is thinning me gradua*lie.*

They expect when I dine
That I'm to confine
My attentions to every cheap dish.
And never to stoop
To such weakness as soup,
Or cast longing eyes at the fish.
(*short melancholy dance to symphony*)
The hour they fix
For the breakfast is six,
The time for the dinner is one,
But it's far from a treat,
For so quickly they eat,
That they've finished before I've half done;
We've the plainest of cooks,
So when to my books,
I return for the rest of the day,
From the manner I've dined
I invariably find
I'm a victim to dyspep*si-a.*
My parents loved me. Neither of them hated me;
And yet, blind fools, they went and educated me.
Made me a lady – pah – a thing of sport
For wealthier dames – a governess in short.
Had they not crammed me with all sorts of learning,
I might, as cook, my living have been earning.
Had not this *nous* made me for work too high,
I might have been a *n'ouse maid* – mightn't I?
On Sunday afternoons allowed to take a
Walk with that most genteel young man the baker.
Where are those torments, doubtless in some mischief.
That Tom, of disobedient children *is* chief.
His sister too is really – (*Looks at watch.*) goodness gracious!
An hour after time – it's *too* audacious.
          (*Music. The* CHILDREN *run in through door roughly.*)
Miss Sarah, on you station don't presume.
Is *that* the way you come into a room?
Go back directly – make a curtsey, Miss.
          (SALLY *runs back to door and drops a hasty little bob.*)
Good gracious me! – No – something more like *this.*
          (*Drops a profound curtsey;* SALLY *imitates her mockingly.*)
Of Master Thomas, I shall tell his aunt.
Go back and bow directly, Thomas.
TOMMY: *Shan't.*
GOVERN: You'll turn my hair grey – thin it now has grown.
TOMMY: Why aunt said yesterday it war'nt your own.
          I heard her – didn't *you* sis?
SALLY: No, she said

You dye it every week, because it's red.

She said, too, you were full of cunning tricks.

TOMMY: *I* heard her say you ate enough for six.

SALLY: She says you're ignorant.

GOVERN: Oh, dear! Oh, dear!

SALLY: Decidedly not worth ten pounds a year.

If to next quarter you should keep alive –

TOMMY: Fully intends to drop it down to five.

GOVERN: This is distracting! Five! Ah, me! Ah, me!

SALLY: She hinted that she thought you stole the tea.

TOMMY: And that whenever she may chance to come

Into the school room, that it smells of rum.

GOVERN: This is *too* much – but I must let it pass.

(*suddenly*) Go to your seats. (CHILDREN *sit on a small form.*)

My poor, poor brains. (*Goes to her desk.*) First class!

(SALLY *rises* (*upsetting* TOMMY) *and goes to* GOVERNESS
lingeringly – GOVERNESS *puts on a pair of green spectacles.*)

Now, say your Pinnock; stand straight up, miss; *so*

Who was, (be still!) Wat Tyler – come!

SALLY: (*abruptly*)   Don't know.

GOVERN: I wonder how to answer thus you dare.

Who was Wat Tyler! think again.

SALLY: Don't care.

GOVERN: I'd like to shake you well, you saucy jade!

SALLY: (*impudently*) Why don't you do it then! Yah! You're afraid.

GOVERN: Sit down! (*aside*) Endure this longer much, I can't.

Sit down!

SALLY: Well, p'raps I shall, and p'raps I shan't. (*Sits.*)

GOVERN: Thomas! (*He appears to be studying hard.*)

Why, deaf the boy must surely be.

Thomas!

TOMMY: Beg pardon, miss, did you call me?

GOVERN: Of course I did, you wretched little dunce!

Come up and say your poetry at once.

(TOMMY *suddenly rises, upsetting* SALLY, *and repeats the lines
commencing with 'Cattle court the zephyrs bland', etc., after the
manner of children who have been instructed – at its conclusion, he
stealthily places a bull's eye in his mouth – the* GOVERNESS
observes his action.)

Give me that bull's eye, sir!

TOMMY: (*speaking with difficulty*) Don't wish m' get it!

GOVERN: (*seizing him*) I'll have it!

Pinnock: writer of school text books and catechisms on a wide variety of subjects during the
early nineteenth century.

'*Cattle . . . bland*': untraced – obviously from a text book, book of verse or alphabet book
much in use at the time. LC contains a simpler direction – 'repeats *some poetry* after . . .'

TOMMY: Will ye? He! He! He! *I've ate it!*
        (GOVERNESS *shakes him violently – a large top falls from his*
        pockets.)
GOVERN: (*picking it up*) Is that a top, that from your pocket drops?
SALLY: Well if he reads too fast, he minds his *s'tops*.
GOVERN: (*pocketing top*) P'raps in arithmetic you'll better be.
    Suppose a –
SALLY: That's a *poser*, I can see.
GOVERN: Suppose a herring and a half should come
    To just three half-pence, pr'ythee for what sum
    Could you a dozen get? Of course he sticks.
TOMMY: I have it! – no I haven't – *two and six.*
GOVERN: Oh! Shade of Cocker! (CHILDREN *chatter.*) Cease this worst of Babels!
    Now, Thomas, do you recollect your tables?
        (TOMMY *commences his multiplication table in a rapid and a*
        parrot-like manner.)
GOVERN: Oh, stop! Stop! There, that will never do.
    You, like a *parrot*, say your *cocker-too*.
    Tis quite disgraceful in a boy so big
        (*Produces large birch twig from desk.*)
    Do you see *that* – I *may* say do you *twig*,
    A present from her Ladyship. See *there*.
TOMMY: (*uncomfortable*) That is a *branch* of study I can't bear.
GOVERN: Your aunt this twig did lop.
SALLY: How very kind!
TOMMY: *She'll op the twig* herself, if she don't mind.
GOVERN: Well, I must do my duty, boy, and so
        (TOMMY *bursts into a violent fit of boohooing.*)
    It causes *me* most pain.
TOMMY: Oh, does it though?
GOVERN: It grieves me you won't do as you are bid –
    It goes *against* me.
TOMMY: Ah, *I wish it did.*
    For most uncomfortable you would find it,
    It goes against *me*, or I shouldn't mind it.
GOVERN: Hold out your hand!
TOMMY: I shan't! – Than you I'm stronger,
    To revolutionise is my intent!
    There! (*Kicks over form.*) I've upset the form of government.
    No longer I'll be treated as a brat,
    Relic of bygone tyranny take that! (*Upsets desk.*)
    Blackguard blackboard, you've bored me often so,
    Sal, ope the window – overboard you go.
        (SALLY *opens the window*, TOMMY *throws out board.*)
    This slate (*Seizes it.*) his late behaviour shall rue;

Cocker: a famous teacher of arithmetic, d. 1675.

This bit of *sleight* of hand I'll treat him to.

(*Sends his fist through it – turns upon the* GOVERNESS.)

If you don't leave the room, mum, by the door –

(*Points to window.*) Remember too, we're on the second floor.

GOVERN: Children, this is the most ill-judged of strikes.

TOMMY: (*making towards her*) The area rails too have such jolly spikes!

    (GOVERNESS *rushes off with a shriek, followed by a book –*
    TOMMY *clutches* SALLY *by the arm, and brings her down*
    mysteriously.)

TOMMY: Sister.

SALLY: Ber-other.

TOMMY: Easy 'tis to see.

    That uncle's getting tired of you and me.

SALLY: I've oft observed my uncle cast, 'tis true,

    An 'eavy eye upon his *nev-vy-u.*

TOMMY: Indeed, we may say without hesitation,

    That nunkey is *an unkey-ind* relation.

    But, Sarah dearest, apprehensions smother,

    Remember that you have a great big brother.

    I'm now, please recollect, a child no more;

    See my last measure on the parlour door;

    My whiskers too – oh, Sarah, I'm not humming –

    Though you can't see 'em, *I can feel 'em coming.*

    I fancy my moustachios will be brown.

SALLY: Of course you're growing up. (*Feels his chin.*) And *growing down.*

    Whiskers are not enough for most men's faces –

    This is the age of 'airs, if not of graces.

    Some soldiers, who looked meek and mild a year hence,

    On the'upper lip have a *most 'arsh* appearance;

    The butcher doth with lard his beard an'int,

    Each publican has his *imperial pint,*

    With more to match upon the upper lip,

    And every betting fellow has his *tip.*

    Soap fixatures, which twist one's curls like cables,

    Have banished bear's grease from our toilet tables;

    Stead of pomatum pots, as once were seen –

    A *band of fat jars* – there's a *band o' lean.*

TOMMY: By which, perhaps, the ignorant democracy

    Hope to be taken for the *hairy*-stocracy.

    (LADY MACASSAR *enters, comes down between the* CHILDREN;
    they run left and right where they are met by the 1ST *and* 2ND

---

imperial: applied to all weights and measures used throughout the UK from 1838; also used to describe a small part of the beard growing just beneath the chin.

fixatures: a gummy preparation for fixing the hair.

pomatum: pomade – a scented ointment for head and hair.

band o'lean: bandoline – a gummy preparation for fixing hair or moustache.

RUFFIANS – *they run up to door, where they are met by* SIR
ROWLAND, *who takes each of them by the hand and brings them
down centre – this is done quickly.*)

SIR ROWL: We think, my dears, a little change of air
Would do you good; and as you are aware,
A distant relative of yours hard by
The forest lives, we think – your aunt thinks – Why
Do I tremble? (*aside*) Wife, I cannot do it;
This hand is innocent – (LADY MACASSAR *slaps it indignantly.*) I'll not
imbrue it –

LADY M: (*in his ear*) You will allow me if you please to state,
That college debtors clamour at your gate,
And swear they *will* be paid. – What little pelf
I have, remember's settled on myself.

SIR ROWL: It must be then. Smile, Sally dearest, smile;
These gentlemen go with you – they'll beguile
The way with pretty stories. Sarah, come?
(SALLY *and* TOMMY *are looking frightened and dejected.*)

LADY M: Your uncle speaks to you; don't suck your thumb.

SIR ROWL: Come, don't be pensive child; you're mostly funny:
Here are some *pence if* you're in want of money.
(*Presses some money into her hand – hands* TOMMY *a large slice
of bread and butter.*)
Here is some bread and butter, Tom, in case
You're hungry. (*aside*) How he looks into my face.

TOMMY: (*in choked accents*) Goodbye, dear hunkle!

SIR ROWL: (*aside*) Tears bedim my sight.
(*Presses bread upon him.*) That *hunk'll* satisfy your appetite.
(*Clutches* LADY MACASSAR *aside imploringly.*)
Don't sacrifice them *both*; let's wait a bit:
My head swims round – I'm going have a fit –
A kind of *Vertigo.* You won't, I trust?

LADY M: (*with immense emphasis*) You said they *vere to go*, and go they must.
SONG – '*I'm leaving thee in sorrow, Annie*'

SIR ROWL: Good even! (*shaking* SALLY's *hand*) Practise your pi-anny.
Good even! (*ditto with* TOMMY) Drop your tears:
Come Tommy, be a little manny,
And recollect your years.
Come, what is it so much thou fearest?
Your spirits pray sustain;
If thus my kindness thou requitest,
You'll ne'er come back again.
(*The air changes abruptly to, 'Sally come up'.*)

1ST RUF: My dears, good children never cries,

---

pelf: money.

So darlings wipe your little eyes;
　Your little noses too likewise,
　　Your infant spirits rally.
We'll look at all the pretty shops;
　I'll buy you hoops, and whips and tops,
And blow you out with lollipops,
　Which I'll divide e-*qually.*

SALLY: (*to* TOMMY) We're on a brink!
TOMMY: (*to* SALLY) I saw him wink!
　　　　　Oh, Sarah, dear,
　　　　　I sadly fear
　Our apprehensions tally.
1ST RUF: Sally look up,
　　　Tommy don't frown! (*Holds out his hands.*)
　　Don't mind my hands
　　'Cause they're rayther brown.
　It's time we were toddling off to town,
　　　Come, Sally, I'll take the middle.
　　(*Universal dance to symphony – the last bar is played abruptly, and
　　the* 1ST RUFFIAN's *manner changes to the ferocious – drags off*
　　CHILDREN, *followed by* 2ND RUFFIAN – SIR ROWLAND *in a
　　desponding attitude,* LADY MACASSAR *drags off* SIR ROWLAND
　　triumphantly.)

SCENE 3.　　*Wood scene*
　　　　(*Enter the* FAIRY-BIRD QUEEN.)
FAIRY: Awake my feathered friends and subjects, all,
　　Let each obey her royal mistress' call;
　　Shake off the drowsy trammels which now fetter her,
　　It is the early bird that – well, et cetera.
　　　　(*Music. The* FAIRY-BIRDS *awake.* OTHERS *enter. Tableau. Grand
　　　　Fairy-Bird ballet, and exeunt* FAIRIES.) (*Enter* 1ST RUFFIAN *and*
　　　　TOMMY. *This scene played in imitation of the one between Arthur
　　　　and Hubert, in 'King John'.*)
1ST RUF: Now stretch your little legs, my little lad.
　　Heigho! Heigho! Heigho! I –
TOMMY:　　　　　　　　　You are sad.
　　Methinks nobody should be sad but *I* –
　　My uncle hates, but I know not why.
　　I have no father now – because he's dead.
　　I would, I would I'd been *your* son instead.
1ST RUF: (*Starts, aside.*) If he goes on like this, I'm safe to rue it.
　　And shall not have the heart to go and do it!
TOMMY: You're not quite well – your knees both knock together.
　　You're changing colour –
1ST RUF:　　　　　　　　Am I? – It's the weather.
TOMMY: (*producing a pie from his pocket*) Here is a tartlet – with it I can part.

1ST RUF: (*rejecting it*) I'm tired of pastry. (*Sighs.*) And I'm *sick o 'tart.*
    Read here, young Thomas. (*Hands him paper.*)
TOMMY: Oh, good gracious *me*!
    A letter from my aunt – what's this I see?
    (*Reads.*)   'Let dogs delight to bark and bite,
              For 'tis their nature *toe*,
              But little boys are different quite,
              Which Thomas ought to know.
              He on a tender nursery maid
              His teeth did exercise,
              For doing which, I'm much afraid,
              That heedless of his cries,
              From out his ill-conditioned head
              You must take all of *them*.
              Dare but to disobey, and dread
              The rage of Lady M.'
    Must you with pinchers then my molars take?
    Have you the heart? When *your* teeth did but ache
    I knit my handkerchief about your brow,
    Every ten minutes said – 'How are you now?'
    And tended you so carefully all day
    When you were suffering from neuralgi-*a*.
1ST RUF: I've sworn to do it.
TOMMY: (*falling against him*) Won't it hurt?
1ST RUF: No doubt,
    But with this iron must I take 'em out.
TOMMY: Ah, you're in fun, you smile although sardonically,
    Admit that you are speaking now *iron*-ically.
1ST RUF: You'd best submit at once, small infant, come,
    For out comes every *tooth* of yours by *gum*;
    I draw them well, if that's a satisfaction,
    Though poor I am of very *good extraction*:
    Come, like a college man, for fame athirst,
    I'll try if I can't take a double first –
    At once, they come out – strong as well as brittle ones
    At one fell swoop!
TOMMY: Oh, oh! what all my little ones!
    Don't get excited – if you really will
    I will not struggle – stone I'll stand as still,
    Or as a mouse, or the proverbial stock,
    Or as the hands of the Victoria Clock;
    Oh, have you never suffered from – you must –
    I wouldn't for a kingdom *you* annoy?
    (*Takes his hand.*) Don't you believe me?

Victoria clock: almost certainly the clock face of 'Big Ben', facing the Victoria Tower in the new Houses of Parliament, completed in 1858.

1ST RUF: (*overcome*)   *I believe you, my boy!*
TOMMY: I think I see the dentist's room (his drawing room) see there –
    There's the deceptive operating chair,
    Prepared with open arms – and there – see, see,
    That smiling little gentleman is he,
    Who shortly means to send a madd'ning pain
    Through your poor jaws into your bursting brain;
    He blandly tells you 'Not to be afraid',
    And drawing nearer to the doomed decayed
    Before you are aware of it – oh, oh!
    Murder! Police! – Ugh! Ooh! Ah! He! *Let go!*
    Ah! Hee! Ugh! Yah! – But as you foam and tear,
    The small man stops you with – '*Your tooth is there!*'
1ST RUF: (*completely overcome*) Come to my arms; I'd not touch one of *those*
    For every farthing that your uncle owes.
        (*Embrace* – TOMMY *over shoulder is met by tooth-extracting
        instrument, is terrified and embraces over the other shoulder.*)
        DUET – *Air, 'The Fricassée'*
1ST RUF: No, small boy, you shall not suffer
            Torture, though I brought you,
            You ought *not* to suffer, ought you?
        I'm not such a bad hearted buffer,
            Though p'r'aps at *first* you thought I *was.*
    You may laugh, you may laugh – Ha! Ha!
    And Sir Rowland may chaff – Ha! Ha!
    But I wouldn't kill this lad for all the *gold* in his exchequer,
    So, my pretty little boy, sustain your pretty little pecker.
        (*dance*)
TOMMY: I hope you will not think me rude, sir,
            But I cannot *find* a word,
            That is any *kind* of word,
        Sufficient to bespeak my gratitude, sir.
        Though 'pon my word, I'm very much obliged,
            And I'm sure that my papa,
            Were he living now,
1ST RUF: Ha! Ha!
TOMMY: Would reward you *liberally*; but alas, in a three-decker,
        He was drowned!
1ST RUF: Come, *as* I *said* before, sustain your little pecker.
        '*The Fricassée Dance*'
        (*a shriek heard*)
1ST RUF: Ha! what is that? a shriek – a female's.
TOMMY: True, man!
        Some one a-molesting a defenceless woman;

---

three-decker: war vessel with three gun-decks.

The man who would refuse to strike a b-low
In her defence –
1ST RUF: Of course, why don't you go!
TOMMY: It may seem strange, it's no less strange than true,
    That's what I was about to say to *you*.
        (*another shriek*)
1ST RUF: (*aside*) They come! 'tis well!
TOMMY: (*Falls against him.*)   Oh, dear!
1ST RUF: (*aside*)   I've saved the brother!
    Now I'll *assist her* – that is, *save the other*!
        (*They hide – enter* 2ND RUFFIAN *dragging on* SALLY. *Hurried music.*)
2ND RUF: You must be mine. Ha! Ha! You understand me.
SALLY: (*melodramatically*) R-ruffianly r-obber, instantly unhand me!
2ND RUF: To finish you at once, your aunt decreed,
    But 'twas thy matchless beauty which –
SALLY: Indeed!
    These nails shall rend that beauty then.
2ND RUFF: Pray mind!
    'Twould render me more dangerously inclined.
    (*Kneels.*) Take up that word again, or take up *me*!
SALLY: No; a policemen shall do that you'll see.
2ND RUF: (*rising and seizing her hand*) Pooh! There are no police about, my dear;
    You're mine!
SALLY: Where *is* there a policeman!
TOMMY: *Here*! (*picture*)
    As N. T. Hicks would say, 'approach her – do;
    And instantly I'll put an *end* to you!'
    I feel a proud contempt for cuts and scars;
    The valour of a dozen 'Coburg' tars,
    Six 'Surrey' pirates – folks who scatter brains
    As trifles – dances up and down my veins,
    Impelling me, although perhaps 'tis rash,
    At once to settle your plebeian hash.
2ND RUF: My *hash*! You fancy you're at *Hashley's*, eh?
    Ha! Ha!
TOMMY: (*imitating him*) Ha! Ha! Come on at once I say,
    And soon your length you'll measure on the ground.
    Why don't you *square* and let us have a *round*?

N. T. Hicks: a popular melodramatic actor at theatres such as the Surrey and the Royal Victoria. Known as 'Brayvo Hicks' on account of the cry that usually greeted his first appearance, he specialised in playing heroes.
'*Coburg*' *tars*: see footnote on p. 46, above.
'*Surrey*' *pirates*: formerly known as the Royal Circus, the Surrey Theatre was situated in Black-friars Road. It was especially famous for its nautical melodramas starring T. P. Cooke.
Hashleys: Astley's was a London Ampitheatre off the Westminster Bridge Road, famous for its spectacular equestrian entertainments and its stagings of famous battles.

2ND RUF: (*contemptuously*) A round with *you*, you stupid little *flat*?

TOMMY: You flat-ter me.

2ND RUF: I'll flatten you – take that!

> (*Hits* TOMMY, *who falls doubled up into* 1ST RUFFIAN's *arms – then recovers and goes to back with* SALLY.)

1ST RUF: (*to* 2ND RUFFIAN) Hit one of your own size! – Pitch into *me*.

2ND RUF: My friend and pitcher, never! As for *she*,
    She's mine, so pitch her over!

1ST RUF: (*Snaps his fingers in his face.*) Pitcher! – *There*!

2ND RUF: To pit *yourself* against *me* can you *dare*.
    (*blusteringly*) Do I not *cow* you? Are you not aware I
    Am strong as bull? How *dare* you?

1ST RUF: Cow! – How *dare I*!

2ND RUF: I'll have that girl!

1ST RUF: She *is* a tempting dear.
    But, in attempting violence, I fear
    You may, by some unlucky mischance, run
    That ugly phiz this ugly fist upon.

2ND RUF: That you and I shall quarrel, friend, is clear.
    (*to* SALLY) Why to my passion turn you a deaf ear?

SALLY: Have you the insolence to ask me why?
    Deaf ear, indeed! – Your threats I do *def-y*!
    I have no wish with you to further talk;
    So make the best of my *def-eat*, and walk.

> (2ND RUFFIAN *makes a rush at her, but is interrupted by* 1ST RUFFIAN.)

1ST RUF: My friend, I recollect the day
    When father's razors I took up in play;
    Lathered my visage well, and said here goes,
    And with one swish sliced off an inch of nose.
    As towards the bell I bawling blindly grope,
    I see my parent looming through the soap;
    Though for a father I'm a touching sight,
    He brutally exclaims, 'it serves me right.'
    Since then, my friend, I count him worst of fools,
    Who cuts himself by playing with edged tools.
    (*advancing*) My razor's keen and cold – ah! How d'ye feel?
    The sort of soap I use is this – (*Draws.*) *Cast steel*!

SALLY: Oh, Tom, they're going to fight, dear, I declare!

TOMMY: Pray don't be frightened, Sal; I'll see all fair.

2ND RUF: Upon this sward this sword shall stretch you soon.

TOMMY: (*confidently to leader*) Could you oblige us with a combat tune?

> (*Music. Fight between the* RUFFIANS. 1ST RUFFIAN *gets the* 2ND RUFFIAN *on his knee;* 1ST RUFFIAN *drops his sword, and*

---

flat: a fool.

Cast steel: Castile – a hard soap, usually mottled, made with olive oil and soda.

*2ND RUFFIAN is about to dispatch him when SALLY snatches a
pistol from his belt in the old Coburg style, and TOMMY snatches
up the fallen sword, and sticks it in the small of 2ND RUFFIAN's
back where it remains, he appears to feel uncomfortable from the
introduction and falls. – Picture.)*

2ND RUF: (*to* SALLY) Maid, you did steal my heart. (*to* TOMMY) And as for you,
Unfortunately you have *steeled* it too.
(*Indicates* 1ST RUFFIAN.) You'll hang ere long for piercing *that ere lung*!
That man that you *be'old* will soon *be 'ung.*

1ST RUF: I wouldn't hurry you; but die, my man,
As soon as you conveniently can; –
It's getting rather late, as you're aware.

TOMMY: Come don't be disagreeable – die.

2ND RUF: Well – *there*! (*Stiffens himself and dies.*)

1ST RUF: I'll come back soon, my pretty little children:
Don't wander far, the paths are so bewild'rin',
And very likely you may lose your way.
Come on, my friend! Remember, dears – good day!
(*labouring under the weight of the* 2ND RUFFIAN) Oh, dear! Oh, dear!

2ND RUF: (*reviving*) What, am I heavy?

1ST RUF: Rather.
Suppose you walk.

2ND RUF: I will – like Hamlet's father.
(*Exeunt. Stage becomes darker – distant thunder.*)

SALLY: It's getting very dark, oh dear! It lightened!
Tommy!

TOMMY: Well, Sarah dear?

SALLY: I am getting frightened:
That fellow's exit seemed to me like slinking off.

TOMMY: Don't talk like that! Oh dear, it won't bear thinking of;
Left in a forest all alone! – I wish you
Wouldn't – ugh! – say such things – ugh! ugh! a-tishoo! (*Sneezes.*)

SALLY: Alas, poor Tom's a-cold.

TOMMY: Oh, Sal, my pet,
I never had enough blackberries yet:
We'll wander through the woods, dear, and employ ourselves,
In gathering a lot – come, let's enjoy ourselves?
DUET – '*Limerick Races*'

TOMMY: Now, Sally, dear, be good?
Come, dontee cry, ha' done now;
Let's wander through the wood,
And have a bit of fun now?
Come, come, be stout and bold;
No nonsense let me see, dear!

SALLY: Oh, Tom, I shall take cold!

TOMMY: Pooh! Pooh! take 'old o' me, dear!
Chorus – Whack, fol, etc.

                    For my part I enjoy
                        A hat full of blackberries,
                    Much more than a tuck in
                        At Farrance's or Verey's.
SALLY: Well, I prefer a bun,
                        A maccaroon, or ice, dear.
TOMMY: But blackberries cost nothing,
                        And they're filling at the price, dear.
                    Chorus – Whack, fol, etc.
                    Irish Jig.

SCENE 4.   *Arched chamber*
                    (*Enter* SIR ROWLAND, *followed by* PHYSICIAN.)
SIR ROWL: Throw physic to the dogs!
PHYSICIAN: That's what my *lady*
                    Also remarks, and yet, without its *aid, I*
                    Am (not to beat about the bush) *afraid* I
                    Shan't be successful, and, Sir R., she *may* die!
SIR ROWL: (*aside*) Die! She is dyed already black as night
                    Or *Day* and Martin's blacking – quit my sight.
PHYSICIAN: Sir, she is troubled with thick coming fancies,
                    And falls at times into peculiar trances!
                    When in the night all's quiet as a mouse,
                    Amina-like, she stalks about the house.
                    Asleep, sometimes she moans, and sobs – she suffers,
                    Sometimes she wildly snatches up the snuffers
                    With suicidal looks, but with a frown, again
                    Appears to change her mind and puts them down again.
SIR ROWL: Away!
PHYSICIAN: Sir Rowland!
SIR ROWL: Quit the room, I say.
PHYSICIAN: (*going*) An MRCS and an LSA, an MD too, addressed in such a tone!
SIR ROWL: Doctor, away! I wish to be alone.
PHYSICIAN: (*aside*) Ah! I shall have to physic you ere long,
                    And p'raps the dose may be a *leetle* strong.
                        (*Is going; is met by* 1ST RUFFIAN, *who has entered quietly –*
                        PHYSICIAN *makes a comically terrified exit.* SIR ROWLAND
                        transfixed at sight of 1ST RUFFIAN.)
SIR ROWL: Returned to *haunt* the children's uncle – eh?
                    (*aside*) Alas, I fear they'll never go away;
                    In summer time, as well as winter p'raps,
                    I, on my *hands*, shall have these dreadful *chaps*.

Farrance's or Verey's: confectioners: Thomas Farrance's shop was located at 67 Charing Cross;
Charles Verey's at 229 Regent Street.
Day and Martin's Blacking: Blacking manufacturers located at 97 High Holborn.
Amina: sleep-walking heroine of Bellini's opera *La Somnambula*.

1ST RUF: My lord, they say five moons were seen tonight.

SIR ROWL: Five moons? Five fiddlesticks! Go quit my sight!

1ST RUF: They say that virtue is its own reward,
        But vice is vice versey – so, my lord,
        That little bill I'll trouble you to settle,
        As yet we've not set eyes upon your metal.

SIR ROWL: (*in* 1ST RUFFIAN*'s ear*) Is the boy gone?

1ST RUF: Gone as the gonest 'coon.

SIR ROWL: Alas! I feel that I shall follow soon.
        (*Seizes* 1ST RUFFIAN.) Thy hand hath murdered him! Poor Tommy –
        gone!

1ST RUF: Thy hand! *I was* a mere au*tomy-ton*!

SIR ROWL: Yes, I had mighty cause to wish him dead,
        But thou hadst none to kill him.

1ST RUF: Want of bread!
        Hunger is –

SIR ROWL: Bother! hadst *thou* not been by,
        A *fellow near* to do a *felo-ny*,
        A wretch from whom a single glance is quite
        Sufficient to destroy one's appetite;
        The sort of vagabond whose constant trade is
        To grab the reticules of fat old ladies,
        Smash some poor struggling baker's window panes,
        Garotte the gouty in the Brompton Lanes,
        To pounce on children paralysed with fear,
        Hadst thou but asked of what I could be thinking,
        Thine eye looked the remotest bit like winking;
        Deep shame had struck me dumb, but no, no, no!
        You gloried in the business – go, man, go!

1ST RUF: Go, go! Besides my pay, ungrateful dog,
        I hoped to get at least a glass of grog,
        But from this strange behaviour, I suppose
        I'm to be satisfied with these *two goes*.

SIR ROWL: The manner of their final exit tell,
        But break it gently to me – I'm not well.
           DUET – *Air, 'Giles Scroggins'*

1ST RUF: I took him down a narrow walk,
        And drew each tooth out like a cork;
        But when I'd taken two or three,
        His piteous howls got over me,
        So I put him out of his miserie.
          With a ri-tol-de-ridy-ray.

SIR ROWL: What would my brother say, were he
        Acquainted with this villanie?

Gone . . . 'coon: a gone 'coon was someone overtaken by disaster; literally, a racoon on the point of capture.

A prey to agony and woe,
Away, away, away I'll go!
But where? – I little care to know.
(*agonisedly*) Ri-tol-de-riddle, etc. (*Rushes off.*)

1ST RUF: (*mysteriously to audience*) Now, who I am you're not aweer; –
I'm not so bad as I appear.
At present I'm unstained by crime;
But, public, at the proper time,
You'll be surprised to find that I'm –
Ri-tol-de-ridy-ridy-ray. (*Exit.*)
('*Lord Lovel*', *played: – Enter* GOVERNESS *and* PHYSICIAN, *on tip toe, à la Gentlewoman and Physician in 'Macbeth'.*)
DUET – *Air, 'Lord Lovel'*

GOVERN: The hour is nigh, when my lady –
PHYSICIAN: Oh, my!
Miss J., I must say my flesh creeps;
For you say, miss, that she
In her habit de nuit,
    Walks about?
GOVERN: Beyond doubt, while she sleeps and keeps
Her eyes close as wax – never peeps.
But though closed are her eyes, yet her mouth –
PHYSICIAN: You surprise
Me – you don't mean she speaks?
GOVERN: Yes I do.
And her words to repeat
I'm a deal too discreet;
    But they're terrible words to list to.
PHYSICIAN: Oh, *you*, would tell me! Oh, tell me them, do.
(LADY MACASSAR, *in a burlesque imitation of Lady Macbeth's midnight toilet, enters, and comes through symphony – her eyes are closed.*)
GOVERN: Her eyes are closed – extinguished is each peeper –
(LADY MACASSAR *seems agitated by some internal emotion.*)
PHYSICIAN: A *train* of thought seems passing o'er that *sleeper*.
This is indeed a very ticklish question.
GOVERN: I think it's *crime*.
PHYSICIAN: *I* think it's indigestion.
(LADY MACASSAR *opens one eye.*)
GOVERN: See, she awakes – for one eye opes to view.
PHYSICIAN: The other one *I 'opes*'ll do so too.
(LADY MACASSAR *commences rubbing her left hand.*)
GOVERN: See how she *scours* her hand, 'tis *dire* to see her.
PHYSICIAN: (*solemnly*) She *is* a *dyer hand scourer*, my dear.
For that however we've no right to snub her;
But let the strange old *card* enjoy her *rubber*.

(LADY MACASSAR *suddenly bursts into song. – Air, 'King of the Cannibal Islands'*)

LADY M: Hokey! Pokey!

PHYSICIAN: This is rum!

LADY M: Husband mine, we must be dumb,
    Our counsel keep. –

PHYSICIAN: Precisely, mum.

LADY M: Hey, what a cannibal *I am*,
    Than Lady Macbeth worse by far
    Am I – she loved her old papa,
    I fancy I resemble. –

PHYSICIAN:⎫
GOVERN: ⎬ *(listening)*   Hah!

LADY M: More Lucretia Borgi*a*!
    I fancy I was born to shine
    As a dramatic heroine,
    With dagger, bowl, and poison'd wine!
    Hey! What a cannibal I am!
    (*She dances the 'College Hornpipe' and exits.*)

PHYSICIAN: *(aside)* We are alone. *(aloud)* List, maiden, while I tell
    My ardent passion?

GOVERN: *(coyly)*   Oh!

PHYSICIAN: *Ma belle!*
    (*Symphony to operatic duet – The* GOVERNESS *and* PHYSICIAN
    prepare to sing after the fashion of Italian lovers, he hands her a
    voice lozenge, etc. – as they are about to commence, a bell heard.)

PHYSICIAN: My bell! (*Rushes off, followed by* GOVERNESS.)

SCENE 5.   *A wood scene. A large gnarled tree, right, with a hollow space in trunk; a bank with brushwood, left.* SIR ROWLAND *lying exhausted on the bank. The* FAIRY-BIRD QUEEN *standing watching him – several* FAIRIES *grouped in an attentive attitude. Soft music.*

FAIRY: An hour has he slept. See, he awakes,
    Sufficiently to sigh: observe he makes,
    An effort now to rise. Begone, each fay;
    Come when I call!

SIR ROWL: *(dreaming)* Dear brother Bill!

FAIRY: *(to* FAIRIES)   Away! *(Exeunt.)*

SIR ROWL: *(Starts up.)* Where am I? Surely – oh – ah, I forget
    Fairies,
    I'm in the forest; Rowland am I not;
    I'm stupid, sorrow-stricken, savage, sad;
    I fancy too I'm going rather mad. (*wind*)
    The tempest's coming on! The Tempest – oh,
    A play of somebody's – I'm Prospero.
    (*with dignity*) My revels now are ended: Leicester Square

Is melted into air – into thin air:
The cloud clapp'd towers of th'Alhambra Palace,
The solemn Shades, e'en the *Great Globe* itself,
Shall all dissolve! Why am I thus inveighing?
Alas, I'm growing wild; and what I'm saying
I know no more about, as I'm a sinner,
Than does an Irish member after dinner.
Feelings of chilly languor o'er me creep again –
(*Yawns.*) A capital idea! – I'll go to sleep again. (*Sleeps.*)
    (*Hurried music* – SALLY *enters, cold with her nose red.*)
SALLY: I am *so* miserable; and, alack,
I'm sure our kind protector won't come back.
Such dismal thoughts my anxious bosom fill:
Poor brother Tommy too has gone *so* ill;
The blackberries with him have disagreed;
Poor fellow! Oh, he's very bad indeed.
    (TOMMY *enters, with a very 'come-to-griefy' aspect, and with the*
    traces of blackberry juice round his mouth.)
TOMMY: Oh dear, oh dear! I'm very much afraid,
That in the dark some slight mistake I've made;
And that I have abused this splendid oppor-
Tunity by eating what's improper.
I feel as oft I've done whan 'pa was living,
And a grand dinner party he's been giving;
Enjoined to hold our tongues and not be pert,
We've been allowed to gorge at the dessert;
With faces full of eagerness and hope,
Shining with innocence and yellow soap,
Amongst the oranges we ran our rigs.
Then dashed off at a tangent into figs;
When my neighbour, asked what we'd have next,
Paused for an instant, puffy and perplexed,
Then gurgled forth – with elevated spoons –
'Some pears, and apples, and some maccaroons!'
Added to which, by slow but sure degrees,
Were olives, almonds, and some damson cheese;
And when no further dishes could be found,
We both were carried to be kissed all round.
SALLY: Oh, every word you say, dear Tom, is true:
But recollect, love, I'm as bad as you.
(*Leans heavily on* TOMMY.) For very full indeed's my sorrow's cup.

Alhambra Palace: originally the Royal Panopticon of Science and Art, situated in Leicester
Square, it was converted into the Alhambra Palace in 1858 as a venue for entertainment. The
'cloud-capp'd towers' were the turrets on either side of the building.
Great Globe: erected in the Leicester Square Gardens in 1851, a project of James Wyld's to
celebrate the international nature of the Great Exhibition; subsequently demolished.

TOMMY: (*struggling with the weight*) Would you oblige me, dear, by bearing up?
    (*suddenly*) Sal! I've a bright idea!

SALLY: Oh! Pray tell *me* it.

TOMMY: Let's die! What d'ye think of it?

SALLY: (*doggedly*)   Don't see it.

TOMMY: (*Clutches her hand – tremulous music all through following speech.*)
    Think of the thousands who will tell our story
    Over the fire o' nights for years – there's glory!
    In the dim future – ages, ages on,
    Parents will ponder well our fate upon,
    And though mayhaps his fondness he alleges,
    Will with their uncle leave no little pledges,
    And into nurseries our tale will creep,
    And little children at our fate will weep,
    And drop (as sobs of sympathy they utter)
    Tears of compassion on their bread and butter;
    To my proposal, girl, you *must* agree,
    Sarah, just cast your eye upon that tree;
    See, he has, scouting at an adage good,
    Hollow'd before he was out of the wood.
          (*Grasps her wrist tightly – she shrinks.*)
    'Twas made for you and me – (*aside*) ha! ha! she shrunk,
    I'll put this little baggage in the *trunk*:
    (*aloud*) Come be a *heroine*.

SALLY: (*emphatically*) I *will*, you'll see.

TOMMY: Brayvo!

SALLY: You shall not *hear a whine* from me.

TOMMY: 'Tis well! – But ere *we enter for the Oaks*,
    Why we must do as do the op'ra folks.
    Express our anguish, dear, for the last time,
    In modern and alas! – *spasmodic* rhyme.
          DUET – *Air, 'Paddy's Wedding'*

TOMMY: Oh, Sally dear, I am so queer, I
        Feel so ill, I do indeed;
      Those blackberries with me very s-
        Hockingly have disagreed;
      I'm an example sad un*to*
        Small boys who blindly gorge and stuff
      When they're allowed, and never know
        When of good things, they've had enough.
      (*spasmodic symphony*)

SALLY: A heroine don't care a pin,
      Whatever her fate in life may be;
        Since there's no way

---

the Oaks: a horse race run at Epsom by three-year-old fillies.

    To end the play.
    But this, of course, I *must* agree;
    But if that fellow I could catch,
     For cruelly deceiving us,
    His good-for-nothing face I'd scratch,
TOMMY: (*faintly*) Oh, Sal, I'm getting wuss and wuss!
    (*They get into trunk of tree melodramatically to symphony.*)
    (*Fairy music. The* FAIRY QUEEN *and* FAIRIES *enter with large leaves.*)
FAIRY: These little children are my special care,
    Of course they only sleep, as you're aware;
    So with this leafy counterpane we'll cover 'em,
    Though we can't help their coming thus to grief,
    Still we can give them this out-door *re-lief.*
    (*The* FAIRIES *cover the children with the leaves –* FAIRY QUEEN *waves her wand, and the* FAIRIES *vanish.*)
SIR ROWL: (*Wakes.*) Give me another horse, bind up my – bother
    As usual, I've been dreaming of my brother.
    This state of things won't do – I can't go home,
    I'll turn weir-wolf, a goblin, imp, or gnome!
    Off to that German mystic mountain fly,
    Where fiends keep up their midnight revelry;
    And there become, mids't storms and lightnings darts,
    A member of the *Society of Hartz,*
    I may say, *brocken* hearts. (*Sinks on bank.*)
FAIRY: That's very true.
SIR ROWL: (*suddenly turning with his glass to his eye*) Excuse me, my dear
    madam, who are *you*?
FAIRY: Queen of the forest fairy-birds am I,
    Birds it is well to be befriended by;
    Heedless of sportsman's gun or schoolboy's stone,
    We look upon this forest as our own.
    You, Rowland, have our fairy footpaths crossed,
    And, as I think that you are scarcely lost,
    And only wandering from the road of virtue,
    I will reclaim you, there (*Offers her hand –* SIR ROWLAND *shrinks.*) I
    will not hurt you.
    (*She clasps his hand – music, piano, 'Still so gently'.*)
SIR ROWL: Oh, gracious, what a pleasant kind of feeling
    Seems gently o'er my seven senses stealing.
FAIRY: What! Art thou penitent?
SIR ROWL: Could you but see
    Into this heart, you would believe in me.
    Would that my brother Bill were here, for I'd

German mystic mountain: the Brocken Mountain in the Hartz range of mountains near Göttingen, the traditional site of Walpurgis Night. Location of a famous scene in Goethe's *Faust*.

Gladly give up his wealth – and with my bride
In meanly furnished two-pair back reside.
Without a hope of ever once again
Indulging in Moselle or Still Champagne,
Port – e'en South African, or e'er again Sherry,
Or without *halfpenny* in the *peni*tentiary.
FAIRY: Dost thou remember him?
SIR ROWL: At school you'd say,
I do indeed, as it were yesterday.
How all my battles manfully he fought,
When overbearing bullying boys sought
My services as servant – two or three
At *school* tried hard to make *a-cad-o' me.*
Once in particular, a dreadful row,
In which he half killed Jones – I see it now.
> (*Corsican Brothers' Ghost Melody played.* FAIRY QUEEN *waves
> her wand, and through transparency a school fight is seen going on.
> The* CHILDREN *grouped in exact imitation of the duel scene in the
> Corsican Brothers – a red-headed* BOY *upset on the ground, and
> 'BROTHER BILL' in the triumphant attitude of Chateau Renaud.
> Exit the* FAIRY QUEEN *and the* 1ST RUFFIAN *glides on, à la
> Ghost.*)

1ST RUF: (*snatching off his wig, etc.*) Rowland!
SIR ROWL: Can I believe my eyes?
1ST RUF: Don't start.
SIR ROWL: Alive!
1ST RUF: Alive – come to a brother's heart. (*wild embrace*)
            SONG – '*Willie we have missed you*'
SIR ROWL: Oh, Billy is it *you*, dear,
                Safe, safe at home!
            Your death then was a 'doo', dear
                For in the billows' foam,
            I heard you met your fate.
                But it makes my heart rejoice,
            To shake your hand again, and hear
                That dear familiar voice.
            At once I will assist you
                Unto a brush and comb:
            For Billy, I have missed you,
                Welcome, welcome, home.

---

two-pair back: apartment consisting of back rooms up two flights of stairs.
Corsican Brothers' Ghost Melody: This piece of music became very popular after it had been
played during the ghost scene in Dion Boucicault's *The Corsican Brothers*, first performed at
the Princess's Theatre on 24 September 1852. At the end of act I the ghost of Louis dei Franchi
glides across the stage in the presence of his twin brother Fabien. A vision then appears to
Fabien of a glade in the Forest of Fontainbleau: Louis lies dead on the ground, whilst Chateau
Renaud, who has just killed him in a duel, stands wiping his sword.

1ST RUF: You thought me dead – I am alive and here,
       To guard the lives of my two children dear
       This habit I assumed – the which did come
       From Nathan's Masquerade *Empo-ri-um.*
       Where are the dears? I'm yearning to enfold 'em
       Both to a parent's – a – heart!
           (FAIRY *waves her feather – the tree splits in two, discovering the*
           BABES *asleep.*)
FAIRY: See, there, behold 'em!
           (*Music –* TOMMY *and* SALLY *go through the business of the*
           Monster when awakened to life.)
TOMMY: What do I see? It cannot be – Ha! Ha!
TOMMY:⎫
      ⎬ It is! It ain't! It is! *It is* our pa! (*All embrace!*)
SALLY: ⎭
FAIRY: Well, now, as things appear to be serene,
       There's nothing left me but to change the scene.
       In *feather's* Tom – to look *down* longer, Sally has
       No cause. – welcome to my feather *palliasse.*
           (*Transformation scene –* FAIRIES *discovered in their feathery nests*
           – SIR ROWLAND *advances to Audience with the hand of* 1ST
           RUFFIAN.*)
SIR ROWL: A brace of brothers – that is *two Adelphi*
       In their new domicile – the *New* Adelphi,
       Trusting you'll recollect their past endeavours,
       Beg humbly a renewal of your favours;
       And that tonight you'll give – to calm our fear –
       A hearty English *old* Adelphi cheer.

           FINALE – *'Skin a ma link'*
SIR ROWL: Ere the curtain falls tonight, say you're not severe, now;
           But that in our hopes we're right-public, please to cheer now.
TOMMY: We ne'er again will naughty be, lessons we will learn, sirs,
SALLY: If we have your clemency tonight contrived to earn, sirs.
1ST RUFF: Give us a lift, oh, public, do; give us a lift tonight, oh –
           We ask it as a favour, which we fear we have no right to.
           (*Repeat.*)

           CURTAIN

Nathan's: L. and N. Nathan, 24 Tichborne St, Haymarket, supplied theatrical costumes and fancy dress for masquerades. Founded in 1790, the firm merged with Berman's in 1972.
business of monster . . . life: probably based on a scene in H. Milner's *Frankenstein* (1823), which was based on Mary Shelley's novel.
New Adelphi: the original Adelphi Theatre had been demolished in 1858. A new theatre was built on its site and opened on 27 December 1858.

II Act IV of *The Lancashire Lass*, Queen's Theatre, London 1868

THE LANCASHIRE LASS; or, TEMPTED, TRIED AND TRUE

A domestic melodrama in a prologue and four acts

First produced at the Royal Ampitheatre, Liverpool, on 28 October 1867; afterwards at the Queen's Theatre, London, on 24 July 1868; with the following casts:

	Liverpool	*London*
ROBERT REDBURN, *an adventurer*	Mr Brade	Mr H. Irving
NED CLAYTON, *a young engineer*	Mr John Wilson	Mr C. Wyndham
JOHNSON	Mr Thompson	Mr S. Emery
SPOTTY	——	Mr L. Brough
DANVILLE, *old man*	Mr Lunt	Mr J. Clayton
KIRBY, *a yeoman*	——	Mr H. Mellon
JELLICK	Mr Hunter	Mr W. H. Stephens
SERGEANT DONOVAN	Mr Cahill	Mr Montgomery
PHIL ANDREWS	——	Mr Charles
MILDER	——	Mr J. Howard
KITELY	——	Mr Keeth Webb
POSTMAN	——	Mr J. Vincent
RUTH KIRBY	Miss Hill	Miss Nelly Moore
KATE GARSTONE	Miss M. Cooper	Miss H. Hodson
FANNY DANVILLE	Miss C. Denvil	Miss Montague

PROLOGUE

SCENE 1.   *A green lane.* REDBURN *discovered, sketching – sitting on camp stool that afterwards folds up and forms a walking-stick. Easel and picture before him.* SPOTTY, *a farm labourer, looking on admiring; music until curtain is up.*

SPOT: Wonderful! Wonderful!

RED: Ah, marvellous painter, that can so astonish a rustic. You have a taste for the fine arts, Spotty.

SPOT: Fine *harts*, indeed. Not I, I don't know nothin' about fine harts; but I never seed anything more naturaller. The picture seems to grow like, and that cow in partickler, she's the very moral of one of master's.

RED: I'm very good at cows.

Spot: So am I, milking 'em.

RED: Now, by taking a few liberties with the landscape, I can contrive to sneak in just one corner of your master's farm; then when it's finished we'll make him a present of it to stick up in his best parlour. It'll please him, won't it?

SPOT: Well, I don't know so much about that, for master don't care so much for what you call the fine *harts*, sir. It ain't much in his way. Master's never had no heddication; and though he's got a good heye for an horse, he don't care much for pictures. Besides, Miss Ruth, *she* draws and paints lovely, and he don't care for no one else's drawings. She's a deal cleverer than you are, sir, ever so much.

RED: (*Looks at him.*) Spotty, I respect you, because you say what you think.

SPOT: Thankee, sir.

RED: I have never seen any of Miss Ruth's sketches, but she is certainly very accomplished.

SPOT: Bless you, sir, she's as clever as she's good, and as good as she's handsome.

RED: Spotty, your sentiments do you honour; she plays beautifully, doesn't she?

SPOT: Well, she seems to me to make the pianny speak. Not as she can't do the reg'lar *firework* business all up and down, picking a toone to pieces and putting it together again, as *I* call it. Oh, yes; but to hear her a-sittin' in the twilight, playing some old simple song sometimes, too, a-singing it in a soft, gentle sort of way! Oh, it's very soothing to the spirits! I've listened many a time, sir, to her, till I was so overcome I had to go and have a reg'lar good cry in the dairy.

RED: (*painting*) Ah, some young fellow will be snapping up such a treasure one of these fine days.

SPOT: Bless yer, she's engaged hard and fast, all's settled.

RED: (*sneeringly*) Of course.

SPOT: But Ned Clayton, *he* ain't worthy of her.

RED: Of course he isn't, whoever he may be.

SPOT: He's a fine young chap, is Mr Clayton, but Miss Ruth's fit to marry a nobleman.

RED: Of course.

SPOT: But I don't know the nobleman as is fit to marry *her*.

RED: Your acquaintance with peerage is probably limited, Spotty.

SPOT: What chance has she of seeing anyone? Her father never takes her to no
parties. Never gives no parties. She'll marry Mr Clayton, and all her accomplishments will go for nothing.

RED: That's the mistake of teaching people too much.

SPOT: Well, you see, master's never been taught to read or write, and when his
daughter was left to him to bring up, he determined to make *her* as clever as
he was ignorant, and he spared no pains and no money on having her brought
up a reg'lar, *downright* lady.

RED: Then it's to be hoped she'll marry a regular downright *gentleman*.

SPOT: If she marries a reg'lar, upright gentlemen, she'll do.

RED: Very smart of you, Spotty; anyone could tell you were from town, and not
a native to the manor born.

SPOT: No, sir, I wasn't born to no particular *manners*, I'm a reg'lar waifer and a
stray, as the saying is. I was born in Seven Dials, I believe, though I don't
remember it myself, being rather young at the time. I did Mr Kirby a good
turn once by accident, and he took me out of the gutter and tried to make a
farm servant of me; but you can't wash a black-a-moor white, can you, sir?

RED: Can't say I ever tried. Now you can carry my easel and camp stool home.
(REDBURN *takes off picture and* SPOTTY *folds up easel. Gives* SPOTTY
painting implements and picture.) There, there, now you are loaded.

SPOT: Yes, sir, like the gun; I'm loaded, and now I'm a-going off. (*Music; exit.*)

RED: What a fool I am to talk about her; my treacherous tongue will be my ruin
some day or other. But she is always in my thoughts, and I can speak and
dream of nothing else. Well, this very day will seal my fate; I have made an
impression on her heart – poor, vain, silly little beauty – which I think she
can't resist. If virtue triumph, and I lose her, farewell the Arcadian joys of
country life, once more to the full round of toil and labour in the ever grind-
ing Liverpudlian mill. But I think she is mine, mine hard and fast – hard and
fast. (*music*)

> (*Enter* KATE GARSTONE. *Looks back, as if watching, then
> hurriedly walks towards* REDBURN. *Places her hand on his arm;
> he turns. Music ceases.*)

RED: Kate, are you sure you are unobserved?

KATE: Yes. No one has seen me come. I have seen Ruth again and the ice is melt-
ing.

RED: Beneath the sun of your influence. Ah, Kate, at first she was cold enough,
but she'll thaw, my dear, she'll thaw.

KATE: Don't speak to me like that, Robert Redburn, ours is a business compact,
nothing more. You are in love with this Ruth Kirby, and you stay at her
father's farm, under pretence of taking rest from overwork, but really with a
view to –

RED: To taking Ruth herself – speak *plainly*, such is my object. I am weary of
your town beauties, all back hair and artificial bloom; this young girl is real,
and once away from the low surroundings of her humble home – once convinced that my love for her is genuine – who knows but that her gentle

---

Seven Dials: a district of London then notorious as a haunt of criminals.

influence may change *my* nature too; may make me something better than I am. Kate Garstone, you think perhaps this passion is nothing better than the lawless love of a selfish man of the world. Not so, I would risk my life for Ruth Kirby. I have fancied that I have loved before, but Ruth Kirby is my fate – my destiny.

KATE: We have met strangely here, and my word is pledged to help you.

RED: And your fear of exposure is my guarantee for your good faith. One word of mine, and –

KATE: No threats; no threats.

RED: Certainly not; but never forget that it would be madness to throw me over. I know your short career in the Metropolis, the accusation of theft brought against you, your mysterious departure –

KATE: The accusation was false.

RED: Of course. They always are.

KATE: It is from no *fear* that I am your willing tool in this vile plot. It is from another motive.

RED: Which is? (*Lights cigar, having thrown away the one he was smoking at the opening of scene.*)

KATE: Revenge! Revenge and hate, Robert Redburn.

RED: Ah! Two strong incentives for evil in the female breast. Revenge and hate, eh? Neither of those unpleasant sentiments are directed against me, I trust.

KATE: No, a woman never hates what she *despises*.

RED: Hem! I'm sorry you *despise* me, Kate, though I see no reason why you should not; still, on the whole, I think I would rather be the object of that feeling than of your *hate*. There's sometimes a flash in your dark eyes, and a quiver of the lip, to say nothing of a grasping action of the fingers that make me uncomfortable. I only notice this when I mention Mr Clayton. (KATE *starts. She twitches her fingers and bites her lips.*) Ah, there it is again. Come, now, is there any motive for revenge in that quarter? (*music*)

KATE: That is *my* story.

RED: Well, let's hear it. (*Sits on stool.*)

KATE: I was a forward, obstinate, self-willed girl from the first; always passionate and ungovernable. No one ever said a kind word to me, when a child; but when I used to sit and sulk at the front gate of mother's cottage I often used to see Ned Clayton passing on his way to the works; and he would give a pleasant nod and a civil word as he passed – the only one who ever did. At last I grew to *watch* for his coming, and he would stop longer and longer each time, and he would talk to me as no one ever talked to me before, aye, or since. I had never cared for living being but I soon learned to love Ned Clayton, and I thought by day and by night of nothing else. My whole being changed for the better beneath the softening influence I felt for that one kind friend. I was a good girl then, Robert Redburn, and mother marked the change and wondered at it. But the dream of joy was short indeed. One day I was watching – watching, oh, so anxiously, for Ned; at length he came, a woman leaning on his arm, and looking in his face tenderly while *he* (*with vehemence*) looked down at hers, as he had often looked in mine. They came nearer, and I saw that it was Ruth Kirby. (*Music louder at* 'RUTH' – RED-BURN *starts slightly and bites his lips.*) 'See, Kate', he said, 'this is Ruth, and she has promised to be my wife.' The earth swam before me; I felt a dull sick feeling at my heart, my brain reeled, and I though I should have fallen, but I managed to gasp forth some broken words, and they passed on. Not one kind soothing word had he uttered, he broke the news to me abruptly, and with a smile upon his cruel face – a smile to think how deep and deadly was the wound. But he little knew me; he little knew that I could *hate* as deeply as I had loved, and that I would never rest until I had my revenge. You now know why I assist you in this business, Robert Redburn, and why I will leave no stone unturned, until I deal him back the withering blow he struck me.

RED: (*Rises.*) It's an ill wind that blows nobody good, Kate, and your revenge once gratified you may settle down into –

KATE: Settle *down*, man? No, there is no peace for me *now* – there will be less then. No matter, there is still the river. (REDBURN *takes up camp stool.*) There is peace *there*, peace for the stormiest spirits, – rest for the weariest hearts.

RED: Don't talk rubbish. Look there, that diamond caught your eye the other day. I saw its sparkle reflected in those dark orbs, Kate. (KATE *gazes at his finger.*) See these, I know you love them.

KATE: (*in ecstasy*) Yes, I do, I do. I love them, the bright and beautiful tempters. (*touching his hand*) What is it worth?

RED: Worth your keeping faith with me, worth your labour in this delicate affair, which involves so much love and so much hate.

KATE: (*still staring at ring*) It's very beautiful, very, very beautiful. (*She is scarcely able to restrain herself from seizing the ring.*) A diamond, and of the first water is it not?

RED: (*folding up stool*) Ruth once mine, it is yours, Kate. Revenge is sweet and so are diamonds. Think of the double triumph.

KATE: What would you say if she was ready to fly with you this very night?

RED (*surprised*) Eh! (*recovering himself*) Well, I should say, great as is the impression *I* have made, greater far must have been your persuasions.

KATE: She is weak and silly at the best.

RED: Kate – I –

KATE: I say what I think – if I offend I'd better go.

RED: Don't be so impetuous – have it your own way.

KATE: She never really *cared* for Ned. Your fine speeches and town manners have dazzled her. I have never ceased to praise you – your generosity, your truth, your *honour*.

RED: (*aside*) He-hem!

KATE: I fanned a jealous feeling that existed into a flame, and made her lover out a deceiver and a cheat. She scarcely believes this, but whatever affection she may have fancied she felt for him exists no longer.

RED: And this fellow – this lover – this Clayton; does he dare to – ?

KATE: To love her? He loves her better than his life, or where would be your triumph and where *mine*? (*music*) He loves her as I know he once loved *me*.

I will break his heart, embitter his whole future even as his false conduct robbed *me* of every trace of happiness. I help you in this business, Robert Redburn, from no liking to you, be sure.

RED: No matter so long as you *do* help me, Kate, and am I to be sure of that to-night —

KATE: This very night I am well nigh certain; but you shall have the *assurance* from her own lips, or in her own handwriting. (*suddenly*) Her own handwriting would be best.

RED: I can scarcely think it possible, but you women are mysteries.

KATE: Yes, strange mysteries, are we not? (*musing*) A letter – yes – that will be well; yes, yes.

RED: (*looking at her*) So, goodbye for the present, Kate. I say, goodbye. She is in the clouds – threatening clouds they are, too. Goodbye.

KATE: Yes, yes, leave me alone – leave me alone. (REDBURN *shrugs his shoulders and after looking at her with interest, exits slowly.*) Now to get her to write but three lines, then the exposure and the triumph. Gold and diamonds and fine clothes are precious in my eyes, and set my gipsy blood aglow, but revenge on one who has basely wronged me is sweeter yet – sweeter yet? Something *more* than a lost sweetheart, Ned Clayton – a public shame, a blight upon Ruth's father's home, and all Kate Garstone's doing – sulky, stupid Kate as they called her once – all her doing, all her doing. (*Exit. Scene changes quickly.*)

SCENE 2.   KIRBY'*s farm. Interior – large fire, right. Door. Staircase with door at top. Window large. Curtains. Round table, and two chairs. Dresser between door and window. Writing material on dresser. Gin and water and pipes on table. [Time evening, but not dark.]* KIRBY *[a stern, hard-featured elderly man] seated right of table smoking.* JELLICK, *an old young-looking man, walking about restlessly.*

KIR: Why man, one would think thou wert training for walking match – up and down, up and down. Wonder thee beant wearied out.

JEL: I would rather not take a seat, I'm obliged to you. A blighted heart, sir, cannot sit down.

KIR: Blighted heart. Bah!

JEL: I have watched her grow up, sir. I nursed Ruth when a child.

KIR: And now you want to marry her that she may nurse you, eh? Why, mun, thou should look for a nice comfortable body, about thy own age. A nice middle-aged sort of party.

JEL: You'll excuse *me*, Mr Kirby, but I don't see because I'm in the sere and yeller, that I should turn my nose up at new potatoes. Besides Ruth would respect one so much her senior.

KIR: Respect! Bother! Don't you want your wife to love you!

JEL: Hem! I flatter myself nobody would know me for long without loving me.

KIR: (*rising*) Well, if thou can'st get Ruth to say yes my consent's ready. (*aside*) She'd as soon think of marrying clown at circus. My pretty, wilful, gentle Ruth, Heaven bless her!

JEL: That's right, that's right, sir, trample on me, sir; you've got me down, sir, you got me down; your head is on me, sir, like the Scotch party in the play: 'Your foot is on your native heath, your name's McGregor.' The quotation's a little confused, but my feelings must be my excuse. (*Walks about.*) Kick me when I'm down, I can bear it. (*Blows his nose.*)

KIR: Pshaw! Be a man. Leave off snivelling. Whoever won a wench by yowling and moping about. Put on a smiling face. (JELLICK *grins.*) That's rect – pull theeself together and stand up like a man. (JELLICK *puts himself in a ridiculous attitude.*) That's better; now thee looks some it like. (*Looks out at door.*)

JEL: Mr Kirby, sir, your words are like brandy and water to a blighted heart. I feel another man, Mr Kirby; your sentiments act like wine, sir, as has often been observed 'inspires us and fires us, with courage, love and joy'; as the poet says, 'Why should I play the Roman fool'. I'll be equal to the occasion. I'll see Ruth and tell her that I am a changed man, that I mean no longer to sue in faltering accents, but to storm the citadel, carry the fortress of her affections by a *coup-de-main*, lay my heart and savings-bank-book at her feet. No more beating about the bush. I feel the courage of the roused lion. (*music*)

KIR: (*at the door*) Here she be coming.

JEL: (*sinking into a chair*) Oh, law!

KIR: A foine lion thee'd make, Jellick, (*advancing to him*) with a heart of straw, loike stuffed fellow in Museum. (*patting him on the shoulder*) Keep up courage, lad, two's company, thee knows. I'm off. (*going*)

JEL: (*in feeble voice*) Don't go, Mr Kirby. As the poet says, 'Fly not yet'; wait a moment or two till 'Richard's himself again'. Mr Kirby, sir. (*Exit* KIRBY, *laughing.*) He's gone – gone like the baseless fabric of a what's-his-name, leaving a wreck behind. (*looking up piteously*) I'm the wreck.

    (*Enter* RUTH. *She appears greatly agitated and walks from one side of stage to the other; music ceases.*)

RUTH: (*not seeing* JELLICK) I know he never loved me, or he wouldn't treat me so. He is unkind, say what he may; no one else ever speaks to me without a compliment, never looks at me but in admiration; who's Ned Clayton that he's to lord it over a girl, and make her frightened to do a thing or say a word! (*Throws down hat on table, and sits on chair, stamping her foot petulantly.*)

JEL: (*Approaches her, timidly.*) The noble girl seems put out. I'm half sorry I stopped. Hem! (RUTH *turns angrily, and laughs at him scornfully.*) Good afternoon, Miss Ruth. Might I say Ruth?

RUTH: Anyone may say what they like, Mr Jellick. It matters little what folks *call* me. Oh, I'm weary of it all. (*Rises and crosses impatiently.*)

'*Your foot . . . McGregor*': a direct quotation from Sir Walter Scott, *Rob Roy*, chapter 34.
'*inspires us . . . joy*': John Gay, *The Beggar's Opera*, II, i, air 19 – 'Fill every glass, for wine inspires us . . .'
'*Why . . . Roman fool*': *Macbeth*, V, viii, 1.
coup-de-main: sudden attack.
'*Richard's himself again*': Cibber, adapted from *Richard III*, V, iii.
'*baseless fabric . . .*': misquotation of Prospero in *The Tempest*, IV, i, 148–56.

JEL: I brought you a little nosegay, Ruth. Would you condescend to accept it? (*Takes a very diminutive nosegay from his hat and presents it.*)

RUTH: (*taking it*) Even this one gives me some flowers and a civil word – but you —

JEL: (*sighing*) Ah, Ruth, I wish you knew how I adored you.

RUTH: (*sneeringly*) You don't mean it.

JEL: Mean it? Simple prose is not sufficient to express my sentiments. 'The rose is red, the violet's blue, carnations' – don't pluck it to pieces, my dear.

RUTH: (*having thoughtlessly pulled some leaves from nosegay*) Oh, I'm so sorry. I was thinking of something else. I was very rude and unkind, too, dear Mr Jellick. (*Takes his hand in hers.*) You'll forgive me this time, won't you?

JEL: Forgive you? I'll bring you a nosegay every morning if you'll only pull it to pieces and ask me to to forgive you in that pretty way. (*Holding her hands and looking ridiculously affectionate at her; she looks down.*) I'm no foolish flatterer, Ruth. I've loved you ever since you were a child. I'd go through fire and water for you. P'raps I talk like an old fool, but I mean what I say, Ruth Kirby, I mean what I say; and if you'll only marry me I'll never say a harsh word to you. I'd never cross your slightest wish; I'd pass my whole time in trying how I could make your life a pleasant one. (*She snatches her hands away and begins to cry.*) I'd – What's the matter, Ruth? What have I said? What on earth have I gone and said now?

RUTH: (*turning to him, and with emotion*) You mustn't think of me. I'm – I'm promised. Heaven help me – promised. I'm no wife for you, Mr Jellick. (*Sits.*) Go – please, sir, go. I'd rather be alone, indeed I would.

(NED *enters at back, pauses on seeing* JELLICK.)

JEL: Turn it over in your mind, Ruth, turn it over. I can wait. I don't grow younger, but I can wait a bit, my dear. I love you very dear – very dear – and – (*Turns and sees* NED CLAYTON *who has advanced a little.*)

NED: Good day to you. (RUTH *turns away from him.*) I fear I'm in the way here.

JEL: N-n-no – no – not at all.

NED: (*at back of table*) Or mayhap *you* don't feel altogether comfortable.

JEL: (*nervously*) On the contrary, never – never more comfortable in my life. Just dropping in to a – to a – Just so. Good day, Miss Ruth.

(RUTH *crosses to him and shakes him warmly by the hand.* NED CLAYTON *sits and betrays annoyance.*)

RUTH: Goodbye, Mr Jellick. I am very much obliged to you for the nosegay. Goodbye.

JEL: (*shaking her by the hand nervously*) Thank you. You're very welcome, I'm sure. It didn't cost me anything.

NED: (*laughing derisively*) Cheap sort of love that, Ruth. (*Exit* JELLICK, RUTH *is looking after him for the purpose of annoying* NED CLAYTON; *pause*) Now, Ruth, why not cease this trifling?

RUTH: What trifling, Edward?

NED: (*roughly*) Don't call me Edward – call me Ned, as usual.

RUTH: Well, then *Ned*, if you wish it.

NED: Not if you don't wish it, lass. Old Jellick's pretty attentive, eh? (*Rises.*)

RUTH: He's not so old –

NED: (*angrily*) Old or not old, he's no right to come dangling after you. Ruth, you're going to be married to me, as you should let him know. I tell you what, it don't look respectable.

RUTH: What'll you bring against me next, Ned?

NED: (*softening*) Come, my lassie, don't quarrel about it.

RUTH: I never wish to quarrel. It's always you. Everything I do wrong. You're always correcting me.

NED: Well, if I do, Ruth, it's for your good. I can't bear to see the girl I love making herself foolish. (*putting his arm round her waist*)

RUTH: Thank you. (*throwing his arm away*)

NED: What have I said *this* time? You flare up at every word?

RUTH: Why, I'm as calm as possible.

NED: Yes, my dear, that's the worst of it. If you flew out and boxed my ears for my impudence, I shouldn't so much mind – nay, I'd like it, lass; but I can't abide to see you cold and still, and biting your lips all the time I'm speaking – (*pause; despondingly to her*) – What, what's come over you of late, Ruth? It's only of late, mind you. You seem a changed girl like, and I'm sure it's not my fault. You used to be a very different girl, Ruth, you used indeed.

RUTH: *You* used to be very different. You used not to chide me and talk to me like a schoolmaster.

NED: Nay, don't say that, Ruth. Why should *I* talk to you like a schoolmaster? It's little enough beyond my trade I can boast of, in the way of knowledge. I'm a poor, ignorant fellow enough, Ruth; and, indeed, there's but one thing I do know thoroughly, and that's that I love *you* truly, and my heart bleeds at your conduct *now*. Why, I'd lay my life down for you; aye, willingly, and well you know it.

RUTH: I wonder if you treated your other sweethearts so?

NED: (*enraged*) How often am I to tell you that I never cared a bit for anyone but you? Why will you so mistrust me? Who's put these notions into your mind? You've picked 'em up maybe in some of those silly story books this gentleman lodger's lent you, and I'd just tell him a bit of my mind, (RUTH *turns upon him sharply.*) if he wasn't an invalid, and my rough way might make him bad. (*Goes towards door – turns.*) I tell you you're not yourself, Ruth, but I hope you'll come to your senses soon (*music*), for make sure of this, my lass, what I tell you is for your good – aye, for your good, Ruth. There's some mystery about your strange way. I'll not try to fathom it, but I'll just wait until you are the old, simple, kind, gentle Ruth, who said she'd be an honest workman's wife, and wished for no higher lot than to share the home of the man who loved her better than all the world besides. (*He walks to her.* KATE *enters and stands at back; gently*) Goodbye, Ruth. Shall I come again by-and-bye? (*Holding out his hand; she takes no notice.* NED *comes down a step or two.*) Say a word, lass – not one? (*putting on his cap*) Nay, then, I'll not come again till you're better tempered. (*Goes out quickly, slamming door.*)

RUTH: (*in a great rage*) Better, better tempered! That is a new complaint against me. Better tempered! And yet I *am* changed, I *am* no longer the same girl.

(KATE *comes slowly down from behind stairs.*) I am fretful, unhappy, wretched. I thought I loved Ned. I – I – scarcely know what I do or say. (*Sinks in chair.*)

KATE: Don't be a fool, girl. (RUTH *starts, and slightly shudders at* KATE's *voice.*) I heard Ned Clayton's remarks, Ruth. I wonder you credit him when he says he never loved another. They all say that, but few of us are such idiots as to believe them.

RUTH: Well, you would have me believe Mr Redburn and he says the same.

KATE: What, in his letter?

RUTH: In his letter? (*Involuntarily places hand to bosom of dress.*)

KATE: Which you carefully carry next your heart.

RUTH: (*suddenly*) Who told you that?

KATE: Where else should you carry the written avowal of a gentleman who has offered to take you from this dull, wretched den and make a lady of you? A gentleman wealthy, accomplished, *honourable*, and one who loves you, Ruth, as dull, jog-trot Ned Clayton couldn't dream of loving. I think I see you as Ned's wife (*Gets writing-case from dresser.*), a poor patient drudge, without one ray of hope to lighten the long dreary days – a cheerless present and a dismal future – work – work, nothing but work, through the long wearisome years. (*Begin to lower lights gradually and increase limelight from window. Lights half down by* SPOTTY's *entrance.*)

RUTH: Don't – don't Kate! (*Sits at table.*)

KATE: Compare it with a life of sunshine and happiness, travelling from place to place, plenty of money, plenty of beautiful dresses; no care for the morrow, all happiness and excitement.

RUTH: But father! It would break his heart.

KATE: What does he care? Has he not consented to your marriage with Mr Jellick, provided you would say the word?

RUTH: Yes, yes.

KATE: You are mad if you miss this chance. There – there (*giving her pen*), write a line – just a line or two – to Mr Redburn to say you will go.

RUTH: I cannot – I cannot, Kate! Ned!

KATE: (*almost fiercely – music*) Have you no pride, no spirit? Do you let consideration for him stand in the way? (*quickly*) Ned Clayton, who has flirted with every good-looking girl for miles round, but who comes with an injured air to you if you give another man a civil word. Pshaw!

RUTH: Give me the pen. (*Writes.*) 'I am acting wrongly – very wrongly, but I will trust to your honour and the love you say you bear me. I will fly with you, but take me away, far away, so that I may never look upon their faces here again. I scarcely know what I am writing. I trust to you; do not let me trust in vain.' Oh, Kate! he has said that he will make me his wife.

KATE: He is a *gentleman*, Ruth, and gentlemen never break their words. Sign it quick. (*Music increases.* RUTH *writes and sinks her head upon her hands.*)

---

limelight: a mode of stage lighting then current, creating an intense white light through heating lime in a flame. Its radiant yet mellow quality was perfect for special effects such as moonlight or lamplight, especially when directed through doors or windows.

KATE: (*snatching up letter; aside*) So far, so good. (*Goes up slowly, wetting envelope.*)

RUTH: (*looking up wildly*) Stay, Kate, give me back that letter. I – I wish you to give it to me. (*Is rushing up to* KATE *when* SPOTTY *enters. Lights half down.* RUTH *retires towards fire.*)

SPOT: Beg pardon, Miss Ruth. (*aside*) Them two has been having no end of a shindy. I'm afraid of that black-eyed girl. She's a Tartar *she* is. When she fixes me with them piercers I'm reg'lar under her control, for all the world like I was when I went to the lecture at Trudberry Town-hall, and a professor chap messer-merised me, and made me look a reg'lar fool on the platform afore all the folks.

KATE: (*in a loud whisper to* SPOTTY) Give this to Mr Redburn. Take care that no one else sees you do it. (*Gives him a shilling. He holds the letter in one hand, and the shilling in the other, looking bewildered.*) Hide it – put it into your pocket. (SPOTTY *does so mechanically; to* RUTH) Come with me, Ruth. (*Fetches* RUTH *from fireplace, and takes her across stage; when they get to foot of staircase* RUTH *is about to ask* SPOTTY *to return the letter, but is prevented by* KATE, *who leads her up staircase and off at door. Music ceases.*)

SPOT: (*Watches them off.*) I don't like that girl's way. There's something up, I'm certain. Why should she give me a shilling? People don't give other people shillings to carry letters unless there's something uncommon secret and important inside 'em. (*Looks round. Feels for letter. Attempts to whistle unconcernedly.*) There's no one about. I was always of a cur'ous natur' – always cur'ous. So was mother; she was cur'ous, too. If I could get a peep now – just a peep. (*Kneels down by fire, to read it by the light of it.*) It's dreadful, straggly writing, too. These sticky envelopes will open if you moisten 'em. I know that well, for I've done it afore. Yes, *there*! (*Begins opening letter,* KIRBY *enters, quietly puts hand upon his shoulder.*)

KIR: Now then.

SPOT: (*starting into corner on ground*) Murder! Murder!

KIR: (*laughing*) Why bless us all, mun, what be matter wi' ye? Hast thee been drinking?

SPOT: No, no sir. (*aside*) Oh, law!

KIR: Be est mad, then?

SPOT: Me mad? Lor bless you, sir, I haven't got the brains to go mad with. (*hands behind him*)

KIR: What's gotten theer?

SPOT: Where, sir?

KIR: Wheer, sir? Theer.

SPOT: (*holding out hat*) Billycock, sir.

KIR: No, t'other hand.

SPOT: (*having passed hat behind him to other hand*) That's billycock too, sir.

KIR: No, that letter thou was trying to read, be it from thy feyther?

SPOT: No, sir, I never had a father, that's only your joke. You know I'm foundling and a horphan. You picked me up in the London streets one November –

Billycock: a hard, felt hat with a round crown, like a bowler.

KIR: Aye, Cattle Show week.

SPOT: You saw as I was hard up and —

KIR: And I brought thee back with me, least I could do when cab-horse knocked thee down, as thee were pulling me from 'neath wheels of omnibus. I thought as 'twere all over wi' me. So 'twould have been but for thee.

SPOT: I was a starving lad and that cab 'oss was my best friend – after you, sir, of course. I haven't been ungrateful, I hope.

KIR: No. (*Snatches letter.*) What has got theer?

SPOT: A le-letter for Mr Redburn. (*aside*) Oh laws! I shouldn't have said that.

(*Enter NED. KIRBY examines letter and turns it about; scratches his head and seems puzzled. SPOTTY retires to fire and sits on stool.*)

NED: (*aside*) I can't rest like this, I must solve this riddle and find out what she means. I shall go wild if this sort of thing's to last.

KIR: A letter for Mr Redburn and thee trying to read it. Noice trusty postman thee'd be, Master Spotty. Ah, Ned! Tell me if this prying chap speaks truth. Thou knowest I was never taught to read, Heaven forgive those that let me grow up like a weed in the world.

NED: Never mind, Mr Kirby, it's too late in the day to regret it now, and you've done pretty well for all that. (*Takes the letter.*) Ruth's handwriting. (*music*)

KIR: (*starting up excited*) What, what, say, mun? Ruth, my Ruth write to him. What's it mean, Ned? Ned, my lad, I'm afeared – I'm afeared —

NED: (*agitated*) No, no, don't be fanciful; it's no doubt nothing, nothing. (*aside*) So she corresponds with him. Oh, Ned Clayton, what a fool you've been all this time, not to see the reason of her changed manner. Here's the explanation sure enough – sure enough.

KIR: (*turning to him*) Ned, you expect summut wrong; don't deny it, I can read it in they face. An honest wench don't write letters to fine gentlemen for now't. There's summut wrong, Ned, and I'll find out what it means.

(*Music – RUTH and KATE appear at top of stairs. They both start. [Turn on limelights . . . SPOTTY makes an action expressive of dismay at KATE.]*)

NED: (*aside*) My heart sinks within me. (*Retires a little.*)

KIR: (*turning and seeing RUTH*) Ruth, coom, lass. (RUTH *comes down.*) This letter be from thee to Mr Redburn – (*She hangs her head; aside to* NED) See there. (*to* RUTH) I've been blind not to see the change in thee of late. There's summut 'neath surface. (*She shrinks.*) Thee cannot meet my eye, Ruth, for first time in my life. (RUTH *sinks her head.* KIRBY *turns fiercely to* NED.) Read that letter.

RUTH: (*with a movement towards* KIRBY) No, no!

KIR: (*waving her off*) I'll have it read.

RUTH: (*aside*) Oh, would that I could sink into the ground.

KIR: Read it. (NED *looks at letter. After having read a portion he crushes it in his hand and sinks his head.*)

KIR: It be as I suspected. Oh, my Ruth, my Ruth!

KATE: (*aside and back*) This is better than I could have hoped. My triumph will soon be complete. (KATE *is about to go.*)

KIR: Dunna go. Listen wi' rest of us to the story of our shame and sorrow. (*Takes

NED's hand. KATE stands by window with limelight upon her.) I see it all, lad, I see it all. But thy heart is young and strong, and there be some other lass, trust me, who will know how to prize the true love of an honest lad. (RUTH sobs.) Read the letter. (Looks sternly at RUTH. NED looks at RUTH who looks at him appealingly; he commences to read in a cold and forced voice, struggling with his emotion.)

NED: (as if reading a letter) 'You ask me if I will go away with you. I will own I have been dazzled by the thought of another home; a higher, grander home than I could otherwise hope for, but if I went away with you, I should break two hearts that love me better than life. (KIRBY turns round. NED immediately looks at letter and as KIRBY again turns his head towards RUTH, NED resumes.) And though you say you love me now, you would change your opinion when you had grown tired of me, when I grow older, plainer, and I should then forfeit your love as I should have long ago lost your respect. Seek not to tempt me further. If I have wavered for a moment I am strong now, and I cannot, will not go away with you'. (Pause. RUTH rushes to her father and kneels. KIRBY utters an exclamation of joy, 'My darling RUTH', and smooths her hair with his hand. NED sinks into chair. REDBURN appears at window when NED is about halfway through letter.)

(Picture. Ring sharp as RUTH is falling on knees.)

SLOW CURTAIN

ACT I

SCENE 1.   Two years are supposed to elapse. REDBURN's office in Liverpool; door with 'private' written on it. Office table, centre; library chairs, left of table. Chair for clerk, right of table. Cabinet. Writing materials and all the paraphernalia of an office on table. Decanter of water and tumbler and Vesta lights on table. MILDER, an old clerk, seated, writing.

MIL: Almost time Mr Redburn had returned.

(Enter SPOTTY, dressed in very shabby black.)

SPOT: No news of Mr Redburn yet, eh, Mr Milder?

MIL: No, Mr Spotty, no news at present. (SPOTTY sits.) By the way, Mr Spotty, it strikes me you appear to be more than usually anxious about Mr Redburn. You're fidgetty, Mr Spotty, deuced fidgetty; and a fidgetty messenger is a nuisance – a confounded nuisance.

SPOT: Well, you see, Mr Milder, some parties is gifted with the power of concealing their feelings; other parties, on the other hand, is not. You are one of those parties as is.

MIL: (Pulls chair a little forward as SPOTTY sits on corner of table.) Mr Spotty, there's more in you than meets the eye. I hate picking an employer to pieces; but come now, what is going on behind the scenes? (coaxingly)

Picture: tableau at end of scene, demonstrative of the dramatic situation at that point in the play.
Vesta lights: short matches, originally made of wax.

SPOT: Oh, now you're growing pleasant; I was coming to this, only you take up a party so.

MIL: That's a very disagreeable phrase, sir, and reminds one of the police.

SPOT: A sore subject with you, eh? Well, now, I happen to know as Mr Redburn's sweet on a certain Miss Danville.

MIL: Not daughter of the wealthy Gregory Danville, the lucky party who realised so large a fortune in so few years?

SPOT: No other, Mr M.

MIL: Oh, he flies as high as that does he?

SPOT: Bless you, I am always carrying billys for him, unbeknown to old Danville, who's as proud of his pedigree as if he was a dook or a favourite for the Derby. Master met her at a ball, and – well, you know he's a captivating sort. Bless you, I could tell you a story about him as 'd freeze the very marrow in your bones.

MIL: (*uneasily*) Don't do anything of the kind, I beg.

SPOT: You see when one's thrown into the society of sociable parties, a fellow likes to do as other fellows do. When in Turkey behave like the Turkeys – you've heard the saying! Now, last night I was at a very small public by the name of the Nag's Head. Bragging was general, everybody was boasting about something or other. So I, determined not to be outdone, announced as a marriage was in course of arrangement between my employer, Robert Redburn, Esq., and the lovely and the accomplished daughter of Gregory Danville, the great shipowner. I was sorry directly I said it, but the fumes of the tobacco and the grog was too much for me, and out it come. Well, no sooner had I said it than up jumps Muggin's clerk, low feller, Muggin's clerk, and he says, says he (*striking the table, at which MILDER starts, this business repeated in appropriate places during this speech*) – 'What,' says he, 'Mr Danville permit his daughter to marry a fellow like Redburn? What, Mr Danville, a gentleman every inch of him, a respectable member of society and a millionaire permit such a match? Rubbish!' says he. I was about to reply, when a gentleman as I adn't noticed bangs the table, and shouts out 'Rubbish to you!' – yes, 'Rubbish to you!' he shouts, quite red in the face. 'Who says he ain't good enough for the likes of her? You?' he says, pointing contemptuous at Muggin's clerk. 'You? Why,' he says, 'I say as he can marry her, if so be as he likes.' And then he bangs the table again, and sinks back into his chair in a half-stupified state, as if he had been taking a soapy-rific.

MIL: Oh, some tipsy fellow anxious for a row.

SPOT: Nothing of the kind. When I left, and was going home, I felt a hand suddenly laid on my shoulder, and when I turned round there was my gentleman. He hooked on, and before I could get rid of him he'd learnt all about what I was going to say. I let it all out as innocent as a child.

MIL: And what appeared the effect upon this interesting stranger?

SPOT: Most extra-ordinary. He snapped his fingers, and cocked his shabby hat on one side, quite defiant like; pleased, too, mind you – *dreadful* pleased! (*music piano*)

---

billys: billets-doux.   *public*: public house.

(*Enter* REDBURN, *quickly.*)

MIL: And his name?

SPOT: Spoke of hisself as 'a party by the name of Johnson'.

RED: (*taking it up*) 'Party by the name of Johnson'.

(SPOTTY *jumps off table and arranges* REDBURN's *chair and stands behind it.* MILDER *resumes writing.* REDBURN *sits and takes up his letters, looks at the direction of one or two, opening others.*)

RED: Bills, bills, bills. (*Reads.*) 'Sir, – We are instructed to commence proceedings' – ah, commence them, by all means. (*Throws letter in basket.*) 'Your well-known generosity of disposition will prompt you to' – will it? (*Throws it into basket; reads.*) Society for the Regeneration of the Abyssinians. Milder.

MIL: Sir. (*Music ceases.*)

RED: You can retire to the bosom of your family, I don't want you any more today.

MIL: Very good, sir. (*Takes umbrella off table and hat off peg.*)

RED: Spotty.

SPOT: (*Comes down briskly.*) Yes, sir.

RED: Get out.

SPOT: (*passing behind table*) Yes, sir.

RED: Stop!

SPOT: Yes, sir.

RED: Wait in the outer office till I call you.

SPOT: Yes, sir.

MIL: (*aside to* SPOTTY) Down on his luck.

SPOT: Oh! 'orrid – 'orrid! (*Exeunt; music piano.*)

RED: (*sitting at table*) It's strange that I cannot shake off this overwhelming sense of depression. Can my lucky star be setting? Is it all up with Robert Redburn? Bob Redburn, who never flinched in his life. Is he going to give in *now*? What! (*rising*) Wrecked in sight of port, Bob? No, my boy. Never say it – never say it. (*Goes to cupboard and produces brandy.*) Brandy, brandy; they say you depress us in proportion to the elevation. (*Takes glass off table, and pours out of bottle.*) Let depression come, we'll elevate you again, Bob Redburn. Faint heart never won fair lady, and Fanny Danville's not to be dazzled by a coward. (*Drinks.*) Ah, Fanny, here's to those bright eyes, my love; here's to –

(*Enter* SPOTTY *suddenly.*)

SPOT: Beg pardon, but a party by the name of Johnson. Couldn't help it, sir – would come in.

RED: *Would*, eh? Show the fellow in, whoever he is.

(SPOTTY *goes to door and shouts 'Hi!' Enter* JOHNSON *remarkably shabby, a vulgar swell on his last legs. Dirty light coat and battered white hat cocked on one side.*)

RED: (*seated*) Well, sir, what's your business? (JOHNSON *indicates the presence of*

---

direction: address.   *swell*: someone dressed ostentatiously in the highest fashion.

SPOTTY.) Get out, sir. (SPOTTY *exits.* JOHNSON *takes off his hat.*) Now
    sir, may I – ?

JOHN: Yes, but how about a chair?

RED: Oh, be seated by all means. (JOHNSON *sits and places hat on table.* RED-
    BURN *looks at him in surprise.* JOHNSON *removes hat and places it on ground.*)

JOHN: Well, but won't you be seated?

RED: Oh, never mind me.

JOHN: I won't. (*pause*) Fine town this – Liverpool.

RED: Glad you think so.

JOHN: Yes; fine go-a-head-put-on-the-steam-never-mind-if-you-bust sort of place,
    eh? Suits me, I'm a go-ahead; suits you, you're go-a-head, ain't you?

RED: Well.

JOHN: Lots of tin to be made in this town, but, bless you, what's the use of wealth
    without love, eh? Like a lantern with the light left out, ain't it? Bless you,
    love! Why it's board and lodgin', washing, and clothes, Sunday noosepaper,
    and summer 'oliday all rolled into one, that's what *love* is.

RED: You're a strange card; but, upon my word, I don't see what on earth you
    want here.

JOHN: You ask me what I want. Absurd! I want what everybody wants, only I
    want it more than everybody. Money!

RED: It's no use you coming to me for it.

JOHN: Make no mistake. I'm a trader, not a begging letter impostor. I've got some-
    thing for sale, it's something out of the ordinary way of business. Oh, don't
    elevate those eyebrows, it ain't smuggled pocket handkerchiefs, and it ain't
    real Havannas for a mere trifle, and it ain't a child's cawl. No, no, I'm playing
    for a big fish, I am, and if *you're* anything of an angler you ought to know
    that it isn't wise to try and land him all in a minute. (*Looks* REDBURN *full
    in the face.*)

RED: You wouldn't dare to come here and talk like this unless –

JOHN: Don't talk to me about what I wouldn't *dare*. It's an unpleasant way of
    putting it, and it gets my back up; don't you get my back – Now, between
    ourselves, there's only two courses open to you – the Court of Bankruptcy or
    the Temple of Hymen! – matrimony or smash – Mr Commissioner Thingamy
    or Fanny Danville.

RED: (*rising*) Scoundrel!

JOHN: Lookee here. If the arguments are going to be as strong as that I'd better
    call in a harbitrator. (*Draws out revolver.*) There – there's my referee.

RED: (*Sits.*) What! What do you mean? In what way can my private affairs concern
    you? Who are you? What are you? What do you mean by mentioning Miss
    Danville?

JOHN: You wish me to come to the point? I've heard all about it; you're on the
    brink of a smash. You're in love with – we won't mention names as you don't

---

tin: money.

child's cawl: a cawl is the portion of the membrane enclosing a foetus, occasionally found on a
child's head at birth. A cawl was considered a good omen or charm against drowning. Cf. *David
Copperfield*, chapter 1.

like it – a certain party – certain party's father objects to you – has great view
for certain party – certain party's spoons on you – extronary thing she should
be, but women do such remarkable things; certain party can't marry without
her father's consent – what's that consent worth? (REDBURN *is lighting a
fresh cigar.* JOHNSON *reaches across and takes one from* REDBURN's *case;
lights up; pause; smoking.*) Now, take your time; don't you commit yourself
to figures if you're flurried, take your time. (*taking bottle and glass*) Thankee,
don't mind if I do take the least dram. (*Helps himself.*) Fortune helps them as
help themselves. Here's towards yer.

RED: Mr Danville is a wealthy and highly respectable gentleman; he comes of an
old and aristocratic family, one of our foremost men. In what way can *you*,
who appear to be, to say the least of it, a shabby –

JOHN: Go it. (*Drinks.*)

RED: Out at elbows –

JOHN: Proceed. (*Drinks.*)

RED: Vagabondish sort of person –

JOHN: Continue. (*Drinks.*) Those are just the sort of words to go with this kind of
liquor. (*Smacks his lips.*) Brandy and vituperation combine capital. Finish up.

RED: In what way can *you* presume to assist me?

JOHN: Do you know how the inventor of Parr's Life Pills made his money?

RED: No.

JOHN: By never telling nobody what was inside on 'em. (*finger to nose*) Now,
what's the consent worth in round figures? Make it up in thousands; it sounds
more satisfactory and counts heasier.

RED: (*rising and sitting on corner of table*) You mean to say you can obtain her
father's consent? (*music*)

JOHN: I mean to say I can try. S'pose I succeed. You know what's coming to her.
Give me a cool five thousand on the wedding morning, and *on* goes my own
particular patent peculiar screw.

RED: But how did you get this patent peculiar –

JOHN: Never mind, that's my business. (*music*) I've heard your character and I can
see it in your face. You're a black-hearted one, you are. I can read it in your
eyes.

RED: (*laughing sneeringly*) Ha!

JOHN: And I can spell it in your laugh. You're one as has what's called an iron will,
ain't you? You're a *cruel party too* – one as wouldn't turn aside a foot to
avoid driving over a dog. When you've said you'll do a thing you'll do it,
'specially if it's bad, eh? You never had a friend, had you? Or if you had you
never let him stand between you and what you wanted. You never gave a
sixpence to a beggar or patted a child upon the head, or felt sorry when you'd
done an unkind act or cared a rush when you see another do one. No tale of

---

spoons: in love with.
Parr's Life Pills: pills based on a recipe handed down by Old Parr, who had reputedly lived for
130 years. According to the advertisements they helped to prolong life and increased the
beauty of women. Herbert Ingram, co-founder of the *Illustrated London News*, acquired the
recipe and marketed the pills in the nineteenth century.
screw: pressure.

sorrow ever touched you, did it? No tears ever came into your eyes unless it was in rage for something that you'd missed. You are a stony-hearted one, *you* are, and I want such a one as *you*, and you want such a one as *me*, and if you'll say the word I'll strike this bitter bargain, and I'll stick to it.

RED: It is a bargain. [Five thousand are yours and freely if by your aid I obtain his consent.] (*Both rise.*) There's my hand upon it.

JOHN: (*looking contemptuously at his hand*) It's a bargain.

RED: What your hold over Mr Danville may be I know not, but something about you convinces me you have a hold. (*Goes to back of table and takes up hat.*)

JOHN: A *hold*, man? A grip – a *grip*.

RED: The bargain's struck then, and when Fanny Danville's mine the money's yours. (*going*) And now I think our interview's at an end.

JOHN: (*giving place*) After you, sir. (REDBURN *crosses and exits at door. JOHNSON watches him off, helps himself to glass of brandy, puts bottle into his pocket.*)

RED: (*without*) Now then, Johnson. (JOHNSON *swaggers out, imitating* REDBURN.)

    (*Clear for livery. Change.*)

SCENE 2.   *Drawing-room at* MR DANVILLE's, *handsomely furnished;* MISS DANVILLE *discovered reading.*

MISS D: (*throwing down book, after a pause*) I can't read with any pleasure. I can't work. Oh dear, oh dear! I don't know what's the matter with me. Well, I'll try and read a little more, for I told papa he should know all the plot of Mrs MacScorcher's last work when he comes home to dinner. (*Recommences reading.*)

    (*Enter* RUTH *plainly but tastefully dressed.*)

RUTH: (*Creeps up behind* MISS DANVILLE, *peeps over her book.*) Is it so very interesting?

MISS D: Gracious, Ruth, you quite startled me; have you done writing letters?

RUTH: Yes, for the present; now I can have as long a gossip with you as you like. [*Sits by her.*]

MISS D: Well, Ruth love, I am dreadfully unhappy.

RUTH: You unhappy. Come, that's rather too good; what have you to make *you* unhappy? Haven't you a beautiful home, a love of a boudoir, lap-dog, birds, the last new novel, all the new music, as much pocket money as you can possibly spend or give away, a doting father, and –

MISS D: And a dear little duck of a friend in you, Ruth. Heigho! (*Takes her hand.*)

RUTH: What a sigh!

MISS D: You say I have everything I wish for; there's an article left out of the catalogue. (*turning aside coquettishly*)

RUTH: And that is?

MISS D: Can't you guess?

RUTH: Why, you puss, I do believe you mean a lover.

---

livery: change-over or scenery (?)

MISS D: (*with a sigh of relief*) You've hit it. .

RUTH: (*seriously*) Well, Fanny dear, you can pick and choose; you must have admirers in plenty. (*Turns away.*)

MISS D: But I don't want to pick and choose. I have picked and chosen —

RUTH: I don't know that.

MISS D: It's the only little secret I've kept from you, for you will think me very strange, Ruth, but I have felt a presentiment you would not like him —

RUTH: (*quietly*) If *you* like him, Fanny, surely that is sufficient.

MISS D: No, no. You must like whoever *I* like. Perhaps after all I'm only frightening myself. *You may* like him very much, too much, perhaps; but you'd better not, for I'm so jealous.

RUTH: But what does Mr Danville say?

MISS D: Won't hear of it; talked about cutting me off with a shilling. Fancy, what *fun* being cut off with a shilling. Ha! Ha! I wonder how it's done. Ha! Ha! Ha! (*seeing* RUTH *looking demure*) Why, how grave you look.

RUTH: (*turning to her*) Fanny, dear Fanny, you know how fond I am of you, how deeply anxious I am that your future should be a bright and happy one. Let me beg, let me implore you not to think of crossing your father's will. I disobeyed a kind and loving father. I was dazzled by one I thought noble and generous, but I learned my error bitterly, Fanny, and lived to loathe the recollection of the time when I deceived my father, and broke the truest heart that ever beat with honest love. (*Rests her head against her hands.*)

MISS D: Dear, dear! That's all very terrible, but *I'm* not going to break *any* hearts, unless it's my own, if I'm not allowed to do as I like. (*tapping her foot half playfully, half annoyed*)

RUTH: Had I not disobeyed my father, and deceived those who trusted me, I should not be here now amongst strangers, and ashamed to show my face in my own home.

MISS D: Come, Ruth, you never need be ashamed to show *that* face, I'm certain. Come, now, did you really break a heart – really now in downright earnest?

RUTH: Yes, in downright, cruel earnest.

MISS D: Oh, how I should like to break a heart; (*pettishly*) but I don't believe the young men I meet have any hearts.

RUTH: Oh, Fanny!

MISS D: No, they've no hearts, they've only eye-glasses; if they have any generous sentiments they seem to think it's the proper thing to disguise them. Why on earth should people take a pride in being cold and distant, and never roused to anything like enthusiasm – in these days, too, of volunteers and oppressed nationalities and I don't know what; but there, how I do rattle on, and what rubbish I talk. What was he like? Not the broken-hearted one, the other. (*music piano*)

RUTH: Well, he was of a tall figure, and he'd a dark piercing eye that seemed to look through one; his voice was low and earnest, and when he smiled it was a smile of conscious power that always frightened me. (REDBURN *enters outer room; does not see* RUTH *and* MISS DANVILLE.)

MISS D: Why, I do declare, you have described my admirer. (RUTH *sees* REDBURN

as he goes off, utters a smothered scream, and hurriedly passes to door. MISS
DANVILLE *rises surprised.*)

MISS D: Why, what —

RUTH: He here, in this house; I must go, Fanny. I am not well. (*Exit.*)

MISS D: Well, of all the strange girls I ever saw —

       (REDBURN *comes in from outer door.*)

RED: Are you alone, Fanny?

MISS D: (*with a half-shriek*) Oh, whatever has come to the people? One goes out
of the room in a faint and the other comes in like a flash of lightning. Oh, Mr
Redburn.

RED: Don't call me Mr Redburn, or else I shall think you don't care for me.

MISS D: And who told you I did care for you, sir?

RED: Your eyes, to say nothing of your lips —

MISS D: Well, now, my lips say I don't.

RED: Look how they're blushing at the imposition. Come, Fanny, I can bear this
suspense no longer. I am determined to see your father to come to the point.
You're all the world to me, and if your father don't consent —

MISS D: Well!

RED: (*with great ferocity*) We'll see if we can't make him.

MISS D: (*flushing up*) Make him, indeed. You little know papa. He's not a man
to be made do anything. You may lead him, but you can't drive him.

RED: Like other patient animals, but I must have his consent. [*contemptuously
aside*]

MISS D: Ah, you know that if I marry without it I shan't have a fortune. Oh, you
avaricious man! I can't bear an avaricious man.

RED: Nay, Fanny, compared to your father, I'm a poor man; but I'm still able to
maintain a good figure in the world, and the woman who becomes Robert
Redburn's wife shall have no cause to call him avaricious. If you never obtain
your fortune, you shall find your pathway strewed with *roses*, Fanny, if I
can't quite afford to make it *camellias.*

MISS D: Then you actually mean to say you'd marry me without my fortune?

RED: Can you doubt the sincerity of my love? Can you doubt my honour?

MISS D: Certainly not; but would you?

RED: Put me to the test, Fanny.

MISS D: Well, I must believe you, I suppose. Did you send me those beautiful love
birds?

RED: I took that liberty, Fanny.

MISS D: Oh, don't think it a liberty. Pa did. I had to tell him such a fib. (*going,
turning to him*) You won't care for me if I tell fibs, will you? It's very wicked
to tell fibs, but it's often done in business, isn't it? But then it isn't fibs, it's

---

MISS DANVILLE rises surprised: the stage direction in LC is as follows: 'The following scene
between REDBURN and MISS DANVILLE to be very carefully acted; the contrast between
the determined REDBURN and the rather vain coquettish girl, MISS DANVILLE, to be very
strongly marked and elaborated.' This direction is deleted in the published version, along with
much of the ensuing dialogue between REDBURN and MISS DANVILLE.
love birds: small birds, of parrot kind, said to pine away at death of their mate.

only like saying you're out when somebody disagreeable calls. Come along
and see how happy they seem. (*music – piano through following speech of*
RUTH's)

> (*Exit* MISS DANVILLE *and* REDBURN. *Door opens slowly;* RUTH
> *appears, pale and agitated. She looks round, and then enters hur-*
> *riedly.*)

RUTH (*wildly*) He's here – here (*behind couch*) beneath the very roof. She – she
loves him, or fancies so, little knowing the depth and cunning of his deceitful
heart; he who would have tempted me away, and whose character I have
learnt, alas, too late, to save my self-respect, but not too late to teach me a
bitter lesson. Villain! The stakes you play for now are high enough, far
higher than the mere love of a simple country girl; play carefully and with
every caution, Robert Redburn, for there's one you little dream of who is
watching your dangerous game. (*Music stops.*)

> (*Enter* MR DANVILLE, *an aristocratic, rather pompous elderly*
> *man.*)

MR D: (*pausing after entering a little way*) I have interrupted you, Miss Kirby, I'm
afraid; you are surely rehearsing a scene from one of Racine's tragedies. I was
not aware that your accomplishments included the art of declamation in so
forcible a degree. Pray proceed. (*This is given with a lofty air of politeness.*)

RUTH: (*confused*) Pardon me – pardon me, Mr Danville – I – I (*with a sudden burst*
of passion going towards him) Will you listen to me?

MR D: (*stepping back, much surprised*) Certainly; what is the matter, Miss Kirby?

RUTH: A man comes here who says he loves your daughter. Perhaps his character
is unknown to you. I wish you to know him in his true colours, even at the
risk of your anger at my presumption and Fanny's grief at the loss of her
lover, who can only bring shame upon this honoured house.

MR D: What does this mean, Miss Kirby? To whom do you refer?

RUTH: Robert Redburn!

MR D: Does he presume to enter this house after the more than strong hint I gave
him, nay, the outspoken assurance that his visits would be considered an
impertinence?

RUTH: This interference of mine must appear strange presumption, but I am urged
to speak thus from knowing too well his real nature, his mean, revengeful,
selfish heart.

MR D: I had already – can it be from instinct? – already conceived the greatest dislike for this Redburn; on inquiries, too, I found he was little known and less
respected. But how is it you know him so thoroughly?

RUTH: Oh, do not ask me now; the story is a long and painful one, but, believe me,
I only speak the truth. Your daughter is dear to you.

MR D: Dear to me! Fanny is priceless; her future happiness is my sole aim of life;
for that I have toiled and laboured, as few who see me now, a wealthy man,
could imagine, Miss Kirby. Dear, too, is the honour of a respected name. I
dare not say what I should do were she to bring disgrace upon it.

Racine's tragedies: the French dramatist, Racine, wrote tragedies that contained long speeches
requiring a very declamatory style of performance.

RUTH: She cannot really love this man. Say, say, that you will never consent for her to be his wife.

MR D: His wife? Never! Not one shilling of mine shall ever be his, and without her fortune a vagabond adventurer will never care to wed her.

RUTH: (*aside*) I hear footsteps returning. Do not forget, sir, do not forget. (*Exit; music.*)

MR D: Presumptuous, insolent cur! But I must reason with Fanny; hers is not a nature to submit to harshness. I must try what change of scene will do to obliterate the recollection of this fancied first love. (*Sits, thinking.*)

> (*Enter* REDBURN, *pauses a moment, not seeing* MR DANVILLE.)

RED: Yes, I will see him this very day — (*Music ceases.*)

MR D: (*Turns, rises indignantly, after a slight pause.*) I'm sorry, sir, you should not have completely comprehended the very decided opinion I expressed regarding you again honouring my house with your presence.

RED: (*aside*) Oh, I see. Excuse me, Mr Danville, but your observations are tinged with such a decided dash of irony that I'm afraid some one must have been maligning me to you. Now my character is quite open to investigation. I have fair expectations, and —

MR D: Pardon me, I have nothing, and wish to have nothing, to do with you or your prospects.

RED: (*biting his lips*) Curse his cold-blooded hauteur! (*aloud*) I love your daughter ardently. My passion must plead my excuse. (*music piano*)

MR D: Harken, Mr Redburn. My credit here is as good as any man's. I am well known and respected, as you are well aware; my honour and good name are dear to me as life. In this great town of Liverpool there is not one living soul who can ever point the finger of scorn at Gregory Danville, or couple his name with anything that is not open, fair, and honest. For years that name has been a bye-word for all that is upright and fair dealing, and the faint breath of suspicion has never sullied it. But I tell you this, I would sooner sink in shame beneath the heaviest load of degradation than that my child should ever become your wife. Should she be mad enough to thwart me, not one penny of my money shall ever be hers. I disown her, disinherit her, cast her off.

(JOHNSON *creeps in slowly, as if he had been listening.*)

RED: (*aside*) This is awkward; can that fellow Johnson have been lying? One final appeal and then — (*Turns and beholds* JOHNSON.) You here!

JOHN: (*placing his fingers to his lips and winking to* REDBURN) You need not announce me, says I to the flunkey. I'm an old friend, and wish to surprise your master.

MR D: I hope this interview will never — (*Sees* JOHNSON.) Who are you, sir?

JOHN: Party by the name of Johnson.

MR D: (*aside*) Can I believe my ears? Surely that voice – Pshaw! (*recovering himself*) Your business. I'm engaged.

JOHN: (*to* REDBURN) Say I'm a friend of yours.

RED: This, this gentleman's a friend of mine. (*Crosses to fireplace.*)

MR D: Indeed. This insolence passes all endurance. Not only do you enter my

---

flunkey: liveried servant or footman.

house against my express wish, but you presume to introduce your acquaintances. I shall at once summon my servants to thrust the pair of you into the
streets, and if you ever dare to present yourselves here again – (*Is crossing to
ring bell when* JOHNSON *intercepts him.*)

JOHN: Don't ring the bell, sir – we're a going directly, we are indeed. (*Looks hard
at him.* MR DANVILLE *looks searchingly at* JOHNSON; *quails before him;
puts his hand to his mouth in indecision.* REDBURN *at back.*) We wouldn't
intrude for the world. We only want to strike a little bargain. Just do a pleasant stroke of business, that's all: we don't want to be turned out; 'cos when
we gets turned out we gets our back up, and when we gets our back up, we
shows our teeth. (*Turns to* REDBURN.)

MR D: Can this be a dream?

JOHN: (*to* REDBURN) Would you oblige me by retiring to another room for a few
moments. Thank you. (*As* REDBURN *goes out* JOHNSON *goes up and closes
door carefully, then turns and comes down.*) You're a leetle surprised at my
appearance, just a leetle bit took aback, eh?

MR D: (*pale and agitated, half turned from him*) I did hope never to see you again.

JOHN: (*Sings.*) 'Hope told a flattering tale' that Johnson would never return.

MR D: How can you trust yourself –

JOHN: (*quickly*) Oh, don't be uneasy on *my* account. I've got my ticket all fair and
square, and 'hon riggle', as the French says. (*Pulls out pocket-book.*)

MR D: What can you want with me after all these years? You see me here wealthy,
respected, an honoured man; my life of long ago had almost faded from my
recollection; your visit brings it back in all its hideous reality. Do not torture
me by your presence; leave me and never let me see your face again. (*Crosses,
and sits down on couch.*) I will make any sacrifice to be rid of you, but do
not come like a black cloud between me and happiness. I have a child who
thinks me all that is honourable and good; for her sake I implore you to name
your price and go. (*Sinks in chair.*)

JOHN: My price.

MR D: (*rising and turning to him*) Yes, I know you can have no other object than
blackmail. It is yours whatever you demand. I own I am in your power. I
admit it freely – at your mercy. The sum, man (*Rises.*) – the sum – name it
and quickly, before I am driven mad, as the bitter memories rise before me –
memories I had hoped were buried in the bitter past. (*Crosses and sits. Music.
Head sinks in hands on table.*)

JOHN: Look'ee here, Gregory Danville; the day before yesterday I was starving –
aye, starving, but I'd sooner a died like a dog in the streets than have taken
bite or sup from you. There's a long out-standing debt between you and me,
but it ain't a matter of money, old pal. (MR DANVILLE *starts.*) Ay, you
don't like the phrase. I don't want to harrow you up by reminding you of

---

'*Hope told a flattering tale*': first lines of song in William Barnes Rhodes's *Bombastes Furioso*
(1811), a popular burlesque on the nineteenth-century stage.
ticket: ticket of leave, the means by which a prisoner was allowed freedom, with certain res-
trictions, after he had served a part of his sentence.

happier days, when you was a dapper clerk with a wonderful knack of copy-
ing other persons' signatures, and letting third parties into the hole along with
you. I wouldn't mention it for the world. You had luck, you was always
clever; I was always a fool. You're a swell, I'm a 'houtcast'. (*in a subdued
tone*) But you don't fancy as I've forgot a deadly wrong you did me. You
don't think I ever thought of anything else through the dismal years of penal
servitude. You don't think I ever dreamt of anything else but a day of reckon-
ing. You don't think I am here for nothing else but my revenge – do you,
Gregory, my old pal, eh?

MR D: (*aside*) This is torture. (*aloud*) What would you have me do?

JOHN: She died after you left her – died in a garret, poor Nell did – died amongst
strangers. You left her to starve. Poor Nell, she was a little blue-eyed, bright-
faced thing, when I first saw her; she raved before she died, and they cut off
all her pretty golden hair, poor child. I've got a bit of it here; would you like
to see it? (*Pulls pocket-book out.*)

MR D: No, no!

JOHN: I wasn't a felon then, Gregory Danville. I was a loose fish enough, nothing
more; and I loved Nell. *You* took her from me. One day you struck her down
in a fit of jealous rage, and you left her all alone with her shame and her sorrow and her broken heart; there was only one thing for the poor lost child to
do, that was to *die*, and she *did* it. Now you know the nature of the debt and
why I am here, and why I don't want your money. I want your peace of
mind; I want the happiness of one nearest and dearest to you; I want my
revenge through your child, and I'll have it, mark my words, Gregory, old pal,
I'll *have* it.

MR D: (*turning to him*) There's a strange mystery in your words, fellow.

JOHN: (*quickly*) No mystery at all, fellow: your whole heart and soul are wrapped
up in your daughter. My friend, Mr Robert Redburn, Esq., which is a waiting
in the back drawing-room, he is one of them parties as 'll chip a woman's
heart to pieces, bit by bit, and I'm determined he shall wed her. (*Slaps right
hand against left.*)

MR D: (*Rises in a rage.*) Man, I defy you, do your worst; I will brave shame, punishment, anything rather than my child shall marry that heartless scoundrel.

JOHN: Here, here, draw it mild – draw it mild – heartless scoundrel indeed! What
are you, Gregory Danville, Esq., millionaire and setterer? Heartless scoundrel
in your teeth.

MR D: Villain! (*about to rush on him*)

JOHN: Don't – don't tempt me to lay a finger on you, don't tempt me to cut short
my revenge by taking your pitiful life; don't tempt me, Gregory, don't tempt
me, old pal, don't tempt me!

       (*Enter* REDBURN.)

RED: What's this?

MR D: Leave my house, fellow, (MISS DANVILLE *enters*.) or I'll call my servants
to thrust you into the streets.

JOHN: Call away, the more the merrier, call 'em that they may hear who and what
you really are. Call away; what shall we tell 'em when they come, eh, old
pal? What, but that the high and mighty Gregory Danville, who brags about

his honour and his spotless name, is no more than a forger and a thief. (MISS DANVILLE *appears greatly alarmed.*) A heartless scoundrel, who sold his pal and left his sweetheart to starve. A cur amongst curs, a felon and a coward.

MR D: (*Rises and is about to attack* JOHNSON. MISS DANVILLE *puts her hand on his shoulder,* MR DANVILLE *shrinks at sight of her, and falls into chair.*) Fanny, oh, shame! shame! (*Buries his head on table.*)

MISS D: (*appealingly*) What's this? – who's this?

JOHN: Party by the name of Johnson.

MISS D: (*crossing to* REDBURN) Mr Redburn, if you have one thought for me – nay, if you possess one spark of manliness, you will at once rid my father's house of this man's presence. Mr Redburn, do you not behold his insolent, defiant manner? Have you not heard his false, outrageous words? Are you deaf and blind?

RED: I am neither, madam. I have seen and heard enough to make me shun association with one so utterly degraded and dishonoured. (MISS DANVILLE *sinks on couch.*)

JOHN: (*leaning over* MR DANVILLE) Gregory, old pal, the tables are turned. The would-be-son-in-law's changed his mind. The lady's relatives don't soot. He'd reyther *not*. Shame and degradation in your daughter's eyes! Portland couldn't be much more of a punishment.

[MISS D: (*looking round with grief and shame*) Can – can it be a dream? No – no. Oh, where, where, shall I find one to help me in this terrible sorrow?
                    (RUTH *enters.*)

RUTH: Here, my darling, here.
                    (MISS DANVILLE *sinks on* RUTH's *bosom.* RUTH *looks over
                    defiantly at* REDBURN, *who is utterly aghast.*)]

             QUICK CURTAIN

ACT II

Eight bars. Curtain. Lights three-quarters down. Goree Piazzas, gas down.

SCENE 1.   *Public house in Goree Piazzas, Liverpool. As curtain rises* MAN *and*
WOMAN *cross.* POTMAN *pushes a drunken* SAILOR *out of the house and off.*
                    (*Enter* NED *and* JELLICK *from public house.*)

JEL: Well, Ned, I'm sorry to see it.

NED: Sorry to see what, Mr Jellick?

JEL: Ask yourself, Ned, ask your shabby clothes, ask your rolling eye, your unsteady gait – you're a changed man, changed for the worst, too. Public houses are doing for you.

NED: Doing for me! What are they doing for me? Making me forget my sorrows, making me forget the day I found that woman, who had said she loved, cared not for me. It's making a man of me once more.

JEL: Yes, but what sort of a man, Ned? You used to be a dapper lad as ever trod shoe leather, but now, now —

Portland: prison.

NED: Now I am a thriftless vagabond. Out with it! I never drank before my troubles came; you know what drove me to it, *you* know.

JEL: Ned, I was as fond as ever you were of Ruth.

NED: Fond of her, man! I'd have laid down my life willingly for her, if she'd have asked me. You can never know the depth of my love for her. And she loved *me* once. But it's all over now – all over.

JEL: (*aside*) I'm glad to hear it. (*Sighs.*) Ah, Ruth, Ruth, I wish I could wipe your image off my heart as easily.

NED: You'll see her soon mayhap?

JEL: Ye-es, I may. She's returned to her father's, poor girl.

NED: Aye, aye! Gone back to nurse the old man. Tell her when you see her, to forget me, if she hasn't done so already. Tell her you saw me in the streets of Liverpool *drunk*. D'ye hear? rolling through the streets, a broken and degraded man. Tell her that I'm trying to drown the recollection of happier days in dissipation, that when the bitter memory of her false love rises before me I drive it away with drink, d'ye hear? Ha! Ha! Ha! I'd like to see her face when she hears that sober, industrious Ned Clayton's turned vagabond; too proud to turn again to the repentant woman who had wronged him, but not too proud to reel about the streets the jest of every passer-by.

JEL: (*aside*) In my present position as a public character I don't think it reputable to be seen about with this misguided young man. (*aloud*) Well, Ned, good evening, good evening. (*aside*) What an escape for the poor girl! Who'd have thought so respectable a young man would so far forget himself? Oh, woman! Woman! If you were permitted to reply to all you've got to answer for you'd never leave off talking till the end of the world. (*Exit.*)

NED: Go back to work? What for? What have I to labour for? Who cares for me? And I could have made my mark as a mechanic. I know it. I had the skill and brain to earn a name, but what's the use? Bah! Where's my friend got to? Oh! Here you are.

> (*Enter* JOHNSON, *very drunk, from public house. He is flashily dressed and has a long pipe in his hand.*)

JOHN: Yes, here we are again. What are you doing out here?

NED: Talking to myself.

JOHN: When a man comes down to talking to himself he must be very hard up for company. I never talk to myself; I talk to the world at large.

NED: Yes, you've a bad habit of blurting out private matters. You'd soon let a whole roomful know your history, aye, and everybody else's too.

JOHN: Who are you correcting – pulling over the coals? I'm as good as you.

NED: If you're not better than I am you're not good for much.

JOHN: Not good for much? I'm good for a pint; I'm good for anything you like to call for. What's that? What's that? (*looking left*)

NED: What – where?

JOHN: Why, a tall figure all in black. (*alarmed and muddled*) Where are we?

NED: Why, a good ten minutes' walk from the pier. Come along. (*aside*) He's afraid of being left by himself. I'll leave him – he'll soon follow. I'll go ahead; follow on, will you. (*Exit.*)

JOHN: (*After looking round pulls a bottle from his pocket; sings.*) Follow, follow

over mountain – follow, follow over lea – and I'll lead you to love's fountain
if you'll – (*Drinks, wipes bottle with his sleeve, tries to cork it, and at last
succeeds.*) It's astonishing what a quantity I can take without its affecting me
in the least. I've known people who've only taken half as much and have been
unable to keep their balance – whereas I'm as firm as a rock. (*Hits his chest
and staggers.*) This is the worst paved town in England, the very worst.

> (*Music piano. Enter* KATE GARSTONE, *her hair untidy, her dress
> draggled, her appearance emaciated, that of an outcast in the lowest
> depths of misery.*)

KATE: No more – no more of this; no more misery, starvation and despair. I knew
that it could end but one way; and that way it shall end tonight. Degraded –
lost, an outcast from my home, I cannot, will not, be dependent on the hand
of charity for bread. Can I return to Fernleigh? return to be the bye-word for
all that's unfortunate and base? I who in happier days flaunted it in the eyes
of my companions, and made many an enemy with sharp and cruel tongue?
No, no! Better the river far than that – the ever-flowing silent river that
sweeps so many secrets to the sea. (*Clasps her hands, her back to* JOHNSON.
Music stops.)

JOHN: There'sh – there'sh a young womans; she's talking to herself. Everybody in
Liverpool seems talking to themselves – it's catching, it's an epi-epi-gram; no,
it's an epi-epidemic – (*to* KATE) Anything the matter? (*going to her*)

KATE: No, sir. (*about to cross*)

JOHN: Don't be in a hurry – how she wobbles about – wish – wish – way to the
landing stage?

KATE: Straight on. (*He detains her.*)

JOHN: Wait a moment – it's all very well to say straight on, but which way's
straight on?

KATE: Let go your hold, sir. I think you had better ask a policeman.

JOHN: (*with offended dignity*) Ask a polisheman! I shall not ask a polisheman, I
don't like polisheman. I consider their manners intrusive, their morals superficial, their utility questionable, and their uniform beastly. Them's my sentiments as regards the constabbley.

KATE: Pray let me go; if you are a man you will not detain me.

JOHN: If I'm a man! I flatter myself there's no mistake about it; you shan't go till
you have given me a kish. (*struggling; music*)

KATE: Let go your hold, man. Beware! if you rouse the demon within me you may
be sorry for it. It would take me but little to do someone mischief tonight –
my blood's on fire, so beware, I tell you.

JOHN: Ah! Ha! What a spit-fire. (*seizing her*) I've got you.

KATE (*struggling*) Help! Help! (*Enter* NED, *who seizes* JOHNSON *and throws him
down.*)

NED: What are you doing? Can't you leave the girl alone?

KATE: (*aside*) Ned Clayton! (*sinking her face in her hands*)

NED: I knew you would get into mischief —

'*Follow . . . mountain*': song composed circa 1823, music by S. T. Smith, words by F. W.
Hohler.

JOHN: (*on the ground*) I don't care so much for myself, but if you've broken the bottle you're no gentleman.

NED: Now, my girl, the best thing you can do is to — (*She turns her face to him.*) Kate!

KATE: Yes, Ned Clayton, Kate Garstone, the girl you once cared for. See what I've come to, and triumph over me if you like.

NED: You did me a cruel wrong, but I feel no triumph, Kate.

KATE: A cruel wrong? Yes, Ned Clayton, I know too well the wrong I did you. I was scarcely my own mistress at the time. I have tried to repent the deed, and I have suffered enough even to satisfy *you*.

NED: Nay, Kate, I bear no malice. Yours was always a strange, wild nature, and unlike the other girls in the village. Tell me; you seem in a poor plight now, lass. Let me assist you. (*Places his hand in his pocket. [She turns upon him almost fiercely.]*)

KATE: Never! Accept alms from you! No, no, Ned. Forget me; at all events, if ever you do think of me, think of me as I was long, long ago at Fernleigh, not as I now am in the cruel streets of Liverpool. Farewell! (*Rushes off.*)

NED: There's a wild way about her that betokens mischief. Kate, Kate! (*Follows her.*)

JOHN: (*reviving*) Kate, Kate, Kitty — Katherine, Empress of all the Rooshians — Catherine de Medecine, here!
       (*Re-enter* NED.)

NED: She is already out of sight. Come on, mate, I'm sorry I was rough just now, but I can't bear to see a woman in trouble. (*Pulls* JOHNSON *on to his legs.*)

JOHN: Who do you call a woman? But, however, I'll look it over this time out of respect for the fearful state of intoxication you are at present in; but if ever you knock me down again (NED *threatens.*) I shall take it as exceedingly unfriendly.

NED: Well, come on. (*Exit; lights down.*)

JOHN: I'm coming. Don't walk so quick; if you are going to your ruin you needn't go so dooshed fast. NB. To send round to old Danville another threatening letter tomorrow to shay I don't find my 'lowance s'ficient to keep me respectably. Ha! Ha! Mr Gregory Danville, Esquire. (*Enter* DANVILLE *in a long cloak.*) Cotton may be shaky and money may be tight, but you'll come down handsome once a quarter to your old pal Johnson, or it will be the worse for your — health. (*Exit. Music.* DANVILLE *follows him off, hiding his face in a long cloak.*)

SCENE 2.   *Lights quite down. The pier at Egremont, Liverpool, seen in the distance; lights in windows of the houses and lamps. One row right along the Docks. The pier extends from left; a shed on pier for* DANVILLE *to hide behind.* KATE *discovered at head of pier. Moonlight full upon her.*

KATE: How I have longed for this night, and it has come at last. Tonight my

---

de Medecine: de Medici.
The pier at Egremont: see appendix for fuller discussion of the setting for this scene.

wearied heart shall cease to beat. My throbbing brow shall rest at peace in the silent, solemn river that has soothed to rest so many a broken spirit. O placid water, how many dark crimes have you hidden! How many aching hearts have quenched their anguish in your peaceful depths! He said that he forgave me! Could *I* have forgiven one who sought to do me a grievous wrong? Did I forgive *him*? No, nor do I forgive myself. Lower and lower have I sunk till *now*. (*clasping her brow*) My brain is burning, but only for a little time. My life seems to pass before me as in a rapid dream. All that I have thought and said and done – my love, my hate, my vengeance, my despair – all – all in hideous reality – oh, let me shut it out! Let me shut it out! (*Throws off bonnet.*) I can – I will – there, there lies my last resource; there lies the welcome resting-place for the wearied heart, the broken spirit, the degraded outcast! (*About to throw herself into the water when a muffled bell is heard off.*) What's this? The late boat? I shall be seen; I'll wait until it has landed its passengers; it is but a few moments after all.

> (KATE *hides behind bulwark at head of pier. Music. Large steamboat with red light on pole and steam from funnel enters and rakes by pier.* MAN *comes on from top of pier.* MAN *on boat throws rope to him; he loops it over post, then places gangway.* DANVILLE, *wrapped in cloak, comes off boat and hides behind shed. Two or three passengers then get out and walk off pier. While this is going on,* NED CLAYTON, *who is on boat, rouses* JOHNSON, *who is asleep at the head of the boat.*)

JOHN: (*waking up*) Holloa! What's the matter?

NED: Come along.

> (JOHNSON *gets to gangway.* NED CLAYTON *passes across first,* JOHNSON *exchanges 'Good night' with* CAPTAIN, *gets on to gangway, and it nearly upsets him, being made on the usual see-saw principle. He turns round and looks at* CAPTAIN *as if he was the cause of it.*)

JOHN: Now, then, what are you doing?

> (MAN *draws up gangway and exit as the boat goes off.* JOHNSON *stands at head of pier waving his hand to* CAPTAIN, *and saying 'Good night', when the boat is well off. A loud rattling of chains is heard as if they were anchoring.* CAPTAIN *places red light at head of boat.* NED CLAYTON *has been leaning disconsolately over rail of pier during this.*)

NED: Now then, Johnson, are you coming on home?

JOHN: No, I'm not coming on home. I tell you what it is, Mr Ned, you're in a disgusting state of intoxication, and I don't think it altogether respectable to be seen with anyone who's in such abominable condition.

NED: Well I can't spend my night *here*. Are you coming?

JOHN: I are not. I'm going to have a smoke here in the moonlight.

NED: Rubbish! You'll be falling into the water, that's what you'll be doing.

Large steamboat . . . enters: see appendix for further discussion of this effect.
rakes: projects its bow or stern.

JOHN: Take care *you* don't come to grief. I shall stay out hereabout and solil – soliloquise.

NED: Once for all are you coming with me?

JOHN: Twice for all, I ain't. (*Staggers to seat.*) Go home, I'll join you soon. (NED CLAYTON *is going.*) Here, Ned, now don't take a mean advantage of my absence and finish the spirits.

NED: If I leave him here he'll get into mischief. (*to him*) You'll find yourself in the lock-up if you don't mind. (*Exit off pier.*)

JOHN: The lock-ups – that for the lock-ups (*snapping fingers, and nearly over-balancing himself*). How deep and black the water looks. (*music*) Aye, and how *still*. That's the cove to keep a secret. No blabbing there. Holloa! There's my pipe gone out and I've got no lights. Wonder if that vessel there would put off a boat and give me a light. (*Gets up and staggers to back of pier.*) By George, a fellow might fall over too; what a magnificent relief it would be to my old pal and private banker if I was to. (DANVILLE *comes from behind shed, gets behind* JOHNSON.) Lor', how I should like to have a bath. (DAN-VILLE *pushes him in, and rushes off.* KATE *screams, staggers forward a step or two and speaks in a weak voice.*)

KATE: Help! Help! I cannot call loud enough, my voice fails me, and I have a pain here, like a knife, in my heart. It's grown worse and worse each day. Help! Oh, if someone would but come! They are putting off a boat from that vessel. Help! (*Takes off handkerchief and waves it.*) I cannot stand. Oh! (*Faints behind bulkhead, her figure almost concealed.*)

(*Enter* NED *from end of pier.*)

NED: Now then, Johnson, here's the pier-man. Here Johnson. (*looking round*) Why where's he got to. What's this? Why here's his pipe and his purse, too, – care-less old fool. (*Pockets them – turns round to near where* JOHNSON *went in.*) Why here's his cap – Oh, horror! Why he must have fallen into the water, – he can't have passed me. Here, help!

(*Enter* KITELY *and another, carrying a lantern.*)

NED: Here, my friend's fallen into the water. See, there's a boat making for the pier.

KITE: Fallen into the river, mate? That's scarcely likely. (MAN *looks over side with lantern.*)

NED: It must be so, I'd only left him a few minutes.

KITE: Where was he when you left him?

NED: Here, far gone in drink and foolish as he is apt to be when he's in that state.

KITE: I've seen him about with you a good deal, flashing about his money pretty free. Not much of a companion for a respectable young man, eh, mate?

NED: But he wasn't –

KITE: Never mind, it don't much matter what he *was* now, poor chap, but here's the boat.

RED: (*who has entered in boat, with* SAILOR *sculling it*) A man's been thrown into the water off the pier.

NED: What?

KITE: Halloa! (*Places his hand on* NED's *shoulder.*)

---

lock-up: a house or room for the temporary detention of offenders.

NED: (*shaking off his hand*) Don't touch me, fellow. What do you mean? What do I see? Redburn? (*Pulls out handkerchief. The purse falls out.* KITELY *picks it up.*)

RED: I saw the thing from the deck of the Dodo. That fellow there flung a man over the pier-side into the water.

KITE: Will you swear that?

RED: I'm almost sure; but still —

NED: Will you swear that, Robert Redburn?

RED: You here? (*aside*) My revenge comes tardily, but it is none the less secure. (*to* SAILOR *in boat*) I shall not accompany you, I'm afraid, to Pernambuco. Important business will detain me at home.

KITE: What was his name?

NED: Johnson.

KITE: Here it is, engraved upon the purse. This looks bad.

NED: It *is* his purse. I found it lying here, and —

KITE: Don't say anything more, 'cos I shall have to use it against you.

NED: Great Heavens! Do you mean that I – I — (*in an agony*) Do you still say you saw me do it?

RED: I swear I did.

KATE: (*Starts forward, and stands erect.*) Liar!

KITE: Who is this woman, and what does she mean?

KATE: Never mind who I am. I – I – (*Staggers, and places her hand on her heart.*)

RED: Will you believe that ragged outcast, who is, no doubt, one of the fellow's gang?

KATE: I was here and saw it all.

NED: Ha! Then you can solve this dreadful mystery. Kate, Kate, speak and clear me.

KATE: (*her hand to her head*) Oh, air, air, give me air! (*Staggers and almost falls.*) What does it mean?

KITE: (NED *catching her*) There, there, you're better now.

KATE: Yes, yes. I'm better now. Oh! What does it mean?

NED: (*in great alarm*) She wanders, and a word of hers can save me! Kate – Kate! Remember your silence may doom me to disgrace – to death – say what you saw and save me, Kate.

KATE: (*with an effort*) I saw – I saw a man flung into the water, (*pointing to* DANVILLE's *hiding-place*) by – by —

NED: Kate! Kate!

KATE: By – (*Screams; places her hand on her heart, and sinks.*)

KITE: (*looking at her*) She'll never speak another word, poor lass, she's gone. (*Kneels and lifts her head.*)

NED: Gone!

RED: Don't let that fellow escape.

NED: My life hung upon her lips, and they are closed for ever!

QUICK DROP

Pernambuco: a port in Brazil, with direct trading contacts with Liverpool.

ACT III

SCENE 1. *Interior of farm. Door.* RUTH *discovered looking over accounts at table.* SPOTTY *standing. Music.*

SPOT: If I was to live to the age of Methoosalem I should never be able to show sufficient gratitude, Miss Ruth, never.

RUTH: Well, show your gratitude, Spotty, by attention, civility, and truth; serve your new employer, Mr Danville, well, and you will have no cause to regret entering his service.

SPOT: Bless you, miss, I'm only too glad to be Mr Danville's manservant. A word from you got me the place. I've no stupid pride; besides, Mr Danville and his daughter's going to travel, and I want to see the world like – like –

RUTH: Like the monkey, eh?

SPOT: Ha, Ha! Had me there. But I like to hear you speak in your old cheery voice, if it's only for a minute. (RUTH *sighs; aside*) There she is again, sighing again; *her* sunshine don't last long. Well, as I was saying, miss, you see, I couldn't go on any longer with that Redburn. (RUTH *shudders.*) Beg pardon, miss, for naming him to you. I know you can't abide to hear his name mentioned. He's given up business; gone abroad among the blacks, I fancy. (*aside*) Hope they'll h'eat him.

RUTH: It's a come down from a clerk to a menial, but now you will be with kind, good people instead of –

SPOT: Instead of a crocodile in coat and trousers. It's my opinion that one of these fine days Mr Redburn will be found out to be somethin' 'orrid. I've often heard him groaning to hisself and stamping about his office, all alone – sometimes too, when I went in sudden, he used to start and turn like a ghost. (RUTH *indicates annoyance.*) There – there, I beg your pardon. Oh, miss, as to being a menial, my opinion is that a flunkey's sitywation is very much superior to a clerk's – that is, the half clerk, half messenger that *I* was. Look at a clerk. He gets precious little pay – he has to keep hisself respectable. He works like a nigger; he can't enjoy hisself, for fear of folks saying he's going to the bad; if he's seen taking a glass of grog he's a confirmed *drunkard*: if he plays a game of billards he's a reg'lar gambler; if he dresses pretty well, he's a robbing of his tailor or a drawing of bills; if he dines at home his landlady starves him; if he feeds at a cook-shop he's pisoned; and if he goes and gets married he's obliged to live up in a top floor in a back street, with nothing but babbies and chimney pots for company.

RUTH: Not a very tempting prospect certainly, Spotty.

SPOT: Which, miss, the babbies or the chimney pots? But look at the position of a flunkey, as his h'enemies calls him. Fed like a h'emperor; dressed like a h'ambassador, mixing amongst the best society, without having his opinions

---

cook-shop: eating house.
h'universal 'sufferings': universal sufferage, the extension of voting right to all adult citizens, had been furthered by the second Reform Bill in 1867. In LC *reform bills* replaces *h'universal 'sufferings'*.

asked. What's h'universal 'sufferings' to him? What does he care about the state of parties – except h'evening parties? What's it to him who's *h'in* or who's *h'out*. His habits is reg'lar, his noo suits of livery is reg'lar; 'appy in 'is mind, affable in 'is manners, and 'andsome to be'old, there is no more h'enviable mortal than your well-clothed, well-paid, well-fed, fullblown British flunkey.

RUTH: Then think of the foreign countries you'll see; why you'll come back quite an accomplished person, Spotty.

SPOT: Well, give me h'old h'England, Miss Ruth; after all, h'English cookery, h'English cornfields, h'English gals.

RUTH: Ah, you'll lose your heart to some French or Italian beauty, I daresay.

SPOT: *Me!* I'd scorn the h'action; give me the home-grown article; none of your foreign produce.

RUTH: Well (*Rises.*) I shall always be glad to hear of your doings, Spotty. I can never forget the service you did to my poor father. Goodbye, Spotty; mind and do my recommendation credit. (*Offers her hand.*)

SPOT: Goodbye, miss, and thankee once mere, and – and (*shaking her hand violently*) – Goodbye, I'm sure I – (*He backs towards door through which* RED-BURN *enters quietly, standing still.*) I'm sure I'll do you credit. Try and keep up your pecker, miss. There's as good fish in the sea as ever – (*Sees himself close to* REDBURN, *shrinks in horror, walks round him quietly, and sneaks out at door, his eyes fixed on* REDBURN.)

RUTH: (*with back towards door*) Poor fellow; I think he'll keep his word.

RED: Ruth!

RUTH: (*Turns, gives a smothered shriek, and recoils.*) You here?

RED: Pardon me, Miss Kirby, pray pardon me. I will not inflict my presence upon you beyond a few moments. I am aware it is unwelcome.

RUTH: It is, sir. *Most* unwelcome.

RED: (*bowing*) I deserve your reproaches. I submit to them most humbly. Miss Kirby – Ruth, (*advancing a step*) pardon me. I came with the determination to speak to you as one who had never dared to address you but in the cold set phrase of distant acquaintanceship, but (*with passion*) your beauty and the recollection it conjures up of days now gone by for ever – days when I hoped to call you mine, broke down my resolution, and I can only see the girl I loved so dearly once, the girl I love far dearer now than ever.

RUTH: Robert Redburn, these words come strangely from the lips of one who –

RED: (*advancing a step, and quickly*) Who said he loved another, you would say. The passion I fancied I felt for Fanny Danville was a passing whim. I never really loved her. I was half wild at the bitter blow my hopes received that wretched night at Fernleigh. I looked around for consolation, and fancied for a little while I should find it in the artless love of Gregory Danville's daughter, but I will admit with shame that my principal object was her wealth. I was poor then. I am poorer now. I come to you now no longer as a well-to-do gentleman, Ruth. I am little better than a beggar.

RUTH: Those who pursue the dishonourable path you have trodden sooner or later must arrive at the goal of disgrace and shame.

RED: You speak very differently to what you did in the old days, Ruth.

RUTH: (*Rises.*) Yes – I am no longer the willing, foolish girl whom a gentleman like you could twist round his finger, whom a few high-flown compliments delighted, and who learnt – alas! too late for her own peace of mind – how worthless words could be. (*Goes.*)

RED: (*aside*) 'Too late for her own peace of mind.' There's something of the old sentiment lingering about her heart yet. (*aloud*) I am about to go abroad, Ruth, for ever. (*She is quite unaffected by the announcement; pause.*) I shall see you no more, unless –

RUTH: (*coldly*) Well, sir?

RED: Unless you go with me. (*seizing her hand passionately*)

RUTH: Let me go. (*Flings his hands off.*) Don't dare to lay a finger on me. Stand there and finish what you have to say.

RED: Ruth, you are a cruel one. There is no spark of pity in those relentless eyes, no tone but that of harsh and bitter enmity in that voice that once was music to my ear. Don't force me, Ruth, to meet scorn with scorn; don't dare me to do that which I *can* and which I *will* do, unless you find some pity for me – some forgiveness for the past.

RUTH: I – I do not comprehend you. What do you mean?

RED: Women are merciful, and forgive much in matters of the heart. They will overlook almost anything except when *another* intervenes, when their fancy turns to a new or reverts to an *old* lover, as, for instance, young Clayton.

RUTH: Do not name him. He and I are separated for ever.

RED: You've forgotten your fancied affection for him, then?

RUTH: (*with passion*) Forgotten my love for him? No, it's only lately I've *remembered* it. I loved him at the first, but it was the fickle, worthless fondness of a weak and silly girl. Then *you* came like a dark shadow between us, and what with *his* coldness, the evil promptings of a wicked friend, and my own wayward, headstrong nature, I was mad enough to listen to a tempter from whom I was saved by the man I had so cruelly and shamefully wronged.

RED: Then you love him still?

RUTH: *Better than my life!* Leave me, leave me. I cannot – will not – listen to you. (*Turns from him.*)

RED: (*advancing*) But you must! for your lover's life hangs upon your reply.

RUTH: What? (*Turns.*)

RED: Your lover's life, I say. I am telling you a fact, Ruth. Clayton is accused of murder –

RUTH: Murder? (*Retreats.*) Oh, it's false –

RED: That has to be proved.

RUTH: Who dares to bear witness against him?

RED: I dare.

RUTH: *You!*

RED: Yes, an awkward witness too, for, unfortunately, I *saw* him commit the crime.

RUTH: (*taking a step or two towards him, and looking intently in his face*) I'll not believe it.

RED: Very likely. But you'll not have to try him.

RUTH: Oh, mercy!

RED: There is no romance in the breast of the British juryman. He only looks at *facts*. I saw him rob and fling into the river a drunken, loafing fellow, with more money than wit. I saw it from the deck of the *Dodo*, then moored a little distance. My evidence will *convict* him.

RUTH: (*Who has looked up in horror, grasping the arms of the chair, turns in an agony to* REDBURN.) But you *won't* give it? You will have pity! Oh, say you will have pity! (*clasping his hands*)

RED: (*seizing her hands passionately*) His life is in your hands. (*seizing her in his arms*) Ruth, Ruth, I always loved you – madly. I do so still. Ruth, Ruth, let us fly to another land, where we will only live for each other's love; where we shall forget the wretched past in the happy present, in the peaceful future.

RUTH: (*breaking from him*) Tempter – base, insidious tempter, I will listen no longer to your entreaties. There is some hideous mystery in all this. I cannot, *will* not, believe him guilty of so foul a deed. (*music*)

RED: I saw it, girl. Refuse me and you sign Clayton's death warrant. Pause, ere it is too late; he is lying now under the tender care of your old friend Jellick, who will have to deliver him to justice tomorrow morning, as sure as you stand there.

RUTH: (*At the mention of* JELLICK's *name a sudden idea strikes her and she betrays it by her manner; aside*) Mr Jellick! There is yet a chance. I will try it. I can but fail, and then –

RED: (*advancing*) You see the horrible nature of his position, and you will fly with me, Ruth?

RUTH: (*waving him back*) Stand off, sir. My place is by *his* side and not by *yours*.

RED: (*recoiling*) You defy me then?

RUTH: I do. That Ned is guilty I will never believe. Do your worst, and how bad *that* is I know full well. But his innocence will triumph over *your* black arts. (*Takes shawl and bonnet from chair.*)

RED: (*advancing and seizing her hand*) Ruth, Ruth, what would you do? Whither would you go?

RUTH: (*throwing him off*) Where should I go but to him – to be near him in his hour of need; to help him, if I can, in his bitter trouble. (*turning fiercely on* REDBURN) Fly with *you* – *you*, and leave *him* to his disgrace and misery! Why, man, the very thought brings the blush of shame to my cheeks to think I ever listened to the words of such a villain. (*Exit.*)

RED: Fine words, Ruth Kirby, but you shall repent them, my lass, you shall repent them. (*Exit slowly after her; music loud, clear.*)

SCENE 2.   *The lock-up. The scene to have a solid look, the doors to be thick and swing heavily. Doors, right, left and centre.* JELLICK *discovered seated at table with* SERGEANT DONOVAN. SERGEANT DONOVAN *smoking and drinking. Table and two chairs. Bottle and glasses on table. Clothes horse, left. Lamp hanging, centre.*

JEL: Hah, it's all very well for you to sneer at this feeling – but I *don't like* it. I repeat, Sergeant, I don't like it.

SERG: Well, the more you look at it the less you'll like it. So leave off looking at it, man. You must accept your position as the saying is.

JEL: So I do – so I do. But he was such a fine young man, and to think that he's locked up *here*. Me his gaoler, Sergeant. I don't like it, and that's a fact.

SERG: Sure leave the young man alone now – he's comfortable enough.

JEL: Yes, I've made it as easy for him as I could for *her* sake, Sergeant, for her *sake*. I know she loved him, and I know she never loved *me*. We was rivals, Sergeant.

SERG: And now you've got your rival under lock and key, what the divil more would you have, man alive? Bah! You're not fit for your purfession, Jellick; you've too much of the milk of human kindness in your composition.

JEL: And haven't you?

SERG: No, not a drop; it's turned to vinegar long since.

JEL: I don't believe he *ever* did the deed, there. (*Slaps table.*)

SERG: That's not your business. Why, you soft-headed old pump, I do believe you'd let him escape if you had your own way.

JEL: (*with fervour*) That I would.

SERG: Oh bedad, if Government only knew your sintiments. If I'm lucky enough to lay my finger on my gentleman, Slippery Dick, as I call him, you won't find me half so merciful.

JEL: It's a different thing, you're on the track of a thief and a rascal. This young man Clayton's neither. Poor Ruth, when she hears of it, it'll break her heart.

SERG: Oh, go along with your flowery feelings; you say she drove him to it; very well, serve her right. Woman, woman, Mr Jellick, woman is the – is the – well, a woman is a woman. Now, there's Slippery Dick as I call him –

JEL: Oh, damn Slippery Dick!

SERG: Very well, then. (*taking up glass*) My sarvice to you. If your whisky was only half as strong as your language, it's rowling to bed I'd be four hours ago this blessed night. I'll give you a toast, Jellick. 'Here's manners', my boy. (*Drinks.*)

JEL: I beg your pardon, Sergeant, I'm upset tonight. You mustn't think much of my strange way.

SERG: *Much!* Sure, I think precious little of you. I'm thinking of my own little job. It's not the reward, it's the honour and glory of the capture. Master Dick's not been heard of these ten years, and now I've got a clue to him at last – not much of a clue, but I'll folly it up, and when I've got him – (*Sees* JELLICK *wrapped in thought.*) That old fool's in the clouds again. (JELLICK *mechanically raises his glass to his lips in a vacant, preoccupied manner.*)

SERG: Now, then. (*Raps the table suddenly.*)

JEL: (*His liquor goes down the wrong way and he chokes in his glass.*) What are you doing? My nerves are all *nowhere* – you made it all go the wrong way.

SERG: Hah! There's only one way whisky'll go when it passes *your* lips, old boy.

JEL: Hah, Sergeant, it's a pleasant sight to see you so cheerful, when I think of that young man lying there a prisoner.

SERG: Well, *don't* think of him. If you *must* think of him, do it to yourself. Don't bother me about him; you ought to feel proud to have such a prisoner. As a rule, you don't soar above 'drunk and disorderlies', with perhaps now and

---

pump: fool.

then a pickpocket or a burglar in a small way of business. Drop the shop,
Jellick, my boy, and let's be jolly. It's unfortunate the prisoner's a friend, but
you can't help yourself.

JEL: Yes, I *can* help myself. (*Takes bottle.*) I'm not quite a child, Sergeant.

SERG: (*Aside; takes up bottle and looks how much is left.*) Faith, I wish you was
a child; you'd ha' been in bed before this. (*Yawns.*) Sure I'll sleep without
rocking this blessed night, that's what I'll do.

JEL: I've given you *my* bed, Sergeant; you don't turn me out, for I can't rest tonight. I shall sit up here. There's the room. (*Points off.*) Pleasant dreams.
(*Shakes hands.*)

SERG: Thank ye, thank ye. (*Yawns.*) If I do trace him out and nab him, I'll send
you a barrel of the rale potheen, that'll make ye feel as if you was walking on
a sunbeam, and'll curl your eyelashes into ringlets as long as your arrum.
Good night. (*Exit.*)

JEL: Good night. Slippery Dick indeed! Cool hand that sergeant. There he's on the
scent, and I'll warrant got all his plans cut and dried, but he takes it all as
quietly as if he was going on a visit to his grandmother. (*knock at door*)
What's that? (*Goes to door.*) Who's there?

RUTH: (*without*) It's I, Mr Jellick. Let me in. I want to see you.

JEL: Ruth here at this hour; she must have heard all. (*Opens door.*)
        (*Enter* RUTH; *she staggers to chair.*)

RUTH: Wait a minute, don't speak to me yet. (*Puts her hand to her heart*.) I am
better now. I was frightened. I fancied someone followed me, but it was only
fancy, perhaps. Are we alone?

JEL: Quite – except – (*pointing to* NED's *room*)

RUTH: (*rising suddenly*) Is he here?

JEL: Yes. (*close to her*) I did all I could to soften down the severity of his position,
Ruth; I did more than I'd any right to do, in order to make him comfortable.

RUTH: (*seizing his hand*) Bless you, Mr Jellick, you are a good man – a kind, generous man – a kind, generous man always. Heaven! Will the truth never be
known?

JEL: It must and will be known some day, Ruth.

RUTH: But when? – When? When he no longer lives to hear his innocence declared? When the law has wreaked its vengeance on the guiltless? What comfort
is that to those who care for him? (*rising wildly*) And that door alone stands
between him and liberty. One turn of the key –
(*Makes movement to door.*)

JEL: (*Moves to intercept her.*) Ruth, what would you do?

RUTH: (*looking round dazed, after a pause, blankly*) Nothing, nothing.

JEL: Heaven knows I would do anything to help him, but I am powerless – completely powerless.

RUTH: Not so – you are all powerful. You can, if you please, save his life and
mine.

JEL: Tell me how, Ruth.

Drop the shop: refrain from talking about the subject/work.
potheen: Irish whiskey from illicit still.

RUTH: (*grasping his arm*) Prisoners have escaped before now. (*music*)

JEL: What? (*starting back*)

RUTH: Within that room there lies one accused of a crime, that, were he guilty, would rightly doom him to an ignominious death; but he is innocent. By cheating the law of its hapless, *guiltless* victim, you will be doing a simple act of common justice. (*hurriedly*) It will *never* be known; people have *broken* out of this place before *now*; *who* is to know that *you* aided his escape? By tomorrow when you discover your prisoner's flight, he will be far away – out of the country. (*Kneeling and grasping his hand; JELLICK is strongly agitated.*) For my sake do this generous deed; dear, *dear* old friend, it will break my heart – it will *kill* me should he suffer for another's crime. Let him escape and my life shall be *devoted to you.*

JEL: Ruth, Ruth, what are you saying? Do you mean to say that if I let him escape *you* will –

RUTH: (*with her hands before her eyes*) Yes, yes; give me but *his* life, and (*after a struggle, almost choking*) and take mine. (*on her knees, her arms stretched forth*)

JEL: You do not know the danger involved in such a course.

RUTH: One turn of the key and he is free! Can you deny me this? (*appealing*) Can you refuse to do a deed of which your own conscience will acquit you, though all the judges in the land should call it crime?

JEL: (*gazing at her intently*) And if I do this, Ruth; if I run this fearful risk, you will keep your word, Ruth? (*Goes to door of room.*) Listen, and be sure the sergeant does not hear.

RUTH: One moment; he must not know that *I* am here; he must not know of our bargain. He would never purchase his liberty at such a price. (*She hides behind clothes horse.*)

JEL: (*aside*) A broken bar and a crumbling brick or two may lull suspicion. (*Turns the key and opens door.*) Ned, Ned Clayton, here.

NED: (*within*) What is it?

JEL: I want you. Step this way.

(*Enter NED: his manner is stern, and almost fierce.*)

NED: What do you want with me?

JEL: Hush, man, don't speak so loud; you are innocent of this crime of which you are accused. I know that, you needn't speak. If you fly now – at once, you may get clear away, leave the country, and escape.

NED: What do I hear? Are you playing some trick upon me? Beware, I'm a desperate man; the mere shadow of this crime seems to have blackened my better nature already. I feel since I have lain in the grim solitude of that dark room that it would take little enough to make a *real* felon of me *now.*

JEL: I mean what I say – you are free to go. If you are quick and careful you may escape notice. Go without another word.

NED: Do you mean it?

JEL: Yes, yes, go; nothing will be known of it till tomorrow, and by that time –

NED: (*grasping his hand*) I'll live to repay you for this. The truth must be known soon; you shall not repent it. (*Going up rapidly to door, is met by REDBURN. Picture.*)

RED: Stay, you! Your prisoner going to escape? I came in the nick of time, it seems.

NED: Stand back, man; I wouldn't have your blood upon my soul, but dare to intercept me, and I'll never take my grip from off your throat until I've laid you lifeless at my feet.

RED: Rash, mad fool! (*to* JELLICK) I call on you with me to seize that man.

NED: What you will, then! (*fierce struggle, during which* RUTH *is strongly agitated,* REDBURN *is thrown violently on to stage, and* NED *escapes through door, which swings to heavily. As* REDBURN *rises to follow* NED, RUTH *flies to door rapidly, turns large key, and stands with back to door. Picture.*)

RED: Woman, would you shield a felon from the avenging hand of justice? stand aside –

RUTH: He is innocent, and were he *not* YOU are no fit instrument of the law – pitiful, vindictive monster! Your wicked plan has failed, and he is free.

RED: He shall never live to enjoy his triumph. Stand away, I say. (*Rushes at her, swings her round too, is about to wrench the key from her with great fury, when –*)

          (*Enter* SERGEANT DONOVAN.)

SERG: Strike a woman! Hands off.

RED: Would you let a prisoner escape?

SERG: (*looking searchingly at him and mechanically putting his hands into his hind pockets slowly*) No, I wouldn't let a prisoner escape, especially if his name was – (*pause*) – Slippery Dick!

          (JELLICK and SERGEANT DONOVAN *rapidly handcuff* RED-
          BURN.)

          (*Picture.* REDBURN *handcuffed.* DONOVAN *shaking his fist at him in triumph.* RUTH *on her knees overcome.*)

          CURTAIN – QUICK

      ACT IV

SCENE.   *A sheep farm in Australia. A kind of built out store, with door; flat set obliquely so that the opening in the upper part of it, which forms a loft, shows a full front to the audience; a common ladder leads up to it. Rude stone. Table with 'Illustrated London News', stool at each side. Small barrel, and bag of tools and bundle by it.* SPOTTY *discovered, smoking.* PHIL ANDREWS *sitting on barrel, and tying up his things.*

PHIL: Don't talk to me, Master Spotty, my mind's made up.

SPOT: Well, trust me, you'll repent it. Here you've got a good master and high wages, what more can you want? Bother the gold, *I* say.

PHIL: Well, you can do as you like. I haven't thrown my master over like a lot more. I give him due notice. I'm off to the diggins. There's many a poor man like me has found a fortune there this few months past, and I shall try my luck with the rest. It's not so bad a look-out for *you* neither. Labour 'll rise

---

ACT IV: see appendix for act IV in LC.

in vally, and you as choose to stick to your masters 'll get anything you like to ask for in the way of wages.

SPOT: Oh, Phil, I'm ashamed of you; your h'avarice is h'already a h'eating into your constitootion. There ain't no royal road to riches.

PHIL: Ain't there? There's the road as leads to Arbour Creek, and I'm a going to try it.

SPOT: Well, if you get murdered write and let us know.

PHIL: I can take care of myself.

SPOT: There's all the scum in creation rushing here to the Antipods. A pleasant party of a dozen passen me only last Saturday. There was 'Burglary' and 'Cold Bath Fields' stamped on every one of their ugly countenances; and the way in which they were rubbing up their revolvelusses and polishing their bow-wowie knives gave me a cold chill.

PHIL: Well, I'm content to risk it; and I tell you what, Master Spotty, for all your palaver about faithfulness to Mr Clayton and gratitoode to his anxious wife, you get a smell of the gold dust, and it's the sort of snuff as 'll set you a sneezing on your road to Arbour Creek in the twinkling of a pickaxe. I shall see you with a cradle yet. (*Gets to door.*)

SPOT: I hope you will, sir, but it'll be one of a domesticated natur' manufactured in wicker and containing of a new addition to the population of the *Antipods.*

PHIL: Well, goodbye, mate, and when I'm a rich man I'll send you a nugget for a breast pin. (*Shakes hands. Music. Exit* PHIL ANDREWS.)

SPOT: Thankee for nothing. I didn't wear a breast pin in old England, and I don't seem to care about jewhillery in the Antipods. Dear, dear, to think how things come about. The idea of me as was a starving lad in the streets of the mighty metropulus a turning up my nose at the gold fields.

(*Enter* NED, *dressed as an Australian sheep farmer;* RUTH *with him.*)

NED: I'm so sorry to leave you dearest, but it is a most important matter and must not be neglected. You needn't be afraid of my running away in search of gold.

RUTH: Oh, I'm not afraid of that, Ned.

NED: (*taking her hands*) There's metal more attractive, as the man says in the play; the mighty metal may have charms for some, but to me the diamonds that twinkle in those bright eyes, Ruth, are worth a world of gold dust.

RUTH: Married these five years and not tired of paying me compliments yet, Ned?

NED: They're no compliments, they're the truth, lass, the honest truth.

RUTH: And how long shall you be away?

NED: Oh! I shall be back again as soon as possible, you may be sure.

RUTH (*both sitting one at each side of table*) But the discovery of the gold at Arbour Creek has brought such a set of rough people quite near to us that —

NED: You're afraid I shall be robbed and made away with by bush-rangers and other ruffians. They're all too much bent on the absorbing task of gold finding to waste time and powder on a poor sheep farmer.

Arbour Creek: place names in this scene are largely fictitious.
bow-wowie knives: bowie knives were long knives, double-edged at the point.
cradle: a trough on rockers used in mining for shaking stones in water.
bush-rangers: Australian brigands (usually escaped convicts), living in the bush.

RUTH: Ned, dear Ned, you mustn't think me foolish and weak, but for the last few days I have been so sadly depressed with a presentiment of some coming misfortune. I have already endeavoured to throw it off, but by night and day the shadow of a coming danger seems to dim the happiness I should otherwise feel at my present lot. You are not angry?

NED: Well, upon my life, I'm half inclined to be so with you, my silly fanciful Ruth. I do believe you half regret that Jellick's better nature triumphed, and that he refused to make you miserable for life. I do really think you regret having joined me here and become my wife, Ruth, though fortune has smiled upon my labours and I'm already half way on to being a rich man.

RUTH: Until your innocence is established in the eyes of the world I shall never know real happiness.

NED: The eyes of the world indeed! I care for no eyes but yours, and mind I don't see a tear in them for twenty years. (*Enter* SPOTTY, *in great glee, tossing up his hat for joy*.) Hooray, hooray! Here's the post! Letters from England! News from home!

    (POSTMAN *enters; he gives letter to* RUTH; SPOTTY *takes up* POSTMAN *and gives him drink out of a stone jar at back*.)

NED: (*sitting on table; aside*) News from home! Oh, welcome words to many an exile in a distant land! To me, alas, they bring no comfort. Every letter that reaches me may bring the terrible news that I'm tracked – discovered – and once more liable to that fearful accusation which I am so powerless to disprove. (*Gas lights gradually go down*.) Pshaw! Ruth's forebodings are affecting her husband. I must set her an example of cheerfulness, and in the black and threatening cloud that hangs above me strive to see only the silver lining that bids me hope.

RUTH: (*who has been looking over letter*) Ned – Ned – read. Oh, this is news that midst its sadness will bring joy to your heart, my husband.

NED: (*taking letter*) What! From Mr Danville – dying!

RUTH: Read on – read on.

NED: What's this! (*Reads*.) 'I would never have let the innocent suffer for the guilty, but whilst your husband was safe I dared not breathe the terrible secret which I knew would break my child's heart. Pity and forgive me if you can – '

SPOT: (*to* POSTMAN) You never bring me a letter. All my old sweethearts have forgotten me. I'll surprise one or two by going back all over nuggets.

POST: Ah! They'll remember you *then*. Well, I must be on my road; weather's threatening and time's a-flying.

NED: I'll ride with you as far as Blackman's Gully. (*taking down hat and whip*)

POST: Glad of your company, master. There's a deal of rough customers about. I saw one poor fellow who'd been robbed and hurt, I fancy, dragging himself along, only a half-a-mile from here, just now.

RUTH: Oh, Ned, Ned. I wish you wouldn't go. There's a storm gathering too.

NED: It's a matter of duty, dearest, and I must. (*Embraces her*.) Why, that letter

---

Gas lights: the stage and auditorium in the 1860s were lit by gas, the intensity of which was usually controlled by the prompter.

alone, removing as it does the foul stain of suspicion from your husband, should be splendid company for you in my absence. (NED, SPOTTY, *and* POSTMAN *exeunt.*)

RUTH: I knew the welcome news would come some day, but never dreamt that Mr Danville had been driven to such a terrible crime. (*Sits on barrel and reads letter.*) 'The fellow dogged my footsteps, followed me like my shadow, threatening me, and making my already wretched life still harder to bear. At last I formed the terrible resolve of ridding myself of his persecution. (*Stage gets darker.*) When once the idea had seized upon my mind, I vainly endeavoured to shake it off. At length the desire for freedom from this state of thraldom became well nigh maddening, and one fatal night –' (*Starts.*) What's that? I am strangely nervous today. How glad I am Ned had a companion, if for only a portion of his ride. (*Reads.*) 'One fatal night I carried out my dreadful resolution. I waited for my tormenter on the pier at Egremont.' (*A loud peal of thunder, repeated at intervals, only at a distance. Knock heard.*)

RUTH: (*Alarmed, goes towards door.*) Who's there?

RED: (*without*) Let me in for mercy's sake – let me in.

RUTH: A strange voice. Who are you?

RED: A poor hunted wretch who seeks for shelter. Let me in, or I shall die here at your door.

RUTH: Some poor creature who has been ill-treated by these terrible men who are about in such numbers just now. (*Opens door.* REDBURN, *dressed as a bushranger, enters, pale, haggard, and dirty, and in rags. He staggers towards stool, right of table, but falls on ground short of it.*)

RED: Close the door; they'll know I'm here. Some drink – anything – my throat's burning. (RUTH *gives him drink from stone bottle in a cup; he drinks it eagerly.*) Hah! That puts fresh strength into me. I'm a man once more. (*Laughs hysterically.*) Ha! Ha! I'll double on them yet. Your health, my bonny hostess. You've sent the blood back to my heart, and given me fresh courage with my life. (RUTH *has been looking at him during all this, and the idea begins to flash across her mind that it is* REDBURN. *She immediately withdraws.*) Why, how's this? do you shrink from me like the rest? Are you so daintily bred in these parts that a poor travel-stained, footsore, harmless fellow creature frightens you, eh? What is there to – (*Recognises her.*) Ruth! (*Starts back; pause.*) Can it be? Ruth Kirby?

RUTH: Ruth Clayton – I am Edward Clayton's wife. Robert Redburn, what evil chance has brought you here?

RED: So my rival won the day after all, and here am I a poor hunted outcast, whilst *he's* rich and happy – still, felon as I am, the crime of which your husband is guilty has never been laid to my charge – these hands are guiltless of murder – Can prosperous and respected Ned Clayton say as much?

RUTH: Yes – he was innocent.

RED: The proof.

RUTH: Is here – here in the handwriting of the remorseful culprit. Ample proof to fully establish my husband's innocence – the confession of the crime, the explanation of the motive urging it all in this paper written on his deathbed by the man who did the deed. (*music*)

RED: (*aside*) She speaks the truth. I can read it in her eyes. Thwarted – beaten every way. Your husband – where is he?

RUTH: On his road to Blackman's Gully, where –

RED: Ha! (*Approaches her.*) No other evidence exists then but the written confession in that paper.

RUTH: What do you mean?

RED: That paper destroyed, and the only slender proof of Clayton's innocence he could produce. (*He makes a clutch at it.*)

RUTH: Would you dare to –

SPOT: (*Enters suddenly, just at the moment; his jacket off.*) Hallo! Hallo! (*Gets before* REDBURN, *tucking up his sleeves slowly.*) You're a pleasant-looking customer you are; reg'lar specimen of the new kind of importation. Comparing the new settlers with the old natives, I gives my vote for the Aboriginals.

RED: (*in a low voice to* RUTH) You'll hear of me again. Meanwhile, I suppose, I may seek the shelter of some out-house or farm-shed until those who would hunt me down have left the neighbourhood. (*Is going up when* NED *enters.*)

RUTH: Ah, Ned! (*Rushes to his arms.*) What has happened?

NED: Why, old Sally fell lame when only a stone's throw from the farm, and I had to lead her back. Spotty, see to her. (SPOTTY *goes off.*)
　　　　　　(*distant shout heard*)

NED: What's that?

RED: What's that! Why those bush-ranging villains have got a grudge against me, and I'm flying for my life. (*shouts nearer*)

NED: (*not recognising* REDBURN) I don't know what you've done out here, but I'm an Englishman and I won't refuse to help a fellow countryman with such odds against him. Take this pistol and defend yourself, poor wretch. (*Gives him revolver.*)

RED: (*Snatches at it.*) Poor wretch! Ay, poor, scouted, luckless wretch truly – hunted down like a cur in the kennel, and assisted in his great extremity by *you* – you, the successful rival, the detested foe who has been Bob Redburn's bitterest curse in life. (RUTH *clutches* NED CLAYTON. REDBURN *goes up ladder and reaches loft.*) My first revenge broke down and you escaped. There are six barrels to this revolver – the first shall be for *you*, my kind preserver, whom I hate! and who has handed me the means to wipe out the long score of revenge I have against you.

RUTH: What would you do?

RED: I've sworn to be revenged on *him*, and I'll be so *now*.

NED: Stand away from me, Ruth. Stand away, I say!

RUTH: Never! Pitiless villain, you shall not harm him. If you do, I too will fall a victim to your heartless treachery. (*clinging to* NED) You shall not stir from me, Ned: whilst I am close to you, even *he* dare not carry out his atrocious threat.

NED: (*struggling with her*) Stand aside, Ruth! Let me go, I say. You do not know what the ruffian may do in his savage fury. Let me go! (*Throws her off. She sinks on ground.*) Mad fool! Remember that there are those about who will take short and summary vengeance on you for this. You will never live to glory in your triumph.

RED: I care not, so that I do triumph. Ned Clayton, I swore to repay you back the wrong you dealt me, and watch how well I mean to keep my oath. (*Is about to fire when a shot is heard, followed by a loud shout of triumph.* RED-BURN's *revolver goes off at the same moment. He falls off platform to a lower one.* RUTH *revives with the report; screams, and rushes into the arms of* NED.)

NED: Ruth! Ruth! Look up – I am unharmed. (SPOTTY *runs on at the same moment, rushes up steps, and looks down where* REDBURN *has fallen. Several diggers enter at door,* BLACK DAN *amongst them.*)

B. DAN: Well done, Grizzly Joe! He'll never live to sell another pal, the false ruffian.

NED: Who are you all, and what do you want?

B. DAN: We've been on yonder scoundrel's track these two days. He betrayed and robbed his brother diggers down at Gully Creek, and sold his pals who'd helped him, like a mean hound as he was; and we vowed we'd hunt him down, and we've done it. (JOHNSON *enters at this moment, looking off, his face averted from audience, a rifle in his hand, beard, etc.*) And Grizzly Joe here's a shot him like a dog, as he deserved. Oh, it's no murder, missus. We're a rough lot; but we're in the right this time.

NED: (*to* JOE) Your timely shot saved my life. You must have some other name besides Grizzly Joe. What is it, that I may remember it?

JOHN: Party by the name of Johnson.

NED: What! Can it be? Not drowned.

JOHN: No; I wasn't born to be *drowned.* On the night I was in liquor, and fell into the water –

NED: (*to* RUTH) *Fell* in!

JOHN: I struck out, being a good swimmer, and I was picked up by the *Nancy Dawson* brig, bound for Australia. Out here I took to digging, and though I haven't done much as yet in that line of business, I've come out all correct and reg'lar as a h'antipodean Nemesis. We don't mind if we *do* – just the least drop as is.

NED: I haven't words to thank you, Johnson. I'll try what I can do in another way. (*aside to* RUTH) He doesn't even know of the attempt upon his life. Look up, my darling, the danger's over; the storm has passed. After your trials and temptations, such as beset few amongst us, Ruth, peace of mind and a happy lot are now in store for you, and the clear Australian sun shines bright and glowing on your future pathway, my own brave, true-hearted LANCASHIRE LASS.

(*Music, 'Home sweet Home'.*)

CURTAIN

III Act II of *Our Boys*, Vaudeville Theatre, London 1875

OUR BOYS

An original modern comedy

First produced at the Vaudeville Theatre, Strand, on 16 January 1875, with the
following cast:

SIR GEOFFRY CHAMPNEYS, *a county magnate*	Mr William Farren
TALBOT CHAMPNEYS, *his son*	Mr Thomas Thòrne
PERKYN MIDDLEWICK, of Devonshire House, *a retired butterman*	Mr David James
CHARLES MIDDLEWICK, *his son*	Mr Charles Warner
KEMPSTER, *Sir Geoffry's manservant*	Mr W. Lestocq
PODDLES, *Middlewick's butler*	Mr Howard
VIOLET MELROSE, *an heiress*	Miss Kate Bishop
MARY MELROSE, *her poor cousin*	Miss Roselle
CLARISSA CHAMPNEYS, *Sir Geoffry's sister*	Miss Sophie Larkin
BELINDA, *a lodging-house slave*	Miss Cicely Richards

Butterman: manufacturer and vendor of butter and other dairy products.

IV Thomas Thorne as Talbot Champneys in *Our Boys*

V David James as Perkyn Middlewick in *Our Boys*

ACT I

SCENE   *Handsomely furnished drawing-room at* MIDDLEWICK's *house.*
French windows at back. Garden backing, Doors, right and left. PODDLES *enters.*

POD: (*after pause, looking at watch*) Half-past two, I do declare, and the young
gents not arrived yet; train's late, no doubt. No wonder master's anxious; I
dare say Sir Geoffry's just as anxious about his dear son. Bless me, to hear
'em talking about 'Our Boys' as they call 'em, one would think there were no
other sons and heirs in the whole country, but these two young gents a coming
home to their governors this afternoon.

(*Enter* KEMPSTER.)

KEMP: Mr Poddles, any news of the young gents yet? Sir Geoffry has just driven
over, and –

POD: They ought to be here by this time. Mr Charles wrote mentioning the time
and –

(SIR GEOFFRY CHAMPNEYS *pushes past him and enters.*)

SIR G: What a time you are, Kempster. Why don't you let me know if Mr –

KEMP: I beg your parding, Sir Geoffry; I were just inquiring of –

SIR G: Yes, yes, get back to the carriage. (*Exit* KEMPSTER.) (*to* PODDLES) Is
your master in?

POD: I'll see, Sir Geoffry. If you will be seated, Sir Geoffry, I'll – (*Exit.*)

SIR G: (*pacing the room impatiently and looking at watch and fidgeting*) Yes, yes.
The train's late; but I suppose they won't – Why hasn't Talbot answered my
letter? Why does he keep me on the rack? He knows how anxious I am.
Haven't set eyes on the dear boy for three years, and I'm longing to hear his
views on men and things. They'll be the same as mine, I know.

(*Enter* MISS CLARISSA CHAMPNEYS – *the Baronet's sister – an
elderly young lady.*)

CLAR: I couldn't refrain from following you, Geoffry. I am so anxious about the
dear boy.

SIR G: (*tetchily*) Of *course* you're anxious. *I'm* anxious.

CLAR: And I've no doubt Mr Middlewick is just as anxious about *his* dear boy.

SIR G: Clarissa, I'm surprised at you. Because these young men happen to have met
recently in Paris, and are coming home in company, that is no reason you
should link them together in that ridiculous manner. My son comes of an
ancient, honoured race. The other young man is the son of a butterman.

CLAR: A *retired* one, remember.

SIR G: Impossible! A butterman *can't* retire.

You may break, you may shatter the *tub* if you will,
But the scent of the butter will hang by it still.

Mr Middlewick is a most estimable person, charitable – as he *ought* to be;
and has considerable influence in the neighbourhood.

CLAR: Which accounts for your tolerating him.

SIR G: I admit it. The dream of my life has been that my boy Talbot should dis-

tinguish himself in Parliament. To that end I mapped out a complete course
of instruction for him to pursue; directed him to follow the plan laid down
implicitly; never to veer to the right or left, but to do as I bid him, like –
like –

CLAR: Like a machine.

SIR G: Eh? Yes, like a machine. Machines never strike.

CLAR: I hope he'll answer your expectations. Considering his advantages, his occa-
sional letters haven't been *remarkable*, have they? (*aside*) Except for brevity
– which, in *his* case has *not* been the soul of wit.

SIR G: Dear! Dear! Clarissa, what a woman you are! What would you have of the
boy? His letters have been a little short, but invariably *pithy*. I don't want my
son to be a literary man. I want him to shine in politics and –

CLAR: Suppose Mr Middlewick's views regarding his son are similar. Supposing he
wants *him* to shine in politics.

SIR G: Clarissa, you seem to take a great interest in Mr Middlewick. A man without
an H to his back. A man who – who eats with his knife, who behaves himself
in society like an amiable gold-digger, and who –

CLAR: Who is coming up the path. So moderate your voice, Geoffry, or he'll hear
you.

SIR G: You're a very irritating woman, Clarissa, and I don't – don't –

> (MR PERKYN MIDDLEWICK *appears at French windows. He is a*
> *sleek, comfortable man of about fifty*.)

MID: Hah! Sir Geoffry, glad to see you. Miss Champneys, your 'umble servant.
(*Shakes hands;* SIR GEOFFRY *shakes hands distantly,* MISS CLARISSA
warmly.) Phew! Ain't it 'ot – *awful 'ot*?

SIR G: (*loftily*) It *is* very *warm*.

MID: Warm! *I* call it 'ot. (*to* CLARISSA) What do *you* call it?

CLAR: *I* call it decidedly 'Hot'.

MID: That's what *I* say. *I* say it's 'ot. Well Sir Geoffry, any *noos*?

SIR G: *No* news.

MID: No noos! Ain't you heard from your son?

SIR G: Not a line.

MID: Oh, *my* boy's written me a letter of about eight pages. He'll be here soon; I
sent the shay.

SIR G: Sent the *what*?

MID: The *shay* – the *shay*.

SIR G: Oh, the *chaise*.

MID: No, only *one* of 'em. They'll be here directly. What's the good of Charley
writing me a letter with half of it in foreign languages? Here's a bit of French
here, and a morsel of 'Talian *there*, and a slice of *Latin*, I suppose it is, further
on, and then something out of one of the poets – leastways, I *suppose* it is,
for it's awful rubbish – then, lor! Reg'lar rigmarole altogether. S'pose he done
it to show as the money wasn't wasted on his eddication.

SIR G: (*with satisfaction*) Hah! Rather different from *my* son. *He* prefers to reserve
the fruits of *his* years of study until he can present them in person. *Your* son,
Mr Middlewick, has followed the example of the strawberry sellers and dazzled

you with the display of the top. Perhaps when you search *below* you may find the contents of the pottle *not* so satisfactory.

MID: (*aside*) Mayhap I may. Mayhap the front tubs is butter and the rest *dummies*. When I first started in business I'd the finest stock in Lambeth – to *look* at. But they was *all* sham. The tubs was 'oller if you turned 'em round, and the very *yams* was 'eartless delooders. Can Charley's letter be? – *No*, I won't believe it.

CLAR: (*aside to him*) Don't, dear Mr Middlewick, don't. (*Goes up in pleasing confusion.*)

MID: (*aside*) That's a very nice, sensible woman. It ain't the *first* time she's been civil to *me*. I'll play the polite to her if it's only to rile old poker-back. (*Goes up to her.*)

SIR G: I knew 'our boys' would drive here first, Mr Middlewick, which must be my excuse for this intrusion, and – (*Noise of a carriage driving up heard.*) Here they are! Here they are!

MID: (*Goes up to window.*) That's them! That's them!

SIR G: I feel actually faint, Clarissa. (*Sinks on sofa.*) The thought of seeing my dear, handsome, clever boy again is – is –

CLAR: (*aside*) Don't exhibit this ridiculous weakness, Geoffry.

SIR G: Before a tradesman too. You are right. (*Rises.*)

MID: I feel a bit of a – sort of a – kind of a fluttering *myself*.
　　　　　　(*Enter* CHARLES MIDDLEWICK.)

CHAR: Father! Dad! Dear old governor! (*Rushes to his father's arms.*)

MID: My boy! My boy! (*Embraces him; they are demonstrative in their delight.*
　　　　CHARLEY *is a handsome, gallant young fellow.*)

SIR G: Yes, but where's *my* son? Where's Talbot?
　　　　　　(*Enter* TALBOT CHAMPNEYS. *He is a washed-out youth, with*
　　　　　　yellow-reddish hair parted down the middle; a faint effort at a fluffy
　　　　　　whisker and moustache; dreadfully over-dressed, and has a limp look
　　　　　　generally; an eye-glass, and a soft namby-pamby manner.)

SIR G: Talbot, my dear boy, I'm so delighted to –

TAL: Yes, yes; how are you? Bless my life, how grey you've got – shouldn't have known you. And – that's not Aunt Clarissa? Dear, dear! Such an alteration in three years – shouldn't have known you. (*Kisses her; they turn aside conversing.*)

MID: Well, Charley, old boy, how do I look, eh? Pretty 'arty for an old 'un.

CHAR: Yes, yes, splendid. (*to him, aside*) *Hearty, dad, hearty.*

MID: Well, I *said* 'arty. And you, Charley – there! Growed out of all knowledge.

CHAR: (*aside*) Growed – hem! (*Seems annoyed at his father's ignorance; aside to him*) 'Grown' governor, 'grown'.

MID: Ain't got nothing to groan *for*. (*aside*) Rum notions they pick up abroad. But, Charley you ain't introduced me to your friend, Mr Talbot. Do the *honours*, do the *honours*.

CHAR: Talbot, this is my father.

MID: Proud to know you, sir.

---

pottle: small wicker basket containing strawberries.

TAL: (*through his glass*) How do? How do?

MID: 'Arty as a buck, and fresh as a four-year-old, thankee. Hope we shall see a good deal of you, Mr Talbot – any friend of my son's –

SIR G: Yes, exactly, Mr Middlewick. Flattered, I'm sure, but our boys' lines of life will be widely apart, I expect. Your son, I presume, will embark in commerce, whilst mine will, I trust, *shine* in a public and, excuse me for adding, a more *elevated* sphere.

MID: (*aside*) Yes, he looks like a *shiner*.

CLAR: But, Geoffry, probably Mr Middlewick and his son would like to be alone a little, so –

MID: Just so. (*aside*) She *is* a sensible woman. (*to them*) I shouldn't mind if you *did* 'get out' for a short time.

SIR G: Exactly. I want a talk with Talbot too, and as the ponies are put up, Talbot, we'll have a stroll through the grounds.

TAL: I don't mind. Only I'm jolly hungry, that's all.

(*Exit with* SIR GEOFFRY CHAMPNEYS.)

MID: (*aside to* CLARISSA) Miss Champneys, what's your candid opinion of your nephew?

CLAR: A *numskull*! (*Exit.*)

MID: She *is* a sensible woman. Charley, not to put too fine a point on it, your friend's a *fool*. I say it deliberately, Charley, he's a h'ass.

CHAR: (*deprecatingly*) Oh, dad!

MID: And his father destines him for a public areer. Ha! Ha! Him ever take the public – why, he ain't got it in him to take a beer-shop.

CHAR (*aside*) Is it that *he* has grown more vulgar, or that *I* have grown more sensitive? Anyhow, it jars terribly. But who am *I* to criticise – what should I have been but for his generosity – his – bah! Ignorant – H-less as he is, I'd sooner have him for a father than twenty stuck-up Sir Geoffry Champneys.

MID: (*sitting*) And now, Charley, that we're alone, my dear fellow, tell your old dad what your impressions of foreign parts were. When I was your age the Continent was a sealed book to them as wasn't wealthy. There was no Cook's Excursions then Charley; leastways, they seldom went further than White Condick Gardens or Beulah Spor, when they in general come back with their bonnets a one side, and wep' when they was spoke to 'arsh. No, no, you've been born when there was the march o' intellect, and Atlantic cables and other curious things, and naturally you've benefited thereby. So of course you're a scholar, and seen a deal. Paris now – nice place, ain't it?

CHAR: Glorious!

MID: 'Ow about the 'orse flesh?

CHAR: A myth.

MID: Railly though! And I suppose frogs is fallacies. Only to think.

---

shiner: someone who is consistently good or able at something, also, boastful fellow.
Cook's excursions: Thomas Cook (1808–92) organised tours at home and abroad from the 1840s onwards.
White Condick . . . Beulah Spor: White Conduit Gardens were a popular place of resort on the outskirts of London – facilities included tea gardens and a public house. Beulah Spa was a fashionable watering place close to London.

CHAR: Paris is a paradise. But Italy – well, there!

MID: But ain't it a mass of lazyroneys?

CHAR: A mere libel. A land of romance, beauty, tradition, poetry! Milan! Venice! Verona! Florence!

MID: Where the *ile* come from.

CHAR: Rome! Naples!

MID: That's where Vesoovius is, ain't it?

CHAR: Yes.

MID: Was it 'fizzin' when you was there, Charley?

CHAR: No. There was no eruption when I was there.

MID: That's wrong, you know, that's wrong. I didn't limit you, Charley; I said 'See everything', and I certainly expected as you'd insist upon an eruption.

CHAR: But, my dear dad, I saw everything else – Pompeii and Herculaneum.

MID: Eh?

CHAR: Pompeii and Herculaneum – they were *ruined*, you know.

MID: Ah! Two unfortnit Italian warehousemen, I suppose.

CHAR: Nonsense! They were buried, you remember.

MID: And why *not*? It'd be a pretty thing to refuse an unlucky firm as went broke a decent –

CHAR: You don't understand.

MID: (*bluntly*) No, I *don't*.

CHAR: But Germany, dad – the Rhine – 'the castled crags of Drachenfels' – the Castle of Erbenbreitstein –

MID: Aaron who? Some swell German Jew, I suppose.

CHAR: And the German women. (*Nudges him.*)

MID: Charles, I'm *surprised*. I'm simply – a – what were they like, Charley? (*Gets closer to him.*)

CHAR: (*Sighs.*) Hah!

MID: Lost your heart, eh?

CHAR: Not to a German girl, oh no – the lady *I* met who –

SIR G: (*Heard without.*) Well, we may as well join our friends.

CHAR: (*Aside; rises.*) Here's Talbot's delightful father. I wouldn't swop parents with him for all his high breeding. Our heart's blood's a trifle cloudy, perhaps, but it *flows* freely – his is so terribly pure it hardly takes the trouble to trickle. No, Talbot, old fellow, I don't envy you your father. (*Goes up and joins* MIDDLEWICK.)

        (SIR GEOFFRY *enters, followed by* TALBOT.)

SIR G: But really, Talbot, you must have *some* ideas on what you have seen.

TAL: What's the use of having ideas, when you can pick 'em up in the guide books?

SIR G: (*pleased*) Ah, then you *are* fond of *reading*? Good.

TAL: Reading! Ha! Ha! I hate it. (*Sits.*)

SIR G: (*trying to excuse him*) Well, well, perhaps *some* fathers set too great a value on books. After all, one's fellow man is the best volume to study. And as one

---

lazyroneys: lazzaroni were the begging population of Naples, so called from the hospital of St Lazarus, which served as their refuge.

'the castled . . . Drachenfels': a quotation from Lord Byron's *Childe Harold's Pilgrimage*.

who I hope may ripen into a statesman – your general appearance strongly reminds me of Pitt, by the by – perhaps you are right.

MID: (*aside, to* CHARLEY) Finest you ever saw. Sir Geoffry, we shall be back shortly. (*Exit with* CHARLEY.)

SIR G: And you actually saw nothing in the Rhine.

TAL: Oh, yes, I *did*.

SIR G: That's well.

TAL: No end of *mud*.

SIR G: But Cologne now?

TAL: Famous for its Cathedral and its smells. Both, I regret to say, unfinished.

.SIR G: But Germany, generally?

TAL: Detestable.

SIR G: Switzerland. Come, you were a long time in Switzerland. There you saw nature in all its grandeur. Your Alpine experiences were –

TAL: Limited – *very* limited. I *admired* those venturesome beings who risked their necks, but it was at a distance. I can't say a *respectful* distance for I thought them fools.

SIR G: No doubt you were right. (*aside*) Prudence, caution, forethought – excellent qualities. (*to him*) Italy?

TAL: *Second-hand* sort of country. Things as a rule give you a notion of being unredeemed pledges. Everything old and cracked. Didn't care for it. Jolly glad to get to Paris.

SIR G: (*with a relish*) Ha! The Louvre, eh?

TAL: Yes. I preferred 'Mabille'.

SIR G: A *public* building?

TAL: Rather. But even Paris palls on a fellow.

SIR G: (*rising and taking his hand*) I *see*, Talbot, like a true Champneys you prefer your native land to all these meretricious foreign places. Well, dear boy, you've a glorious career before you, and it only rests with you to follow it up. I have arranged a marriage –

TAL: A what!

SIR G: Not *arranged* it exactly, but it *can* be arranged – *shall* be.

TAL: (*quietly*) Provided, of course, I approve of the lady.

SIR G: Eh! *You* approve! What have *you* got to do with it?

TAL: Quite as much as *she* has, and rather more than *you*, considering *I* should have to live with her and *you* wouldn't.

SIR G: (*annoyed*) Talbot, I'm afraid you have picked up some low Radical opinions during your residence abroad. I expect obedience. I have done all a father can for a son. You will wed, sir, as *I* wish; you will espouse my politics, be returned for Lufton by *my* influence, and –

TAL: Unless Charley Middlewick chooses to *stand* –

SIR G: (*in horror*) Charley Middlewick chooses to stand?

TAL: In which case I –

SIR G: Yes?

Pitt: William Pitt the younger (1759–1806) first became Prime Minister in 1783.
Mabille: Jardin Mabille – notorious and lively pleasure garden in Paris.

TAL: Should *sit down.*

SIR G: (*Sits back.*) Talbot Champneys, you surprise me – you wound me. You have received every advantage that money could procure – you have come back after your lengthened foreign experiences, *not* – I must admit with pain – *not* what I *quite* expected. Possibly I looked for too much, but surely it was not an extravagant hope to indulge in that you would obey me in the one important step in a man's life – his marriage. The lady I have selected is wealthy, young, and handsome. She is on a visit to your aunt, so you will have ample opportunity for ingratiating yourself. You will not thwart me in this, my dear Talbot? (*taking his hand*)

TAL: Well, before promising anything you must trot her out.

SIR G: Trot her out?

TAL: Yes, yes, put her through her paces – let's judge of her points. You don't expect a fellow to buy a pig in a poke?

SIR G: Hem! (*aside*) Very remarkable language. If anybody else spoke so, I should say it was vulgar, but *my son*! It's – ha! ha! – eccentricity; his great-uncle Joseph was eccentric – he – (*Looks aside at* TALBOT *and sighs deeply.*)

TAL: (*aside*) Married whether I like it or *not*. Not if I know it. I'm going to 'go it' a bit before *I* settle down. I *have* gone it a *bit* already, and I'm going to 'go it' a bit *more*. It's the governor's fault; he shouldn't have mapped out my career with compass and rule. A man's not an express train, to be driven along a line of rails and never allowed to shunt on his *own* account. There's Charley's father let him have his fling and no questions asked. The governor's had his hobby – let him pay for it – he can *do* it.

    (CLARISSA *has entered, spoken briefly aside to* SIR GEOFFRY *and is now down beside* TALBOT.)

CLAR: Talbot, it is so delightful to have you back again. I shall now have such charming evenings with you at chess.

TAL: At what?

CLAR: Chess – the king of games.

TAL: Do you call it a *game*? Ha! Ha! No, thankee; life's too short for chess.

CLAR: Well, well, we'll say backgammon.

TAL: I don't mind *saying* backgammon, but you don't catch me *playing* backgammon.

CLAR: Well, then, we must even continue our usual cosy evenings. *I* do my woolwork whilst your papa reads us the debates. That's our regular evening's programme.

TAL: (*aside*) They must have had a rollicking time of it. The debates! A dozen columns of dullness filtered through your father. Not for Talbot.

CLAR: But now we have music. Miss Melrose plays charmingly. Do you like music?

TAL: Ye-e-s. I don't like *pieces*, you know – five-and-twenty minutes of fireworks. I like anything with a good chorus.

CLAR: Ah, so does Miss Melrose's *cousin*.

SIR G: (*at* CLARISSA, *to stop her*) He-hem! He-hem!

CLAR: (*aside*) I forgot.

TAL: (*suspiciously, aside*) Halloa! Why did he make that elaborate but utterly ineffective attempt to cough down the *cousin*? (*Looks at* SIR GEOFFRY *and* CLARISSA.) I see it *all* at a glance. The heiress is to be flung at my *head*, not the cousin at my *heart*. Future, luck, destiny, and all the *lot* of you, I see my fate. I marry that cousin.

SIR G: (*aside to* CLARISSA) Mary Melrose, the cousin, must be sent away.

CLAR: (*aside*) But she won't *go*.

SIR G: Talbot is a – Talbot is a –

CLAR: Talbot's a fool.

SIR G: (*wounded, yet proud*) Clarissa Champneys, Talbot is *my* son.

CLAR: Geoffry Champneys, Talbot is *my* nephew. I only wish I could exchange him for young Mr Middlewick.

SIR G: You irritate me – you incense me – go to the *deuce*, Clarissa!

CLAR: Ha! Ha! Come along, Talbot; let's go and see Mr Middlewick's pigs, perhaps *they'll* interest you. (*Takes his arm.*)

TAL: (*Has been taking out a large cigar.*) You don't mind my smoking?

CLAR: Not a bit.

TAL: D'ye think the pigs'll object?

CLAR: (*aside*) He's an idiot.

TAL: (*aside*) She's a nuisance. (*to her*) Tell us all about the *cousin*. (*They go out.*)

SIR G: Of course women can never hold their tongues. Mary Melrose *is* pretty – penniless though. Mischievous too as a girl can well be. And no taste – goes to sleep when I read the debates. Wakes up when it's time to say 'good night', and wants to play billiards. A very dangerous young woman. (VIOLET MELROSE *heard without.*)

VIO: Now, Mary, you must promise to behave yourself, or you shall *not* come out with me again.

SIR G: That's Violet, that's the *heiress* – and of course her cousin Mary with her. Confound it! They're as inseparable as – I'll try and walk off Talbot. He must see and love *Miss* Melrose. Yes, why not 'love'? My father commanded *me* to love, and I was too dutiful a son not to obey him on the *instant*. I *loved* madly – *to order*. (*Exit hastily.*)

        (*Enter* VIOLET MELROSE.)

VIO: Where can they have got to?

        (*Enter* MARY MELROSE – *the poor cousin; both dressed in the best taste.*)

MARY: What a handsome place. Looks awfully new though, doesn't it? Seems as if it was painted and decorated yesterday, and furnished in the middle of the night – in order to be ready for visitors this morning. I seem to smell the hay and sacking that enveloped the legs of the chairs and tables. Don't *you*, Violet?

VIO: Certainly *not*. Mary, don't make remarks.

MARY: Why not? I *like* to make remarks.

VIO: Yes, you like to do a great many things you *shouldn't* do.

MARY: So does everyone. If one's always to do what's proper and correct, life might as well be all rice puddings and toast and water. I hate them *both*, they're so dreadfully wholesome.

VIO: I don't know what excuse we shall make for coming here. It looks as if *we* were impatient to see the young men.

MARY: So we are. At least I am. We've seen no one of the male sex at old Champneys'.

VIO: Mary!

MARY: Begging his pardon. Sir Geoffry Champneys – *Bart's* – no one, under the age of fifty.

VIO: Why, Mary, there's Mr Sedative, he isn't thirty.

MARY: Oh, Sedative's a curate and don't count. Besides, he blushes when you speak to him, and, altogether, he's a muff. He's awfully good and devoted to his mother and all that, but – well, there, he isn't my sort.

VIO: I don't know who *is* your sort, Mary.

MARY: Oh, it's all very well for *you*, you know; you can pick and choose – if you haven't picked and chosen.

VIO: Mary, you – how can you?

MARY: Violet, my dear, don't try to impose upon *me*. I know the impression young Morton made upon your susceptible heart. I tried hard to ensnare him, but you beat me. Oh, you *quiet* ones, I wouldn't trust you out of my sight – (*aside*) or in it for the matter of that.

VIO: You're always thinking of love and marriage and all that nonsense.

MARY: Of course I am. There's nothing else worth thinking about. It's all very well for *you* – you're rich, and you have your tenants, and your pensioners, and your dependants, and I don't know *what*, to interest you. I've nothing. (*Sighs.*) I wish I was rich.

VIO: Then marry someone with money.

MARY: Never! (*after a slight pause*) Unless he's *nice, then* I will – oh, yes, I don't go in for 'love in a cottage'. I never could understand the theory of 'bread and cheese and kisses'. I *hate* bread and cheese.

VIO: (*with admonitory finger*) And –

MARY: (*Sighs.*) I know nothing about the rest.

VIO: You mercenary girl. Mark me, you'll marry a rich man.

MARY: Certainly – if I like him.

VIO: But as for a *poor* one?

MARY: I'll marry him if I like him better.

VIO: I can't make you out; you're simply the most –
    (*Enter* CHARLES MIDDLEWICK *quickly.*)

MARY: (*aside*) Morton!

CHAR: Why, Miss Melrose!

VIO: Oh, can I be – (*Sinks into chair.*)

MARY: If anybody'd catch me I think I could faint.

CHAR: Let me. (*Catches her in his arms.*) My dear Miss Melrose, I –

---

muff: a duffer or fool.

'*love in a cottage*': a common saying, cf. George Golman, *The Clandestine Marriage*, I, ii: 'Love and a cottage! . . . Ah, give me indifference and coach and six!'. Byron may also have had the following lines from Keats, *Lamia*, Part II, in mind: 'Love in a hut, with water and a crust, / Is – Love forgive us! – cinders, ashes, dust.' N. P. Willis's poem 'Love in a Cottage' was published in 1829.

'*bread and cheese and kisses*': quotation from Swift, *Polite Conversation*, Dialogue i: 'Bachelor's fare: bread and cheese and kisses'.

VIO: (*Recovers suddenly.*) Mr Morton!!

CHAR: Miss Melrose! (*Leaves* MARY *and goes to* VIOLET.) Can I – *can* I believe my eyes? What are you doing here?

VIO: What are *you* doing here?

CHAR: Morton isn't my name. I assumed it at Bonn, like a fool, because of a scrape I got into with an offensive and warlike student, which resulted in his being rather severely wounded – an insolent hound. No, I've come back here to my home, to my father, and –

VIO: (*aside, romantically*) Come back to his father, to his home! Mary, is – *is* this destiny?

MARY: (*aside to her*) If it *is* destiny, dear, don't you think I'd better go away for a short time?

VIO: No, no, Mary, don't go by any means.

MARY: I wouldn't *dream* of such a thing. (*Exit.*)

CHAR: Life's made up of surprises. Only to think of meeting you here.

VIO: You took no particular trouble to find out *where* to meet me, did you?

CHAR: You left Vienna so abruptly. You wouldn't have had me advertise?

VIO: Really!

CHAR: Lost, stolen or strayed, a young lady, etc., etc. Anyone restoring her to her disconsolate admirer, Charles, – a –

VIO: Mr Morton, upon my word, I –

CHAR: (*ardently*) And upon *my* word this is the happiest moment of my life; no, it's run hard by the *other* moment, when under the shadow of the trees, with the wild river rushing at our feet, you half – *half* whispered a word or two that led me to hope. Oh, Violet, I swear by – by – by those eyes – and what could a man swear by *truer* (*or, query, bluer*) – I've never ceased to think of you, to *dream* of you –

VIO: To *dream* of me? What, not when you've been awake?

CHAR: I've never been awake; life, since we parted, has been one long sweet siesta in which your image was ever foremost. The chief cause, the *only* cause of my hastening home was to search *you* out. I knew your wandering ways, and meant to track you. You said you intended staying the summer at Biarritz. But fortune has favoured me as she never yet favoured man and placed the prize in my arms.

VIO: (*pleased, but trying to be severe*) In *where*?

CHAR: (*throwing his arm round her*) There! (*slight pause*)

VIO: Mr Morton, I'm *ashamed* of you.

CHAR: Miss Melrose, I'm *proud* of you.

VIO: Really, I –

CHAR: You wouldn't have me think you a flirt – a coquette?

VIO: Indeed, no

CHAR: You *would* be one if when you breathed those half-dozen delicious words, you only meant to trifle with me. I've lived upon that sentence ever since –

Biarritz: a fashionable resort in southwest France; very popular with the English during the nineteenth century.

looking ardently forward to the day when I could present myself in *propria persona* as I do now. Violet, don't turn away, for —

(SIR GEOFFRY *coughs without.*)

VIO: (*rather agitated*) There's somebody coming.

CHAR: Confound it! In this life there always *is* somebody coming. (*Goes up.*)

SIR G: (*Enters.*) I can't find him – he isn't with the pigs. (*to* VIOLET) I regret that my son —

VIO: Why, Sir Geoffry – you must have intended it as a wicked surprise. Your son and I are acquainted.

SIR G: Has he, then, already –

VIO: Oh, before –

SIR G: Good gracious! You must not mind his being a little bashful and retiring.

VIO: Oh, I didn't find him so at *all*.

SIR G: (*aside*) The deuce she didn't! Met before?

VIO: At Vienna.

SIR G: (*aside*) Is it possible? And you don't – don't dislike him?

VIO: Oh, who *could*!

SIR G: (*aside*) I can't believe my — The young rascal! All his opposition was *assumed* then – a deep, young dog. Ha! Ha! Well, he took me in. Ha! Ha! Yes, he took me in.

CHAR: I hope, Sir Geoffry, we shall –

SIR G: Yes, yes, young gentleman, all in good time, but just at present you see we –

VIO: I should like to hear, though, what your son was about to say.

SIR G: (*seeing with horror the mistake*) My – my son! *This* person – he's no son of mine.

CHAR: (*half aside*) No – thank heaven!

VIO: (*Shrinks from him; bitterly*) *Twice* an impostor!

CHAR: Violet, I —

(*Enter* MIDDLEWICK *and* MISS CLARISSA; MARY *and* TALBOT.)

MID: It's true, mum. Every one on 'em was agin me doing it. Halloa – who's the gals?

(*At hearing the intensely vulgar voice of* MIDDLEWICK, VIOLET *has shrunk, and, evidently shocked, assumes a cold look.* CHARLEY *perceives it, and by his expression shows he resents her manner.*)

TAL: (*to* MARY) D'ye know I feel as if I'd known you *ever* so long?

MARY: And I've quite taken to *you* – fact —

(SIR GEOFFRY *who has observed this with suppressed rage, takes* TALBOT *by the arm, with a slight wrench, brings him to* VIOLET.)

CHAR: (*aside*) I could read a volume in her altered look.

SIR G: This, Violet, is – is *my* son!

CHAR: (*seizing* MIDDLEWICK's *hand with a grasp of affection; proudly*) And *this*, Miss Melrose, is *my father*!

ACT DROP

ACT II

SCENE.   *Drawing-room at* SIR GEOFFRY CHAMPNEYS'. *Doors right and left, and French windows to conservatory.* KEMPSTER *discovered.*

KEMP: Well, things are coming to a pretty pass when we have such visitors to dinner as Mr Middlewick, *senor.* Three 'elps to soup, and his napkin tucked
round his neck for all the world like a carver at a *café* – a common *café.* And
yet, somehow, I fancy his 'art's in the right place; I know his 'and is (that's
his pocket) a precious deal oftener than the governer's. I've heard, too, as the
servants at his place are fed on the fat of the land. Hem! *We* ain't. There's a
deal too much *show* here. Three mutton cutlets for four people, who've the
consolation of knowing the dishes is 'all marked, though when a party's
hungry silver ain't satisfying.

   (*Enter* SIR GEOFFRY *and* MIDDLEWICK, *in evening dress,*
   MIDDLEWICK*'s a little old fashioned and extravagant – large, double-*
   breasted white waistcoat and plenty of necktie.)

SIR G: Yes, yes, Mr Middlewick, you are perfectly right. (*to* KEMPSTER) Send our
coffee in here.

KEMP: (*aside*) They're a-getting thick, they're a-getting uncommon thick. (*Exit.*)

SIR G: You enjoyed your dinner?

MID: (*Sits.*) Fust-rate. *Hay one.*

SIR G: Good! And you don't mind leaving your wine for a chat?

MID: Not a bit. Can't abear claret, and port pays me out. I never knew what gout
was when I had my shop.

SIR G: He-hem!

MID: (*aside*) He always shies at the shop. Well, I won't tread on his aristocratic
corns; it ain't fair, for after all, *they're* tender, and *I'm* 'eavy.

SIR G: I'm delighted, Mr Middlewick, to welcome under my roof so successful a
representative of the commercial spirit of the age. Champneys Hall, as a rule,
has been honoured by the visits of people of birth *solely.* Your presence here
is a pleasing exception.

MID: Sir Geoffry, you do me *h*onour. Of course money's always a –

SIR: Not *wholly.* I anticipate your remark. Personal worth must count for something.

MID: Fust-rate theory – *phy*lan*tropic* and all that – but it don't wash, Sir Geoffry.
Take *yourself,* for instance. When you stroll about 'ere, everybody you meet
touches his 'at. How many does so when you walks down Fleet Street?

SIR G: Everybody touches his hat to *you,* Mr Middlewick.

MID: Not a bit of it. See here; *that's* what they touches their 'ats to. (*Slaps his
pocket, which rattles with the sound of money.*) Money makes the *mare* to
go – the *mare* – rubbish! It sets the whole *stable* a gallopin'! If I go into a
shop shabby the counter-skipper treats me familiar, pre-aps 'aughty. If I
wear new broad cloth he calls me 'Sir'. There you 'ave it in a nutshell.

SIR G: Mr Middlewick, I admit that money exercises an undue influence in the
world and to an extent with vulgar – I repeat, *vulgar* minds – elbows birth,
worth, virtue and – a – all that sort of thing a little out of the way. That is
why so many of us – I say *us* – live in the country, where – where —

MID: Jes' so. *I* know. You're somebody 'ere – nobody there. Quite right; that's why *I* settled in the country.

SIR G: Your career has been a remarkable one.

MID: Extry-ordinary. I was lucky from a baby. Found a farden when I was two years old, and got a five-shilling piece for 'olding a 'orse when I was playing truant at the age of six. When I growed up everything I touched turned up trumps. I believe if I'd purchased a ship-load of Dutch cheeses, the man with the van 'ud a' delivered me Stiltons. I believe as the Government went to war a purpose to give one a openin' for contracks. Bacon! Well, there – bless your 'art, what I made out of bacon alone was a little independence. I never meet a pig in the road that I don't feel inclined to take off my 'at to him.

SIR G: Ha! Ha! Ha!

MID: Every speculation proved a success. It seemed as if I was in the secret of life's lucky bag, and had been put up to where I was to pick out the prizes. Some folks said "'old 'ard, Perkyn, my boy, you'll run aground'. Well, I *didn't* "'old 'ard' I "'eld on', and here I am, Sir Geoffry, at the age of fifty-three able to buy up any 'arf a dozen nobs in the county.

SIR G: (*aside*) Nobs! He *is* a *pill* for all his gilding.

MID: But if *I'm* not a gentleman, there's my boy.

SIR G: Who, I have a sort of suspicion, admires Violet Melrose.

MID: What! The stuck-up rich gal. No! No!

SIR G: (*eagerly*) You think *not*?

MID: Certain. My son knows better than to thwart *me*. Miss Melrose snubbed me when we fust met – has cold-shouldered me ever since. Do you suppose my boy Charley would have anything to say to a young woman as despised his father?

SIR G: (*shaking hands*) My dear Middlewick, you delight me. Of *course* not. I was foolishly suspicious. I want *my* son to marry Miss Melrose. He will do so of course – for he has never disobeyed me; he has been brought up strictly to acknowledge my authority and –

MID: And *won't*, I'll warrant. Your system's a mistake – *mine's* the correct one. I've always given my boy his fling – never baulked him from a baby. If he cried for the moon we give him a Cheshire cheese immediate – *that* being the nearest substitute 'andy. *Now* he'd obey my slightest wish.

SIR G: Will he! Ha! Ha! Let us hope so.

> (*Enter* VIOLET MELROSE.)

VIO: Interrupting a *tête-à-tête*, I'm afraid.

SIR G: Not at all, Miss Melrose.

MID: Oh, no, not at all – not at all. (*Rises; aside*) 'Taturate' – always coming out with her *I*talian. Ha, she's not a patch upon the cousin; she's the gal for *my* money.

SIR G: (*aside in an undertone to* VIOLET) Miss Melrose – may I say *Violet* – I trust Talbot's manner, modest as it is, has impressed you. You must not take him for the foo – I mean you mustn't imagine he is the less ardent because he doesn't talk poetry like young Mr Middlewick, or —

---

pill: objectionable person or bore.

VIO: (*with temper*) Oh, don't mention *him*, Sir Geoffry – *that* young gentleman seems to ignore my existence.

SIR G: (*aside*) Good. Son sees father's snubbed and retaliates. (*to her*) Ha! Ha! Do you know – pardon my absurdity – at first I actually imagined there was some trifling tenderness in that quarter. But I see by your face I was mistaken. You are above being dazzled by good looks.

VIO: (*with a natural burst*) And he is good-looking, isn't he?

SIR G: (*a little haughtily*) He-hem! He's *long* – but nothing *distingué* – Talbot now is not what one would call a striking figure, but there's a concealed intellectuality – a hidden something or other – you'll understand what I mean but I'm at a loss for the word at the moment – that is none the less effective in the long run – (*with pleasant earnestness*) a – then, my dear Violet, he's the heir to a baronetcy. He's an embryo statesman, and he *adores* you. Didn't you observe him at dinner? He ate nothing – drank nothing – which – and I say it at the risk of being considered a too observant host – is *more* than can be said of young Middlewick.

VIO: (*aside*) That's true, for I watched him.

CHAR: (*heard without*) Ha! Ha! Ha! *You* play billiards! Why, you know as much of the game as the King of Ashanti knows of –

TAL: (*heard*) Ha! Ha! Play *you* any day in the week.

MID: I say, Sir Geoffry, them boys are going it, ain't they?

VIO (*aside*) 'Them boys!'

MID: (*aside*) I see her sneer.

SIR G: (*aside*) Every time he opens his mouth improves Talbot's chance.

> (*Enter* CHARLEY *and* TALBOT. CHARLEY *is a little excited with wine, but not in the least tipsy – he has been helping himself freely to drown his annoyance at* VIOLET*'s hauteur and evident horror of his father.* TALBOT*'s manner is of the same washed-out, flabby nature as previously shown.*)

CHA: Ha! Ha! Ha! Here's Talbot Champneys trying to argue with me about billiards. Why, man, you can't see as far as the spot ball.

SIR G: The fact of being short-sighted is scarcely a happy subject for jesting.

VIO: (*with suppressed temper*) I quite agree with you, Sir Geoffry.

CLAR: (*Has entered.*) It's aristocratic; double eye-glasses look rather *distingué*, I think.

CHAR: (*at* VIOLET) Yes, those who are *not* aristocratic may sometimes suffer from the affection. There are short-sighted fools in the world who are *not* swells.

VIO: (*aside*) He thinks that severe.

MID: Bless your 'art yes; we had a carman as was always driving into everythink; at last he run over a boy in the Boro', and that got him his quietum.

CHAR: Yes, yes, you told us before about him.

MID: (*aside*) Don't, Charley, don't. If you only brought me out to shut me up, I might as well be a tellyscoop.

SIR G: (*aside to* VIOLET) Charming papa-in-law he'll make to somebody.

Ashanti: kingdom on the Gold Coast of West Africa.

VIO: Don't, don't. (*looking at* CHARLEY) He's looking daggers at me, and I've done nothing.

TAL: It's rather rich your talking of beating me at billiards, considering that I've devoted the last three years to billiards and nothing *else*.

SIR G: (*aside*) The deuce he has! That's pleasant for a father to hear. Oh, a – exaggeration.

TAL: It's rather amusing your bragging of rivalling *me*. And when you talk about my not being able to see the spot ball, all I can say is –

CHAR: Ha! Ha! Ha! If you *can't*, you've a capital eye for the *pocket*. (*At* VIOLET. VIOLET *shows she sees the thrust.*)

MID: Ah, well, *bagatelle's* more in my way. When me and a few neighbours used to take our glass at the Peterboro' Arms, we –

CHAR: Yes, yes, father –

MID: (*aside*) He's bit. That gal's bit him. It'll be an awkward day for Charley when he shows he's ashamed of his governor.

CLAR: I agree with Mr Middlewick – bagatelle's charming.

VIO: So it is, Miss Champneys.

CLAR: So innocent.

SIR G: (*rising*) Come, who's for a game of billiards then? I never touch a cue, but I'll play you fifty up, Mr Middlewick, and my sister here and your son shall see all fair. Come, you shall see that there is even a worse player in the world than yourself. (*aside*) There couldn't be a better opportunity for leaving Talbot and Violet alone. (*to him*) What say?

MID: I'm agreeable – you must teach me though.

CLAR: *I* will do that, if you will allow me.

MID: Only too 'appy. (*Goes off with* CLARISSA.)

SIR G: (*aside to* TALBOT) Now's your time, bring matters to a crisis.

VIO: (*taking* SIR GEOFFRY's *arm the other side*) Sir Geoffry I'll back *you*.

SIR G: (*annoyed – aside*) Confound it! (*to* VIOLET) You really are most – a – I can't play a bit –

> (*As they exit* VIOLET *gives a sort of half sneering, half mischievous laugh at* CHARLEY, *who can with difficulty restrain his annoyance. When they are off, he turns, finding himself face to face with* TAL-BOT. TALBOT *is bringing out a pipe, and filling it.*)

CHAR: Well.

TAL: Well.

CHAR: What are you going to do?

TAL: What are you?

CHAR: I don't know.

TAL: I do. I'm going to have a smoke in the stable. Also a good think.

CHAR: A good what?

TAL: Think. I'm in love.

CHAR: *You!*

TAL: Why shouldn't I be? You tall chaps always think you can monopolise all the love-making in the world. You can love *short*, just the same as you can love *long*. I tell you I'm *gone*. D'ye hear? *Gone*.

CHAR: (*bitterly*) I'm happy to hear it. I shall be happier when you *prove* the fact.
(*Moves away.*)

TAL: I'm off. When you want a *weed* you know where to find me. (*Exit.*)

CHAR: In *love*, is he? I don't wonder at it – she'd entice a hermit from his *cell* –
and – send him back *sold*. She can't have a heart. (*Enter* MARY.) Ah, women
are all alike.

MARY: What a frightful observation! And at the top of your voice too.

CHAR: I mean it.

MARY: No, you don't.

CHAR: If I don't may I be –

MARY: Jilted?

CHAR: Jilted. The foolish phrase for one of the cruellest *crimes* – I say it advi-
sedly, *crimes* – that can disgrace *female* – I won't say *human* – nature.

MARY: Dear! Dear! Dear!

CHAR: (*with feeling*) Hearts are not playthings to be broken like children's drums
just to see what's inside them. A man's feelings are not toys to be trifled
with and tossed aside. Love in a true man means *love* – love pure and simple
and unselfish – the devotion of his whole mind and being to one in whose
weal or woe his very soul's wrapped up. With women –

MARY: What a pity it is Talbot Champneys can't talk like you – and going into
Parliament too.

CHAR: Talbot Champneys – yes – *his* relatives are well-spoken, well-born *some-
bodies*, and so she favours him.

MARY: She? Who?

CHAR: Absurd! There's only *one* she.

MARY: That's very polite to *me*, I'm sure.

CHAR: Oh, you know what I mean. In *my* eyes.

MARY: Exactly. But you don't monopolise all the visual organs of the universe.
There are *other* eyes that may have looked *elsewhere*.

CHAR: Why, what on earth –

MARY: (*modestly*) I don't think Talbot *does* admire Violet.

CHAR: Eh?

MARY: Not so much as he does – a – somebody else.

CHAR: Why, *who* is there he could –

MARY: Well, upon my word – considering that *I* – (*Pauses awkwardly.*)

CHAR: Why, what a fool I've been!

MARY: And are.

CHAR: But – oh, impossible!

MARY: Thank you.

CHAR: No, I don't mean *that*, because, of course, you are a charming young lady,
and –

MARY: Thank you again.

CHAR: I mean it's impossible on *your* side. I really believe Talbot to be not half a
bad fellow in the main, but his manner, his appearance, and –

MARY: Oh, handsome men are like the shows at the fairs, you see all the best
outside.

CHAR: There's some truth in that, perhaps.

MARY: Talbot Champneys isn't either the fool he looks or affects to be. He's wonderfully good-hearted, I *know*, for I watched his manner only yesterday towards a crippled beggar boy when he thought no one saw him; and – and he snubs his pompous old father like a – like a –

CHAR: A young cub.

MARY: Well, a young cub's better than an old bear. I don't believe in surface – I like to know what's inside. You've often noticed confectioners' tarts, with their proud uppercrust – hollow mockeries – delusive shams; when the knife dives into their dim recesses what does it disclose? Fruit, occasionally; syrup, seldom; flavour, *never*. Now, Talbot's *not* a confectioner's tart!

CHAR: No, I should say he was more of the *cake*.

MARY: Never mind, I *like* cake. He may be eccentric, but his heart's in the right place.

CHAR: That means *you've* got it.

MARY: He hasn't told me so.

CHAR: Until you make him I –

MARY: Make him! Well, you *are* –

SIR G: (*heard*) Don't mention it – a trifle.

MID: (*heard*) 'Pon my word, I'm downright –

SIR G: (*heard*) No, no; not at all.

CHAR: (*earnestly*) You will – you *will* make him declare himself, Mary Melrose, and make me the –

> (*Enter* SIR GEOFFRY *and* MIDDLEWICK, *followed by* VIOLET; MARY *and* CHARLEY *sit up.*)

MID: I declare I wouldn't have done such a thing for any money. (*aside*) I knew I should come to grief at them billiards.

SIR G: (*blandly*) My dear Mr Middlewick, commonest thing with beginners. Cutting the billiard cloth with the cue is a trifling accident that might happen with any one. Don't mention it any more. (*aside*) An awkward brute. Treated the table like his confounded counter.

MID: (*aside*) Serves me right, trying to play billiards, and poker-back pretending *he* couldn't, and him all the time a regular dab. He's up to these grand games, but one of these days I'll *loore* him on to *skittles* – and *astonish* him.

SIR G: (*aside to* MIDDLEWICK, *pleased*) Middlewick, look my dear sir. (*Points to* CHARLEY *and* MARY, *in conversation.*) D'ye see that? Ha! Ha! Seem rather interested in each other's conversation, eh? (*Nudges him.*)

MID: Why, anything more like spooning I –

SIR G: I hope, for *your* sake, it may be so; that girl is worth a thousand of her haughty cousin.

MID: (*seizing his hand*) You're right, Sir Geoffry. And I'm proud to hear a swell as *is* a swell give vent to such sentiments – they do you *honour*.

VIO: (*aside*) He means to wound me – to insult me. Mary cannot willingly have lent herself to so mean and poor a trick. *She* is honest – but he – (*Enter* CLARISSA; *goes to* MIDDLEWICK.) How taken up with each other they seem. There isn't an atom of jealousy about my disposition, but I'd give the *world* to know what they're talking about. (CHARLEY *and* MARY *laugh*.) Now they're laughing. Perhaps at *me*. Oh, how I wish Mary wasn't poor – I'd have *such* a quarrel with her.

MID: (*aside; has been talking with* CLARISSA) A more sensible woman I never come across.

CLAR: (*aside*) A delightful person *if* a little eccentric.

MID: (*aside*) I'll find out what *she* thinks of my sentiments regarding Charley's fancy.

CLAR: (*aside*) I hope his evident attentions to *me* have not been noticed by my brother.

MID: (*seated by her*) Miss Clarissa – nice name Clarissa.

CLAR: (*coquettishly*) Think so?

MID: Yes – I wouldn't change it for no other. Your other name I *would* though.

CLAR: (*aside*) What can he mean? These successful commercial people are so blunt and business-like – can he possibly be about to – (*Sighs.*) Well, I must say I consider him rather a fine man.

SIR G: (*To* VIOLET, *who has been and is watching* MARY *and* CHARLEY; SIR GEOFFRY *has sat beside her.*) Depend upon it, ill-assorted marriages are a mistake. For instance, we'll say, young Middlewick there – the poor lad's in a false position.

VIO: (*aside, in temper*) He *is* – sitting by *her*.

SIR G: A husband's relations, too, should not be ignored. Should the young man marry a lady, imagine her humiliation at the periodical visits of 'Papa'.

VIO: (*turning to him, a little nettled*) And yet *you* tolerate him here – make much of him.

SIR G: My dear Violet, in the country one is obliged to swallow one's feelings occasionally. I take good care no one shall ever meet him for whom I have the least – a – he-hem! (*aside*) Nearly putting my foot in it there.

(MIDDLEWICK *and* CLARISSA *have been very earnestly conversing*.)

MID: Of course – of course; when people get to a certain time of life they ought to settle.

(CHARLEY *and* MARY *stroll off.*)

CLAR: My sentiments precisely.

MID: And after all high birth's all very well, but if the other party has the *money* –

CLAR: Certainly – certainly. It may be radical and all that sort of thing, but give me intellect before mere family. And I am worldly enough to revere success – such as *yours*, for instance.

MID: (*aside*) She certainly is one of the most sensible women I – and after all they'd make an uncommon handsome couple –

CLAR: Eh?

MID: Charley and –

SIR G: (*abruptly, and annoyed*) Clarissa, my dear, where on earth has Talbot got to?

CLAR: (*rising, enraged at discovery of her mistake in* MIDDLEWICK) How should *I* know where he's got to!

SIR G: (*astonished*) Why, gracious me! My dear, I – (*aside to her, but aloud*) Remember, Clarissa, if you please, there are visitors present.

CLAR: Visitors indeed! Such canaille! (*Exit.*)

MID: (*aside*) I heard you my lady. So the old *one's* going in for snubs as well as – It's the last time me or Charley sets foot in *this* 'ouse.

VIO: (*who has gone up to conservatory; looking off*) How mean I feel, watching them. I'll – I'll leave this house tomorrow.

SIR G: (*aside*) What on earth's the matter with the woman? Something's annoyed her, but she mustn't be rude to my guests. I have one system with my son, my servants, and – yes, and my *sister*. She must come back at once and – Miss Melrose – Middlewick, excuse me a moment or two. (*Exit.*)

MID: All alone with Miss High-and-Mighty! Hang me if I don't tackle her! You'll – you'll excuse *me*, miss but –

VIO: (*in horror*) Oh, pray don't say 'Miss'.

MID: (*softened*) Eh? (*aside*) not 'Miss'? (*to her*) Well, then, we'll say 'Voylet'.

VIO: (*disgusted, but unable to restrain her amusement*) Mr Middlewick, you really are *too* absurd!

>   (*She moves towards door, and exits; as she does so* CHARLEY
>   *enters and is about to follow her.*)

MID: (*aside*) If ever I set foot in this house – (*Catches* CHARLEY *by the arm, and turns him round abruptly towards himself.*)

CHAR: Why, dad, I –

MID: Charley, where are you going of?

CHAR: (*annoyed*) Oh! Father, I really –

MID: (*severely*) Charles Middlewick, you're a going after that young lady.

CHAR: Well, sir, if I *am*?

MID: Charley, I don't want you and me to fall out. We never have yet. All's been smooth and pleasant with me hitherto, but when I *do* cut up rough, Charley, I cut up *that* rough as the road a being repaired afore the steam roller tackles it is simply a feather bed compared to your father.

CHAR: I don't understand you.

MID: (*with suppressed passion*) Obey me and my nature's olive oil; go *agin* me and it's *still* ile, but it's ile of *vitterel*.

CHAR: If, sir, you're alluding to my feelings towards Miss Melrose, I –

MID: I *am*. Think no more of her. Between you and her there's a gulf, Charles Middlewick, and that gulf's grammar. Perhaps you think I'm too ignorant to know what pride means. I'm *not*. If you ever cared for this stuck-up madam you must forget her. (*determined*) She ain't my sort; never will be, and she shan't be my daughter-in-law neither.

CHAR: You have always prided yourself on allowing me my own way in every-thing – it was your *system*, as you called it – and *now*, when it comes to a matter in which my whole future happiness is involved, you are cruel enough to –

MID: (*sharply*) Cruel only to be kind, Charley. You wouldn't marry a woman who despised your father? (CHARLEY *moves aside, ashamed; pause.*) If you would, if you do, I'll cut you off with a shilling. I – I – (*in a rage*) Why don't you meet me half way and say you'll *obey* me, you shilly-shally numskull!

---

canaille: rabble.

CHAR: (*in a passion*) You have no right to speak like this to me, if you *are* my
    father. (*pause;* MIDDLEWICK *astonished*)

MID: (*in softer voice*) He's right, he's *quite* right; calling names never did no good
    at any time. (*to him*) Leastaways *not* a numskull, Charley, of course; that was
    a 'lapsy lingo', a slip of the pen, you know. I'm speaking for your good.
    You're her equal in everything except *one*, Charley – I'm rich but I'm a com-
    mon, ignorant man. Wait, anyhow, until – until I – I – ain't here to disgrace
    you. (*Turns aside, breaks down.*)

CHAR: (*after slight pause*) My dear, kind dad, there's nothing in the world I
    wouldn't sacrifice to please you –

MID: (*Turns to him, pleased.*) Ah?

CHAR: But in this instance –

MID: (*turning back grumpily*) Hah!

CHAR: I can never be happy without Violet Melrose.

MID: Then make up your mind to be miserable.

CHAR: The appearance of superciliousness which you imagine you –

MID: *Imagine* – but it ain't for you to bandy any further words with *me*. If you
    disappoint me, *disobey* me, *defy* me, take the consequences. Say goodbye to
    your father, live on Violet Melrose's money, but don't be surprised when
    your grand lady wife taunts you with your mean position and flings your
    vulgar father's butter-shop in your teeth. (CHARLEY *attemps to speak.*) Not
    a word – I've said my say, and what I *have* said, Charles Middlewick's my
    ultipomatum. (*Exit.*)

CHAR: (*distracted*) Every word he said was true, and cut like a knife! How can I
    tell him that I know Violet's apparent supercilious manner is only on the sur-
    face? That – but is it? Am I fooling myself all the while? Does my blind
    admiration make me – I'll speak to her, learn the real depth of this seeming
    pride, and – (*Is going.*)
          (MARY *enters.*)

MARY: Oh, such fun!

CHAR: (*disgusted*) Fun!

MARY: Yes, I've completely taken in the old gentleman.

CHAR: I believe you're *capable* of it.

MARY: With half-a-dozen joking remarks in admiration of *you*. I've completely put
    him off the scent. He firmly believes that we're awfully spoons, and that his
    son's only to ask Violet to be accepted.

CHAR: So you did *that*, did you?

MARY: Yes, I did, and Sir Geoffry's simply in raptures at the success of his system,
    as he calls it, and *Violet* the –

CHAR: (*in rage*) You've made matters ten times worse with your meddling inter-
    ference. You – you've widened the gulf, and still further estranged us. But
    come what may I'll speak out and bring her to the point, if it's under the
    baronet's very nose! I – ugh! (*With an exclamation of intense vexation at*
    MARY, *exit.*)

MARY: (*after a blank look*) Moral! Mary Melrose, my dear, for the rest of your

---

'*lapsy lingo*': lapsus linguae, Latin for slip of the tongue.

natural life never attempt to do anything kind for anybody. I'll become supremely selfish, and settle down into a narrow-minded and highly acidulated old maid.

(*Enter* TALBOT.)

TAL: Who's that talking about old maids?

MARY: I was.

TAL: Why, you're all alone.

MARY: Yes, I like to be alone.

TAL: That means I'm to –

MARY: Oh, *no*, you're –

TAL: Nobody. Don't count. Thanks.

MARY: I didn't *say* that.

TAL: No, but you *meant* it.

MARY: Why?

TAL: Because you didn't *say* it. (*pause*)

MARY: What do you mean?

TAL: What I say.

MARY: What's that?

TAL: Nothing.

MARY: Then you mean nothing.

TAL: On the contrary, I mean a lot, but I can't say it.

MARY: Then I wouldn't try.

TAL: I won't. (*slight pause*) I say, Miss Melrose, do you know I'm dreadfully afraid of you.

MARY: Am I so very terrible?

TAL: You're so fearfully sensible, you know – so satirical and cutting, and 'awfully clever', and I'm *not*, you know.

MARY: Not *what*, you know?

TAL: None of *that*, you know. I'm a – a – muff, that's what I am. I haven't got a second idea. I don't believe I've got a *first*, but I'll *swear* I haven't a second.

MARY: Well, at all events, you're not conceited.

TAL: What on earth have *I* got to be conceited about? What are *my* accomplishments? I can play a fair game of billiards, though I'm too short-sighted for cricket. I can stick on the maddest horse that ever gladdened a coroner, and I can smoke like – like Sheffield. Not much to recommend oneself to a woman, eh?

MARY: I don't know. Miss Melrose, for instance, my rich and handsome cousin, has a great admiration for the the Guy Livingstone virtues.

TAL: Don't like her – at least, don't *admire* her.

MARY: Why not?

TAL: Because I've been commanded to. Private feelings ain't private soldiers – you can't order them about and drill them like dolls. Human nature's obstinate as a rule. Do you know how they get the pigs on board?

MARY: No.

Guy Livingstone: a novel by G. A. Lawrence, published in 1857. The hero, Guy Livingstone, was very handsome and displayed great physical prowess.

TAL: Put their noses towards the vessel and then try and pull them away, *backwards*. The result is that they run up the plank into the vessel *immediately*. *I'm* a pig.

MARY: You don't say so?

TAL: And *my* sentiments are *pig-headed*, my governor's are *pig-tailed* – that's to say, old-fashioned – the old 'school', strict obedience, marry according to *orders*, you know, eh? (*Nudges her.*) Ha! Ha! Some of us know a trick worth two of that eh?

MARY: Ha! Ha! Ha!

TAL: (*Laughs with her.*) You're a *sharp* one, *you* are. (*Nudges her.*)

MARY: So are *you*.

TAL: *Am* I, though?

MARY: Only in the *elbow*. Suppose you sit a little further off; you never crowd up so closely to Violet.

TAL: No, I'm not given to *poaching*.

MARY: Poaching! *Eggs*?

TAL: Eggs be – *hatched*! Haven't you seen Charley Middlewick loves her as much as – as – (*aside*) I'll *go* it now – I'm wound up *to* go it, and go it I *will*.

MARY: As much as *what*?

TAL: As I love *you*.

MARY: (*rising*) Mr Champneys!

TAL: (*rising*) No, no, no, I don't mean *that*.

MARY: *No*!

TAL: Yes, yes, I *do*, but in another way. I mean he doesn't love her *half* as much as I love *you*.

MARY: You don't know your own mind.

TAL: Don't want to. I want to know yours.

MARY: You don't mean half you say.

TAL: No, I don't. I mean it *all*.

MARY: Your father'd disown you.

TAL: So he might if I owned *you*.

MARY: You silly boy, what are you talking about. I haven't a penny in the world.

TAL: Even if you did possess that humble but heavy coin, it could scarce be considered *capital*, could it? A start at housekeeping on a ha'penny a-piece would be a trifle rash, not to say risky.

MARY: Housekeeping, indeed! Well, I like your impudence –

TAL: I *adore* yours.

MARY: I never was impertinent in my life.

TAL: Then don't contradict. When I say, 'Be mine', don't say 'Shan't'.

MARY: I won't.

TAL: Won't *what*?

MARY: Say 'shan't'.

TAL: (*delighted*) Do you mean it?

MARY: Talbot, you've had too much wine.

TAL: I admit it.

MARY: You *have* admitted it. If your father suspected this he'd cut you off with a shilling.

TAL: That's fivepence a piece better than your penny. We're getting on.

MARY: You quite take one's breath away – I don't know what to say.

TAL: Let me say it for you.

MARY: No, no, I never was proposed to before.

TAL: How do you like it?

MARY: But I've *read* about people proposing and – and – (*innocently*) They've always gone on their knees.

TAL: I'll go on my *head* if it'll only please you.

MARY: No, no, don't, it might give way.

TAL: Well, as far as a knee goes – *here* goes – there! (*Kneels.*)

MARY: And then the lover always made a beautiful speech.

TAL: *I* know. Most adorable of your sex, a cruel parent commands me to love another – I *won't* – I *can't* – I adore *you* – you alone. I despise heiresses, I despise Parliamentary honours, a public career, and all that *bosh*. (SIR GEOF-FRY *and* MIDDLEWICK *have appeared;* SIR GEOFFRY *now staggers and supports himself on* MIDDLEWICK*'s arm.*) I prefer love in a cottage. I *like* love – I like a cottage, where a fellow can smoke where he likes, and –

SIR G: (*bursting out*) You shall have your wish, sir. You shall have your love and your cottage, and your smoke and – and – (*breaking down*) Talbot – Talbot, what does this mean?

TAL: It means that I've made my own bargain – you can't call it an ugly one, can you? (SIR GEOFFRY *overcome*)

MID: (*almost unable to control his amusement*) Never mind, Champneys, it might have been worse. She's a proper sort, is Mary.

SIR G: Don't 'Champneys' *me* sir. I'll – I'll turn him out!

MID: Well, he hasn't turned out *himself* quite as you fancied he would, eh? Ha! Ha! Ha! Who was right in his system *now*, eh? Ha! Ha! Ha! (*As he is laughing,* CHARLEY *is heard.*)

CHAR: (*without*) My darling, I'll put the whole matter right in a moment.

> (*Enter* CHARLEY, *holding* VIOLET*'s hand; pause abruptly on seeing the others.*)

MID: W-w-what's *this*, Charles Middlewick? Who is this you are –

CHAR: This father, is *my* wife, or *will* be, when I have your consent.

MID: (*overcome with rage*) Why, you confounded –

SIR G: (*taking up the same tone*) Insolent, presuming young upstart, why, I –

MID: (*in rage, to* SIR GEOFFRY) Don't bully my son, sir; don't bully my son – that's *my* department.

SIR G: Ha! Ha! Ha! Finely *your* system has succeeded, eh? Ha! Ha! Ha!

MID: We're insulted, defied, both of us. (*excitedly*) Turn your disobedient cub adrift if you've the courage to stick to your principles.

SIR G: And kick out your cad of a lad if your sentiments are not a snare and a delusion.

> (CHARLEY *and* VIOLET, TALBOT *and* MARY, *all in a state of suppressed excitement, have been earnestly talking in an undertone during the blustering row of the fathers.* CLARISSA *enters.*)

MID: So I will sir, so I will. Charles Middlewick, madam, that boy's no longer any son of mine. If you accept him you blight his prospects.

CLAR: Mr Middlewick, are you aware that Miss Melrose is –

SIR G: (*violently*) Don't you dare to interfere, madam.

VIO: I *have* accepted him sir, and I will not blight his prospects.

(MIDDLEWICK *overcome with rage.*)

SIR G: (*to* TALBOT) And as for *you*, you imposter!

TAL: That'll do. I won't trouble you any longer. I'm off.

SIR G: Off, sir! Where?

TAL: That's *my* business.

CHAR: (*taking* TALBOT's *hand*) Yes, *our* business.

MID: Oh, yes – you can go with him if you please, and a good riddance.

SIR G: Go – go and starve.

TAL: *That* we can do without your permission, anyhow. You've kicked us out remember, father, because, being grown men, we've set our affections where our hearts have guided us – not your *heads*. And – and – Charley, finish it. I'm not an orator, and don't want to be.

CHAR: (*to girls*) We'll prove ourselves worthy of you by our own unaided exertions, and will *neither* of us ask you to redeem your promise till we've shown ourselves worthy of your esteem. We can get our living in London, and rely upon it *you'll* never hear of our distress should we suffer it.

CLAR: (*distressed*) Talbot, my dear nephew, you –

SIR G: (*violently*) Hold your tongue!

VIO: (*half crying; to the fathers*) You're a couple of hard-hearted monsters, and I don't know which I hate the most.

MARY: No – nor which is the uglier of the two.

(CHARLEY *taking farewell of* VIOLET, *kisses her hand.* TALBOT *tries to get at* MARY; *intercepted by his aunt.*)

SIR G: (*aside; violently shaking* MIDDLEWICK's *hand*) You've acted nobly, sir – you – you're a downright Roman father.

MID: (*reciprocating*) You're another.

(*The two old men shaking each other's hands violently overcome by mingled emotions.* TALBOT *pushes his aunt aside, and flings his arms round* MARY, *kissing her audibly;* CLARISSA *falls on to otto-man; on the movement of the scene,*

CURTAIN

Second picture – CLARISSA *discovered fainting;* VIOLET *holding scent bottle to her nose.* MARY *at back waving handkerchief on terrace, off;* SIR GEOFFRY *in easy-chair, overcome.* MIDDLEWICK *with hands thrust deep into his pockets, standing doggedly.*)

ACT III

SCENE.   *The third floor at* MRS PATCHAM's. *A very shabby sitting-room in a third-rate lodging-house. A door left. A door leading to landing; a door right; fire-place and mantel-shelf; a shabby old arm-chair by fireplace; a table on which are remains of breakfast – very common teapot with broken spout, small stale remains of a loaf, two egg-cups, with the shells of eggs in them, brown sugar in a cup, etc; small table, with penny bottle of ink, pens and paper; a few books. A tapping heard at the door, repeated, and then* BELINDA, *a slatternly lodging-house servant, puts her head in.*

BEL: Was you ringin? Please, was you a – (*Enters carrying an empty coal box.*) Neither of 'em here. Bother them cinders, if I had my way with 'em I'd chuck 'em out of winder instead of having to carry 'em downstairs as careful as coals. Coals! Precious few of *them* the young gents has, and prices a rising dreadful. For they *are* gents, if they do buy only kitchen ones and has 'em in by the yunderd. What a fire! It's as pinched up as – (*Is about to give it a vigorous poke when she is restrained by the entrance of* TALBOT. *He is shabby, and a great contrast to his former showy self.*)

TAL: (*sharply*) Now then!

BEL: (*Turns with the poker in her hand.*) Eh?

TAL: What are you going to do?

BEL: Only going to –

TAL: Of course. Strike a little fire like that, it's cowardly.

BEL: Shall I put some more coal on?

TAL: Certainly not.

BEL: You wouldn't let it go out?

TAL: Why not? It's a free country.

BEL: (*aside*) Sometimes I think they're both a little – (*Touches her head.*) It's too much study, that's what it is. (*Sweeps up the hearth.*)

TAL: (*aside*) Capital girl, this; simple and honest. A downright daughter of the soil, and carries her parentage in her countenance. Perhaps you had better put a pinch or two on. Mr Middlewick will be in directly. (*She goes into room.*) He'll be cold, poor fellow, though, of course, he'll swear he isn't. I'm getting uneasy about Charley. Ever since I was seedy, and he sat up so much with me, I've noticed a change in him; if he doesn't improve I shall – (*crash of coals heard*) There's a suspicious, not to say a shallow, sound about those coals. (BELINDA *enters with shovel of coals.*)

BEL: I tell you what, sir, your coals are dreadful low.

TAL: Low! *Blackguardly*, I call them!

BEL: I can easily order some more when I go to Loppit's!

TAL: Just so. Whether Loppit would see it in the same light's a question. There is already a trifling account which –

BEL: Oh, Loppit can wait.

TAL: He *can* – *short* weight. By the way, I saw some boxes in the hall.

BEL: Yes, missus has gone out of town for a fortnight, and – (*Is about to put on the lot of coal.*)

TAL: Gently – a bit at a time. (*Takes up a piece with his tongs.*) There – there – (*business*) I say, Belinda, if Loppit were to call his coals 'not so dusty' it would be paying them a compliment, wouldn't it?

BEL: Ha! Ha! Ha! Well, you *are* a funny gent, you are.

(*As* TALBOT *makes up the fire* CHARLEY *enters. He too is shabby, and looks worn. He carries some papers, and MSS.*)

CHAR: Halloa! Talbot, old man, what are you doing now?

TAL: Giving Belinda a lesson in domestic economy – you know a severe winter always hardens the coal-merchant's heart!

CHAR: Yes, yes. (*Takes off gloves and hat.*)

TAL: And they're simply going up like – like –

CHAR: Smoke!

TAL: There! (*Has done fire, stands before it, facing* CHARLEY*:* BELINDA *takes back shovel into room.*) I consider I make a first-rate fire.

CHAR: Yes, you don't make a bad *screen*.

TAL: I beg your pardon. (*Moves aside.*)

CHAR: Don't mention it. The attitude and position are thoroughly insular and Britannic. It is a remarkable fact that an Englishman who never turns his back on the fire of an enemy invariably does it with his friends.

TAL: (*aside*) We've got our 'sarcastic stop' on this morning, eh? Well, Charley, I suppose you did no good with Gripner?

CHAR: I had a highly interesting interview with that worthy publisher. I thought *you* thought that the poem I commenced at Cologne for amusement had some stuff in it!

TAL: *Stuff*! Ha – *full* of it.

CHAR: Exactly. Partial friends have declared I had a real vein of poetry, but Gripner – Ha! Ha! *He* – well, he disguised his sentiments by assuring me poetry was a mere drug in the market. He'd also thrown his eye on those social sketches I'd thought were rather smart, but he said he knew at least fifty people who can roll out such things by the ream. However, he's given us a dozen pages a-piece for his new gazetteer. We begin in the middle of M – you can start at Mesopotamia, and work your way on at ten shillings a column. (*Hands him papers.*) It's bread and cheese!

TAL: I should think so. Ten shilling a column. (*Unfolds papers; printed sheets.*) By Jove, they *are* columns though. Regular Dukes of York. Penny a lining's coining compared to it. I can't say at the moment I know *much* about Mesopotamia, but –

CHAR: I remembered old Mother Patcham had a dilapidated gazetteer downstairs, so I borrowed it, and you can copy the actual facts.

TAL: Just so. Put it all in different language.

CHAR: Yes, the more indifferent the better.

TAL: Her book's about twenty years old; never mind – I'll double the population everywhere – that'll do it.

CHAR: Talking about population, I've had an interview with the agent for emigration to Buenos Ayres – he rather pooh-poohed us as emigrants. They don't want gentlemen.

TAL: We don't appear in particular request anywhere. It seems absurd to be hardup in the Cattle Show week.

CHAR: Our governors are up in town, I'll swear.

TAL: Mine never missed the show for forty years. I can see him critically examining

---

stop: manner of speech.
Dukes of York: reference to Column of the Duke of York, erected in Waterloo Place, conspicuous for its great height.

the over-fed monsters – punching the pigs and generally disturbing the last hours of the vaccine victims.

CHAR: Whom I envy. What a glorious condition is their's fed on the daintiest food – watched and waited on like princes – admired by grazing – I mean gazing crowds, and –

TAL: Eventually eaten, don't forget that. I'll go as far as the *sheep* with you, they *can* do what *we* can't.

CHAR: What's that?

TAL: Get a living out of their *pens.*

CHAR: Beginning to joke now. You're a changed being, Talbot.

TAL: Yes. Genuine 'hard-upishness' is a fine stimulant to the imagination. The sensation of four healthy appetites a day, with –

CHAR: The power of only partially appeasing *two* –

TAL: Exactly – makes a fellow –

CHAR: *Thin.* Our cash is assuming infinitesimal proportions, Talbot. We must still further reduce our commissariat. I've been calculating, and I find that henceforth bacon at breakfast must be conspicuous by its absence.

TAL: Bacon – the word suggests philosophy, so with many thanks for past favours, 'bye-bye, Bacon'.

CHAR: When we first parted with our convertible property, we had hope in our hearts and cash in our money box. Now things don't look rosy we must bow to circumstances. 'Tempora mutantur'.

TAL: 'Nos et mutamur in illis'.

CHAR: Which being loosely translated –

TAL: Means that we must give up *The Times* and take in *The Telegraph.*

CHAR: We've parted with a good many things, Talbot, but we've stuck to *one* – our word. We've never appealed to a relation.

TAL: Except, of course, a certain avuncular relative who –

CHAR: Shall be nameless. Just so – but our governors must have discovered by this time that our determination was no empty boast, and Violet and Mary have never heard a word from either of us. No one can say we've shown the white feather.

TAL: One minute – I *must* clean my boots. (*Takes up boots, and brings blacking-bottle from corner with a bit of stick in it, and boot brushes.*)

CHAR: Why on earth do you always begin to –

TAL: (*blacking boot*) Always begin to clean my boots when you talk about Violet and Mary? Because I feel it's necessary at the mention of their names to work off my superabundant and irrepressible emotion. I feel if I don't have a go in at my boots, I shall do some awful – (*Begins to brush violently.*) Now go it!

CHAR: Do you know, Talbot, I could almost swear I saw Violet today?

TAL: You don't say so?

CHAR: And I *vow* I saw Mary.

TAL: Hah! (*brushing with tremendous violence*)

CHAR: I don't *think* they saw *me*, but –

TAL: (*at the boot*) What a shine there'll be in a moment!

Tempora . . . illis: the times change and we change with them.

CHAR: For I dodged behind a cab and –
        (*Enter* BELINDA.)
TAL: And got away without –
BEL: (*brusquely*) What are you doing of? Drop them boots.
TAL: Belinda!
BEL: *I* clean the lodgers' boots. And it's my place to clean *yours* – if you are a third
        floorer. (*Takes boot and brush from* TALBOT.)
TAL: (*aside*) A third floorer!
CHAR: Belinda, don't talk as if you were reporting a prize fight.
        (BELINDA *cleans boots.*)
TAL: And deal gently with the *heels*; they won't be trifled with.
CHAR: I've got a deuce of a headache, Talbot, and as I want a good afternoon's dig
        at the gazetteer, I'll go and lie down a bit in my den.
TAL: Do. I heard you walking up and down the room half the night; you're getting
        ill!
CHAR: Not a bit, old man, not a bit. (*Goes towards door.*) Nerves a little shakey,
        that's all – that's all. (*Exit.*)
BEL: I tell you what – it's my opinion *you* wasn't half as ill as you'll soon have Mr
        Middlesex!
TAL: Middle*wick*, Belinda. It's the natural obstinacy of your nature to call people
        out of their names. My name being Champneys, you call me Chimneys – *had*
        it been Chimneys you'd have had it Chimbley, of course. (*aside*) She's right,
        though. I'll go and ask Barnard to come round and see him. (*Takes up hat.*)
        I shall be in soon. By the way, those breakfast things are *not* an ornament –
        if, in a lucid interval, you should feel disposed to take them downstairs, I
        shall *not* feel offended. (*Exit.*)
BEL: He's a queer young gent, that; so are both of 'em. But, somehow, I've took to
        'em – took to 'em *tre*mendous. I wonder who they are. I'm sure they're
        gentlemen 'cos they can't do nothing for a living. Then they don't bully a
        poor lodging-house slavey. 'Slavey' – that's what they call me, but, somehow,
        it don't seem rude like from *them*. Missis says they're 'under a cloud', she
        thinks, and she's always in a regler fluster every Saturday till they've paid
        their rent. Ha, well, they knows their own business (*The door opens and* SIR
        GEOFFRY *enters, then* MIDDLEWICK. BELINDA *is placing the things on a
        tray.*) best, I suppose. Couldn't stand by and see him a blacking his –
SIR G: He-hem! (BELINDA *starts.*)
MID: (*other side of her*) He-hem!
BEL: Bless us, who are *you*? (*Retires a little.*)
        (*The two old gentlemen look round the room with a rueful expres-
        sion of countenance, then they look at each other blankly.*)
MID: Well!
SIR G: Well!
MID: A – here we are.
SIR G: Confound it, sir, don't talk like a clown.

Here we are: here we are again – the traditional greeting of the clown in nineteenth-century
Harlequinades.

MID: I won't (*aside, miserably*) I don't feel like one. Pantaloon, and a worse treated one than ornery's more in my way a deal.

SIR G: Why – why it's a mere garret.

MID: Where did you expect to find 'em? At Claridge's Hotel? Or the Langham? Perhaps you hoped to see 'em driving mail *fee*atons in the Park, or a lolling out of a swell club winder in Pall Mall. Garret as you call it, *I* don't see as it's so oncomfortable.

SIR G: (*in broken voice*) I'm glad you think so, sir, I'm glad you think so.

MID: (*aside, in tone of pity*) Poor dear boy, to think he should have come to this!

SIR G: (*affecting harshness*) Not that I relent in any way. Oh, no, no.

MID (*assuming same tone*) Nor I, nor I! As they make their beds so they must lie.

BEL: (*overhearing*) Bless your 'art, sir, they never make their own beds.

MID: He-hem! (*aside*) The servant. The very image of the gal as waited on me when I lived in a attic in Pulteney Street. It's my belief as nature keeps a mould for lodging-house servant gals and turns 'em out 'olesale like buttons. She's the identical same gal – same to a smudge. (*to her*) These young men here, are they pretty comfortable and all that?

BEL: (*aside*) Pumping! Who are they? (*to them*) Pretty well.

MID: Do they – do they *dine* at home?

BEL: No – they breakfusses!

SIR G: Oh, they breakfusses. Is that – or rather *was* that their breakfast?

BEL: Yes.

MID: (*aside; taking up egg*) Shop 'uns. Sixteen a shilling. *I* knows 'em. (*Puts it down.*) To think Charley should have to – (*Breaks down.*)

SIR G: (*through his glasses*) Good Heavens! What dreadful looking butter!

MID: (*faintly*) Dossit – dear sir – inferior Dossit! (*aside*) *Precious* inferior.

SIR G: *Dorset*, man. *Dorset*.

MID: (*in rage*) Come here, I say, you know – you may be at home in all matters of *h*etiquette, and gene*h*allogy – and such like, but dammy, *do* let me know something of butter. I tell you that it's *Dossit – Dossit* – that's what it *is* – and what's more it's a two *h*ounce pat!

SIR G: (*stiffly*) On such a minute matter of professional detail I cannot, of course, attempt to argue. (*Goes up.*)

MID: (*aside*) Now that's all put on. Inside he's a suppressed *h*earthquake. He's a longing to throw his arms round his boy; but he wants me to give in first. (*Talks aside to* BELINDA.)

SIR G: (*aside*) His rage is only a safety valve for his pent-up affection; poor fellow, he'd like me to propose a truce, but it's not for a man in my position to succumb to sentiment. I've only to wait, and his feelings, which are stronger – I may say *coarser* than mine, are sure to melt.

MID: (*to* BELINDA) And how's their appetites – pretty 'arty?

BEL: Fine. I often hear 'em telling one another what they've had for dinner, but when I see the way they devours their tea – do you know, I sometimes fancy –

MID: Yes?

---

feeatons: phaetons – light, fashionable, open four-wheeled carts.

BEL: As they've had no dinner at all.

MID: (*after slight pause, in a low voice*) No – no dinner at all. (*Turns aside, and places his hand at his heart for a moment, shading his eyes with his other one.*) Here – you seem a decent young woman – here's a half-sovereign – not a word. We're friends of *friends* of these young men. Speak out truthfully. Did you ever hear them speak of – of their relations?

SIR G: Yes, yes, *friends*, belongings – a – speak out!

BEL: Oh, yes, and more than once, by *accident* – for I ain't got time for listening – I heard 'em say they's rather *starve* than write to 'em.

MID: (*overcome*) Did they – *did* they?

SIR G: (*proudly*) That was firmness – pride!

MID: From *your* point of view. Being a tradesman, *I* call it obstinacy.

SIR G: Fostered in *your* case by a system of absurd laxity.

MID: (*aside*) And that to the man as he called a Roman father!

BEL: But at one time – when one of 'em was taken ill –

SIR G: } What!
MID: }

SIR G: Ill! Ill, girl – not *very* ill?

MID: (*almost fiercely*) Which was it?

SIR G: Yes – speak, woman – which – not – not – the shorter one, the one with the light hair, who –

BEL: Yes, him.

SIR G: (*overcome, in broken voice*) But he – he *got better*?

BEL: Yes. Thanks to the other gent, who waited on him hand and foot, and never took his clothes off for a week, looking after his friend and attending to him for all the world as if he'd been his brother.

> (SIR GEOFFRY *goes to* MIDDLEWICK, *grasps his hand, with a sob aside.* MIDDLEWICK *silently returns the grasp, each holding head down.*)

MID: (*after pause; low voice*) And – and the other – who – who helped his sick friend so – so noble.

BEL: Well, it's *my* opinion he's in a worse way than the other, though he won't own it.

MID: (*very faintly, and in grief*) No – no – (*Staggers slightly back.* SIR GEOFFRY *supports him.*)

SIR G: (*gently, aside to* MIDDLEWICK) Come – come, old friend, be a man, (*giving way*) be a man as – as *I* am – don't give way. I'm firm – firmer than – than ever. (*Blows his nose to hide his emotion.*)

MID: What – what makes you fancy so?

BEL: Well, when he first come he was cheerful and happy, but bit by bit – as he got shabbier – he grew quieter like – and sometimes I've spoke to him three or four times afore he seemed to know I was a speaking, and –

MID: (*aside*) Poor boy! Poor boy!

SIR G: (*aside*) And *he* helped and nursed Talbot – I wish I'd come here sooner.

BEL: (*aside*) Who *can* they be? I don't like leaving 'em here, and all the lodgers' private papers about. There's a sort of County Court look about the short one. I've seen bailiffs enough in my time, and it ain't a bit unlikely as –

SIR G: Middlewick, something must be done. We – we mustn't *forget* ourselves and become *maudlin*, you know.

MID: (*pulling himself together*) No, no, certainly not.

SIR G: After all, we did everything for *them* and they showed a shameful return.

MID: (*convincing himself*) Yes, yes, so they did, so they did.

SIR G: Defied us.

MID: No mistake about it, and when you turned 'em out –

SIR G: *You* turned them out.

MID: You suggested it first.

SIR G: Well, well, they've eaten the leek.

MID: Ye-es, there ain't much nourishment in leeks, though I admit, *relishy*.

SIR G: I see you're giving way. (*sharply*) You're *thawing*.

MID: *Me* 'thawing'! Not *me*. But you was saying as something must be done, and I says ditto. Anonymous, of course.

SIR G: Quite so; permit *me* to arrange it. Young woman there's something in your face thoroughly honest – the frequent contact with cinders, or whatever it may be, cannot conceal your innate truthfulness; you face is a picture, and I am old-fashioned enough not to object to a picture in a black frame. I prefer it.

BEL: (*aside*) Soft sawder. Something's a coming.

SIR G: In the first place, you mustn't say anything of our visit, and when the young men come in you must give them an envelope.

MID: Two – *two h*envelopes.

BEL: (*standing back*) Not if I know it. (*aside*) A summons, of course. (*to them*) I don't know neither of you gentlemen, but I wouldn't do nothing as would bring harm to our third floorers for nothing as you could offer me. And, perhaps, you'll be good enough to take back your 'arf crown.

SIR G: (*aside*) Remarkable! But I never *could* understand the lower classes.

MID: (*aside*) If that 'arf sovereign doesn't blossom into a fi-pun note before the day's out my name ain't Middlewick.

SIR G: But whatever you do don't mention that – what's that? Someone coming up the stairs?

BEL: Yes.

SIR G: We mustn't be seen.

MID: Not for the world. What's this? (*Goes to door.*)

BEL: That's what the gents calls their *h*omnium gatherum – where they keeps –

SIR G: Is this Talbot's – I mean, Mr –

BEL: Chimneys' room? Yes, but you mustn't –

(SIR GEOFFRY *bolts into door, as a tap is heard, and shuts door.* MIDDLEWICK *is peeping into room when a tapping is heard and a loud* 'He-hem'.)

MID: Get us out of this without the lodgers seeing us and I'll – (*Bolts into room as door in flat slowly opens; he does not see who it is. Enter* MISS CLARISSA, *dressed in walking dress and carrying a reticule.*)

CLAR: Young woman, are the gentlemen who lodge up here both out?

BEL: Yes'm. (*aside*) One is, and 'tother's a lying down and don't want worrying.

CLAR: Phew! (*Sits; aside*) This is the servant, the young woman, Mr Warrington, the detective, told me was 'a good sort' – an odd phrase, but expressive. If I hadn't employed him the poor young men might have done something dreadful, with their pride and their sense of independence and all that.

BEL: Was you wanting to see either of 'em?

CLAR: Well, no, not just now. (*aside*) Geoffry, after discovering everything by shamefully intercepting one of Mr Warrington's letters, thinks to frighten me with threats of even stopping my allowance and turning me out of his house if I communicate with Talbot. Bah! He's my own nephew, and he shan't starve whilst his Aunt Clarissa's got a penny in the world. His father may act like a brute, and so may Mr Middlewick, but – ugh! *Cattle Show*, indeed. Coming to stare at a collection of adipose sheep, all sleep and suet; at islands of lean in oceans of obesity, called by courtesy cows; and a parcel of plethoric and apoplectic pigs, their own sons all the while wasting away to shadows. (*Brings out fowl, ready trussed, from reticule.*) Mrs Patcham's out of town, isn't she?

BEL: Yes'm.

CLAR: Then there won't be any one in the kitchen?

BEL: Not a soul, 'cept me and the beetles.

CLAR: Very good. Your fire's in, of course?

BEL: Trust me. Missus and the fire ain't never out together.

CLAR: Very good – then follow *me*. (*Exit, carrying the fowl; leaves bonnet on a chair.*)

BEL: Here I say – (*Goes to the front door.*) *She* don't mean no harm. She's a relation of one of the gents, *she* is. (*Listens.*) She skips down them kitchen stairs like a – (*a distant knock heard at front door*) These breakfast things 'll be here all day. Bother the knocker! (*Takes up things on tray; a door slams.*) Oh, Mrs Radcliffe's opened the front door for me. A nice woman that. Always ready to save a poor girl's legs. Bless my 'art, I forgot all about them two parties in ambush. Well, they must wait until I –
(*Enter* VIOLET, *then* MARY.)

VIO: This is the third floor, I believe. That very nice old lady who opened the door said that – (*both girls timid*)

MARY: Oh, if you please, is Mr Champneys in?

VIO: Or Mr Middlewick?

BEL: No miss.

BOTH: How are they?

BEL: Well, really – a –

VIO: They are not ill – Mr Middlewick is not *ill*?

BEL: No miss.

VIO: (*aside to* MARY) Isn't it a dreadful place?

MARY: Poor dear Talbot!

VIO: Oh, Charley! (*to* BELINDA) Are they likely to be long?

BEL: Can't say.

MARY: Are the gentlemen out much?

BEL: Yes, miss.

VIO: Late?

BEL: Don't know. They both has latch keys.

VIO: Mary, we'll wait till they come in, and surprise them.

MARY: If it's *proper*. (*to* BELINDA) I suppose they never have any visitors?

BEL: Well, as to *that*, you see –

VIO: (*aside*) The girl seems confused. I almost wish I hadn't come. I always was of a suspicious nature. I can't help it. Mary believes in everybody, but I – (*noise in room*) What's that?

BEL: N-nothing miss – It's a printing machine next door. When it's at work it throbs like a reg'lar 'edache.

VIO: Whose room's that?

BEL: Mr Middlesex's.

MARY: Middle*wick*. I've a very good mind to – (*Moves towards door.* BELINDA *hastily jumps before it.*)

BEL: You mustn't go there.

MARY: (*aside to* VIOLET) Do you see her alarm?

VIO: Am I blind?

MARY: No, but perhaps we both *have been*. (*Screams at sight of bonnet on chair; in a low voice to* VIOLET.) Look – look there!

VIO: (*in horror*) A human bonnet. Girl! (*Seizes* BELINDA *by arm.*) Don't prevaricate. Speak the truth and I'll give you more money than you ever had in your life!

BEL: (*half crying*) I don't know what's a coming to everybody this blessed day – I wish missus would come back.

VIO: Who's is this?

BEL: A lady's of course.

VIO: You hear, Mary.

MARY: (*tearfully*) Oh, don't speak to me!

BEL: But she's a nice sort of woman as ever lived and she says she's as fond of –

VIO: Of which?

BEL: Of *both* of them.

MARY: The wretch!

VIO: This is no place for us, Mary. (*noise heard in room; with a half scream*) That's not a printing machine.

MARY: I will see who – I mean *what's* in that room. Stand aside girl.

BEL: 'Scuse me, that's the gent's private apartment – their dominum gatherum, and –

VIO: Come, Mary. We've been two fools, dear, and we –

> (*As they go towards front door* CHARLEY *and* TALBOT *enter; slight pause.*)

TAL: Mary!

CHAR: Violet! Can I believe my eyes!

VIO: *I* can. *And* my ears. So can Mary.

MARY: Implicitly.

CHAR: But, Violet, this is so unexpected –

VIO: (*sarcastically*) Evidently.

CHAR: So – so bewildering. So inexplicable, and –

TAL: So jolly rum!

MARY: (*coldly*) Quite so.

CHAR: But how – how did you –

TAL: Did you find us out?

VIO: Never mind. Suffice it to say, Mr Middlewick, that –

MARY: That we *have* –

VIO: '*Found you out*'. (*The girls curtsey; the men dumb-founded.*)

CHAR: You saw me in the street.

VIO: Probably. We were foolish enough to think you – we thought your silence proof of your truth – we deceived ourselves –

MARY: Don't, Violet! Where's your spirit? Let us leave them to their own consciences, if they *have* any. This is evidently a well-trained confederate. Henceforth we are strangers.

VIO: *Utter* strangers. (*They exit.*)

TAL: (*after slight pause*) What have you been saying to those ladies?

BEL: Nothink. But they called me a 'coffederate'. Now a 'coffederate's a man as knows the conjuror and says he doesn't', and I'm not a going to bear it. Look here ladies, I – (*Exit.*)

　　　　(CHARLEY *and* TALBOT *look at each other.*)

CHAR: This is some conspiracy. Somebody's been vilifying us – they shan't leave without one *word* of explanation though. (*Exit.*)

　　　　(TALBOT *goes to fireplace, his back to the door of the room where his father is.*)

TAL: The girls don't mean it – can't mean it. Unless our determined silence has seemed suspicious, and – slightly altering the poet – suspicion ever haunts the *female* mind – always admitting there *is* such a thing as a female mind, which I'm beginning to doubt – (*Leans head on arm on mantelpiece.*)

　　　　(SIR GEOFFRY *opens door a little; it hides him from* TALBOT.)

SIR G: (*to himself*) They've all gone. Not one syllable could I distinguish; but women's voices, and at high words, were only too evident. This comes of leaving two head-strong lads to the temptations of town. Oh, Talbot, I knew you were not a genius, but I did hope you would never forget you were a gentleman!

　　　　(CHARLEY *re-enters quickly; as he does so* SIR GEOFFRY *steps back, nearly closing the door; the side of the room is set obliquely so that he is perfectly visible to audience, though unseen by those on the stage.* MIDDLEWICK *enters a little way.*)

CHAR: Well, upon my life, they're a pretty pair.

MID: (*aside*) Ah, I was sure I heard two of 'em.

CHAR: (*flinging himself into a chair*) A couple of beauties, I *do* think.

MID: (*aside*) So do I. A nice noisy couple whoever they were. Pretty acquaintances for two young chaps as bragged of their fidelity!

TAL: Fact is they've got tired of waiting for us. They see we're poor – and are likely to keep so. What a confounded draught there is from that – (*Goes to close door of his room,* SIR GEOFFRY *advances;* MIDDLEWICK *enters further simultaneously; both indignant.*)

'*Suspicion . . . mind*': a misquotation of 'Suspicion always haunts the guilty mind', from Shakespeare's *Henry VI, Part 3.*

MID: Sir Geoffry, you heard, of course.

SIR G: Not a word could I distinguish, for my hearing is utterly failing me. But you heard women's voices?

MID: Distinctly – even through the row of some confounded machine – a printer's, I fancy – next door.

SIR G: Though we could not distinguish a word your female friends said, some of *yours* reached us, and but too plainly indicated the familiar terms which – Oh, Talbot, I had hoped there would be still something of dignity and self-denial to qualify your absurdly Quixotic conduct, but I was mistaken. From your birth I mapped out your future, and hoped and prayed it should be a bright one, and now I find my son, my only child, who should have been my joy and pride, prove himself not only wilful and wrong-headed – I could have looked over *that* – but a *profligate*, and that, Talbot Champneys, I never will forgive.

CHAR: Don't speak, Talbot; let *me*. So, sirs, you have been playing the spy upon your sons.

MID: Don't exasperate me, Charles Middlewick, and no smug-faced shamming. We'd hunted you out, ready to forgive everything, but – a – there – I knew you were thoughtless, careless, *reckless* even, but I never dreamt you had a bit of vice in your whole nature.

CHAR: (*aside*) This is too much; the last straw breaks –

TAL: Who knows this *is* the last straw? After what I've heard recently I'm prepared for an entire stack.

CHAR: *You* are not the only people who have misjudged us.

TAL: No; others who were here but recently actually –

SIR G: Pray, sir, spare us the opinions of such persons. Talbot I – I blush for you.

MID: There's no shame in you. You're worse than your companions who were here just now.

TAL: (*sharply*) What do you mean by that?

MID: Eh?

TAL: Ladies whom you will mention with respect, if you please. If we have been ill-treated by them it is not for you, no, sir, nor *you* (*to his father*) to speak slightingly of them *before us.*

SIR G: (*aside*) Brazening it out. To think that six months in this abominable city should have obliterated all sense of shame, all sense of self-respect. Oh, London, what a lengthy list of such sad cases lies at your debasing door!

MID: Don't mention her. (*aside*) How dare he speak of that reg'lar lady and true woman in the very teeth of such – bah!

CHAR: I am sorry to see you still bear a resentment in that quarter.

TAL: And as I should never care for any woman but Mary –

SIR G: (*indignantly*) You insult me by mentioning her name at such a time.

TAL: And as all is over between us –

SIR G: Ha! Ha! I should think so. Eh, Middlewick?

MID: Depend upon it, the cousins know *all.*

SIR G: Ay, ay, trust a woman for finding out all she wants, and sometimes a deuced deal more. *This* accounts for their departing for the Continent last week.

MID: Of course; where no doubt they're endeavouring to dispel their sorrow.

SIR G: Just so. In the vortex of Parisian society.

MID: Strolling up and down the bully-vards and the bore de boolong. Showing them saller-faced foreigners what good, 'olesome looking English gals are.

SIR G: Yes, yes. (*warningly*) I can see them.

MID: (*working it up*) So can I.

SIR G: The dear creatures! That puss, Mary, has quite wound herself round my heart. An artful, winning little beauty.

MID: And as for the 'aughty one, we've got that friends I wouldn't see her wronged or insulted for – ugh!

SIR G: Aah! (*With exclamations of disgust, they go up stage.*)
> (CHARLEY *and* TALBOT *gaze blankly at each other, both stupefied.*)

TAL: Charley, does your father drink?

CHAR: No. Is lunacy hereditary in your family?

TAL: Never heard of it. I say, football's a capital game, for the *feet*. But the ball has a somewhat invidious and one-sided sort of place of it, hasn't he. I don't care for any more abuse.

CHAR: Nor I. (*to the fathers*) As we appear by some unfortunate means of which we know nothing to have grievously offended everybody, explanations are, of course, impossible. (*with solemnity and decision*) But as – before such an undertaking as –

TAL: Hear! Hear! Such an undertaking as we are about to – in short, to undertake.

CHAR: Quiet and uninterrupted companionship is desirable in order to finally settle our plans regarding emigration. (*Both the fathers start.*)

TAL: Just so. And *you*, having once turned *us* out, must not feel surprised, if we – (*Shrugs his shoulders, and hands* SIR GEOFFRY *his hat.*)

MID: Em-emigration!

SIR G: Are you mad, sir? Do you know the time of the year – winter?

MID: Why, confound it, Charley – I mean, *Charles* – you're not going to leave me – to leave England, I mean? What are you both dreaming of?

TAL: Nothing *now*, we've woke up.

SIR G: And where would you –

CHAR: Queensland, or else, perhaps –

MID: Charley, I can't bear this; you're a driving me desprit. If – if you go you'll – you'll *break my heart*! Dammy, I can't play the Roman father no longer! (*Sinks into a chair.*)

SIR G: (*aside*) He's given in – I knew he would. If he *hadn't I must* have done, and it's best as it is. He-hem! We have been – a – *hasty* perhaps, when we were concealed in those rooms – a – (*Breaks down.*) Talbot – Talbot – (TALBOT *looks at him – he immediately becomes frigid.*) In *my* case much is at stake. You are my *son* – my heir – (*with severity*) I – I *command* you to give up this mad notion. (*He is standing in a proud and authoritative attitude – a contrast to* MIDDLEWICK *who is sitting crushed and tearful.*)

MID: Charley – I – I – *implore* you! (*slight pause*)

TAL: (*coldly*) I regret my inability to obey you.

CHAR: (*same tone*) Talbot has replied for both.

SIR G: (*almost overcome*) And this – *this* is the result of our much vaunted systems. Even a rod of iron will –

(VIOLET *and* MARY *have entered.*)

VIO: Will *rust*, Sir Geoffry.

MARY: And the truest steel may fail you when most you may rely on it.

VIO: Oh, Charley, forgive me – we know *all* now.

MARY: And we're *so* ashamed of ourselves!

(*The young couples talk eagerly.*)

SIR G: (*Looks amazed; to girls*) Why – why aren't you on the Continent?

MARY: Why aren't you at the Cattle Show?

VIO: (*to* CHARLEY) I never imagined you saw me in the street.

MID: Here, what's this? Why ain't you abroad? Yes, abroad. (*to* SIR GEOFFRY) I'll be hanged if *we* ain't.

VIO: Fancy the two old gentlemen hiding themselves so absurdly, and our having such horrible –

MARY: But highly *natural* –

TAL: No, no, *un*-natural –

MARY: Suspicions.

MID: We can't have been, and yet they seem to be. Ha! Ha! (*Gives a violent start on seeing* CLARISSA'*s bonnet.*)

TAL: Upon my life, Charley, that jolly old firework, your father ought to be *put out.*

MID: What's that, eh?

SIR G: (*seizing it*) Yes! No *lady* was seen in such a monstrosity as *that*. Combining as it does the concentrated incongruity of Covent Garden Market with the accumulated imbecility of the Burlington Arcade.

(*The girls look surprised at the young men, who can't explain.*)

VIO: It *is* a bonnet.

MARY: And a hideous one.

MID: The question is, whose is it?

(*Enter* CLARISSA.)

CLAR: Mine, if you please – don't crush it. (*Comes down, takes it.*)

GIRLS: Miss Champneys!

TAL: Aunt!

SIR G: (*severe again*) So, Clarissa – madam, you not only come up to town against my express commands – but – but in an article of attire which is simply –

MID: *Loud* – oh, yes, you're a highly sensible woman, but it *is* loud.

CLAR: That's *your* opinion. *I* paid Mr Warrington to discover my nephew, and notwithstanding your threats, Geoffry, I preferred to brave your anger rather than share your regret, when you had perhaps found your son – the victim of a severe father's system – either in the streets or gone Heaven knows where. My dear nephew – Mr Middlewick, (*Shakes hands.*) I've heard how you behaved to him. But you're two scarecrows. I've got a fowl at the kitchen fire, and as it's only enough for two, we'll all go round to luncheon at Sir Geoffry's hotel, whilst *you* –

MID: Polish off the poultry. Brayvo!

SIR G: (*severely*) *What*, sir?

MID: It's no good, don't look severe, Sir Geoffry. (*Goes to him.*) It don't suit you.

SIR G: (*chafing*) But my own sister – a Champneys, cooking a fowl in a lodging-house kitchen, and I'm positively certain *spoiling* it – defying my authority and –

VIO: (*Has slipped her arm through his.*) Sir Geoffry, *dear* Sir Geoffry, don't you think we've *all* been a little wrong?

SIR G: (*pleased*) Eh?

VIO: *You*, especially?

SIR G: (*huffed*) He-hem!

VIO: And that we all ought to beg each other's pardons?

MARY: (*other side*) Yes, dear Sir Geoffry, and promise to forget the past, and never do so any more?

VIO: Eh, Sir Geoffry? (*squeezing his arm*)

MARY: Eh, dear Sir *Geff*? (*same business*)

SIR G: (*pleased, and unable to deny it*) Ha! Ha! Sir *Geff* indeed! (*Looks at each admiringly.*) You're a couple of syrens. I feel you would make me forgive *anything* – except that bonnet.

CHAR: I must own it staggered *me*. I knew it couldn't be Belinda's.

BOTH GIRLS: (*Drop* SIR GEOFFRY's *arm.*) Who's Belinda?

TAL: Ha! Ha! A slave.

SIR G: What?

TAL: Slave of the *ring* – comes when you pull the *bell*, you know. (*Enter* BELINDA.) One of the best girls in England, and the best nurse in the universe, as *I* well know.

BEL: That fowl's a frizzling itself to reg'lar fiddle-strings. Why, everybody seems to know everybody else.

MID: (*Beckons her to him.*) Here. Have you – have you got a young man? A sweetheart, you know?

BEL: A young man! He! He! And me two-and-twenty!

MID: Just so. What *is* he? I mean, what's his business? How does he get his living?

BEL: He's a butterman.

MID: *Is* he though? Tell him to call round tomorrow at that address, and I'll buy him the best business in the Boro'. (BELINDA *goes up, dazed.*) Sir Geoffry, they're our own again – our boys.

SIR G: No, no, somebody else's. (*Points to the young couples spooning.*)
(CLARISSA *is explaining to* BELINDA.)

MID: All in good time. (*laughing*) *You* and your rod of iron, bless your 'art, it wasn't a bar of soap.

SIR G: (*shaking hands*) Ha! Ha! I'm afraid so, and *you* – *you* a father of ancient Rome! Ha! Ha! *Greece* is more in *your* line.

VIO: (*to* CHARLEY) Yes, yes, Charley, I know I was blind to my own shortcomings, and was haughty, headstrong, and capricious, whilst *you*, Mary –

MARY: I don't think I've been anything in particular, and if I *have* I'm not going to admit it.

TAL: Quite right, Mary, nothing like being thoroughly satisfied with *yourself*, unless it's being *more* than satisfied with *me*.

SIR G: Clarissa, I was foolish just now. I beg your pardon. Talbot, dear boy – (*Shakes hands.*) Charles – (*Shakes hands.*) I – I see my error.

MID: Ha! Ha!

SIR G: (*stiffly and abruptly at him*) And other people's. (*aside*) I'm so happy I – but I *mustn't admit it* – a – *yet*. (*to them*) We haven't understood each other, borne with each other, we haven't shown sufficient of the glorious old principle of 'Give and take'. Sister, boys and girls, old friend, (*to* MIDDLE-WICK) hot tempers, hasty judgements, extreme crotchets, thick-skinned prejudice, theory and rule run rampant, ignoring the imperfections of poor human nature – these henceforth, we throw overboard and rise to brighter realms, even as the aspiring aeronaut flings away his heavy ballast and floats serenely through the cloudless sky.

(*Melody in orchestra swells as*

CURTAIN FALLS ON PICTURE.)

VI *Gulliver* at the Gaiety Theatre

THE GAIETY GULLIVER

A comic operatic spectacular extravaganza in prose and verse

First produced at the Gaiety Theatre, London, on 26 December 1879, with the following cast:

LEMUEL GULLIVER	Miss E. Farren
SCOWLYGROWLS	Mr Edward Terry
SMUGGINS	Mr E. W. Royce
OLD GROGBLOSSOM	Mr Salisbury
OLD CALICO	Mr T. Squire
THE MUTINOUS MATE	Mr W. Elton
PRETTY POLL OF PLYMOUTH	Miss Kate Vaughan
KING TEENYWEENY	Miss Lilian Linfield
QUEEN PETSYWETSY	Miss Baby English
FIELD-MARSHAL LITTLEMITE, KCB, ABC	Miss Carrie Coote
[THE EARL OF POPPET	Master Bertie Coote]
[ICKESING	Miss Ettie Waldron]
[TINYTROT	Miss Addie Blanche]
BROBDINGNAGIAN DWARF	Mr Le Clerq
BROBDINGNAGIAN BABY	Mr De Voy
BROBDINGNAGIAN PA	Mr Longithiarm
BROBDINGNAGIAN NURSE	Mr Butler
THE CRIER	Mr T. Squire
KING TOLDEROL	Mr W. Elton
PRINCESS TRALALA	Miss Wadman
[TIDDYWIDDI	Miss Gilchrist]
THE SPIRIT OF CHRISTMAS CHEER	Miss Louis
[CAPTAIN	
LORD CHAMBERLAIN	
SAMBO	
OFFICER	
PRESSGANG, PRENTICES, LASSES, SAILORS, GUARDS, COURTIERS]	

ACT I

SCENE 1. *Plymouth. The Jolly Skipper public house right. The draper's shop left with practicable door and window. 'Calico, tailor and draper' over the door. Practicable lattice window up above shop. As scene opens, prentices, lasses and crowd carousing,* OLD GROGBLOSSOM *serving the liquor.*

OPENING CHORUS
'Come, landlord fill the flowing bowl'.
As says the good old stave,
Here's to the lasses all,
The short likewise the tall;
We'll laugh and sing, and sorrow fling
Aside, the arrant knave,
And none of us must shrink,
From taking of his drink;
And toasting all our sweethearts gay,
Yes, all, every fair;
And thus our time we'll pass away,
We lads devil may care.

GIRLS: We take the compliment as meant,
For every one is quite the gent.

LADS: We are aware that we're the cheese,
And bound the sex to please.
(*All repeat.*) Come landlord, etc.

GROG: That's right my brave lads, nothing like good liquor to clear the throat. Well sung my sucking Sims Reeves and budding Santleys. What says the philosopher? 'Claret for boys, port for men, and brandy for heroes'. Good, as you're not 'heroes' at present and only 'men', why stick to port – the Port of Plymouth.
(*All laugh; music.*)
(*Enter from house* OLD CALICO.)

CAL: Silence you shouting vagabonds. You're ruining my business. I shall indict the Jolly Skipper as a nuisance.

GROG: Shut up!

CAL: That's what I must do. My customers can't get measured in comfort for you. I'll have your sign taken down and you taken up. A respectable tradesman can't get his forty winks in peace for the howling you keep up.

GROG: Come, come, neighbour Calico, don't make a goose of yourself if you *are* a tailor. That would be *sheer* waste of time. Take a drink at my expense.
(*handing tankard*)

CAL: You know I *never* drink – never-a-nev. (*Takes tankard.*) Well, *hardly ever.* (*Drinks.*) But what's the cause of all this hubbub, eh?

GROG: What's the cause? Why Master Lemuel Gulliver to be sure. It's his birthday, and he's treating all his friends.

Sims Reeves and Santleys: popular singers of the day.

CAL: It's a pity he doesn't pay his tradesmen first. An extravagant young ne'er-do-well. Runs through his property, runs into debt, runs up bills, runs down my ready-made clothing, and tries to run off with my daughter. Hang me if I don't run him in.

GROG: That's a good lot of runs for an old 'un. Grace at cricket's nothing to you.

CAL: I never *saw* any grace at cricket. Parcel of fools bowling at each other's legs. Don't admire *bowl-legs*. Gulliver indeed! I'd like to – (*All hurray.*) What's that row about?

1ST PREN: It's Gulliver, I knew he wouldn't disappoint us.

> (*Music.* GULLIVER *runs in – all surround him.*)

GULL: There, there, lads and lasses. One at a time. How are you? Drinking my health – that's right. Well old Grogblossom, the family nose in preservation I see. It's a credit to your brewer, and a standing advertisement for your distiller. Thank you, my boy. (*Takes tankard.*) My banking account's at a low ebb, but I can honour *this* draft anyhow. Here's all your jolly good healths, dear boys.

> (*Drinks. All hurray – then go up with* GROGBLOSSOM.)

CAL: You ought to be ashamed of yourself.

GULL: So I ought, but I ain't.

CAL: There's no credit about you.

GULL: No, nor about *you,* or I'd have a new suit of clothes tomorrow.

CAL: You're the biggest rake in Plymouth.

GULL: Yes, I am. I'm not the biggest Hoe though.

CAL: The man who'd make a pun would pick a pocket.

GULL: Not *yours*, for there's nothing in it.

CAL: Just so, for I'm always giving to the poor.

GULL: Are you? Then hand *me* over a trifle.

CAL: Not a penny. And Harkee, if I catch you hanging about my premises looking after my daughter Polly – I'll *turn her out.*

GULL: All right, and I'll take her in. Turn her out indeed. There's *one* thing you'll *never* turn out.

CAL: What's *that*?

GULL: Why a decent suit of clothes.

CAL: Do you intend to pay me what you owe me?

GULL: No, I don't.

CAL: Why you're a swindler.

GULL: Most certainly.

CAL: Look to your bill, Master Grogblossom, look to it – and I'll – I'll look to my daughter. Here, Polly.

> (*Exit into shop – others come down.*)

GULL: How that old fellow does *go on*! When he *goes off* it's positively refreshing; But there, boys, he's proud of his daughter, and so am *I*. Come, a cup all round to the health of Pretty Polly of Plymouth.

Grace: W. G. Grace (1848–1914), outstanding batsman and bowler who played cricket for England.

SONG

GULL: There's not a girl in Plymouth with my Polly can compare,
    She's elegant, she's beautiful, she's spruce, she's debonnaire,
    She sings like any nightingale that carols on the tree,
    And she's just about the sort of girl one dreams about at sea.

ALL: And she's just about the sort of girl,
     The sort of girl, the sort of girl;
     She's just about the sort of girl
     One dreams about at sea.

GULL: She dances like an elfin sprite with light and airy tread,
    You wouldn't hear her footfall were she jumping overhead;
    Her smile is like the sunshine when it's bursting from a cloud,
    And she laughs at her old dad who says 'no followers allowed'.
     Pretty Poll, pretty Poll,
     None in Plymouth is her equal,
     Marriage sure shall be the sequel;
     Oh! my sweet pretty Poll,
     Pretty, pretty, pretty Poll.

ALL: Pretty Polly, pretty Poll,
     None in Plymouth, etc.

GULL: I'd marry her tomorrow if her dad would consent,
    But I cannot quite get over that respectable old gent;
    He has one notion in his mind, that notion's LSD,
    Which is just about the sort of thing you dream about at sea.
    (*Repeat.*)

GULL: Now my dear boys and girls, fascinated as I am by your company, as some-thing tells me my pretty Polly is about to gladden the eyesight of her unworthy Lemuel Gulliver, I should not feel the least annoyance if you were one and all to clear out. (*Music. All repeat chorus and exeunt.*) I am alone. I always am when everybody else has retired. The situation demands one remark – which remark is – 'She comes'.
    (*Ballet, music and action – enter* POLLY *from house.*)

GULL: My Polly!

POLLY: My Lemmy! (*They embrace.*) Oh, Lemmy dear, I fear I must be another's.

GULL: Another's! Perish the thought! What other's?

POLLY: Nay, I know not.

GULL: You know not. Then *no knot* shall tie you to him. Is it Scowlygrowls?

POLLY: Possibly.

GULL: Or Smuggins?

POLLY: Perhaps.

GULL: (*melodramatically*) They die!

POLLY: No, dear, unfortunately they live. One or the other is to marry me.

GULL: Let it be the 'other'.

POLLY: Neither! Sooner than wed either I'd –

GULL: So would I – *what*?

POLLY: Run away. Are you game?

GULL: *Game?*

POLLY: Oh, yes, say you *hare*.

GULL: Yes, I *ham*.

POLLY: Ham! Ham suggests beef, beef suggests junk, junk suggests ships – I have it. We'll take our passage for a distant land, and away, away to the mountain's brow.

GULL: Good. What proper⁺ᵧ have you got?

POLLY: A fourpenny piece, a silver thimble, two odd numbers of the *Family Herald*, grandfather's clock without the works, three pass-out checks to Drury Lane and a shoe-horn.

GULL: Good. I, too, am not without means. I possess two signatures of the Poet Close, a photograph of the Thames Tunnel, *Whittaker's Almanack* for the last year but one, three returned telegrams and a button hook. Not much, but the world lies before us. A few moments for an interchange of vocal and terpischorean ideas, and then – Hey for freedom and the blue waters.

POLLY: Stay dear – a thought strikes me.

GULL: Does it. Then hit it again. What is it?

POLLY: You have been flirting lately.

GULL: *Very* lately. So have you.

POLLY: I own it.

GULL: Then all is over between us?

POLLY: Quite so.

GULL: If you do so again.

POLLY: Which I shall.

GULL: So shall I.

POLLY: Very well.

GULL: Very well.

>   DUET

GULL: You think I'm blind – you'll discover that I'm not.
                I shall flirt whene'er I please,
                Flirting with this chap agrees,
                And you will find I'm aware of what is what;
                And the nicest girl about
                Always does this chap pick out.

POLLY: You always were an unkind and cruel boy,
                And I never loved you, there!
                Now I hate you I declare,
                With new sweethearts, Lemuel, I wish you joy,

---

pass-out checks: small metal tokens, issued by Drury Lane, Covent Garden and Theatre Royal, Haymarket, as tickets in the late eighteenth/early nineteenth centuries. These were undated and used again and again.

the Poet Close: John Close (1816–91), printer and poet, whose doggerel rhymes won him a civil pension in 1860, which was withdrawn in 1861.

Thames Tunnel: a brick, arched roadway under the Thames, built by Brunel and opened in 1843. From 1865 it was used as a tunnel by the East London Railway Company.

terpischorean: used of dancing.

	Never speak again to me
	With familiari*tee*.
GULL:	Come, now Polly, don't be cross,
	Forgive your Lemu*el*.
POLLY:	That overwhelming swell.
GULL:	Polly, no dark cloud our path should cross;
	Come smile again ma belle,
POLLY:	Go back to your hotel. (*At end of dance they exeunt.*)

(*Melodramatic music.* SCOWLYGROWLS *enters pacing stage like a heavy ruffian. Music changes to a light air.* SMUGGINS *runs on with a boyish trip.*)

SCOW: Ha! Ha! She must be mine – ah!

SMUG: Nothing of the kind. She must be mine – ah!

SCOW: Yours – you miserably good boy.

SMUG: Yes mine, you abominably wicked one.

SCOW: I am! Ha! Ha! I glory in being a bad boy. I come of a bad lot – Pa was bad – so was ma.

SMUG: *My* ma was good – and my pa was a better.

SCOW: What a man who lays on horses? A pretty pa that!

SMUG: I love Polly.

SCOW: So do I.

SMUG: She loves *me*.

SCOW: So she does *me*.

SMUG: Excuse me I –

SCOW: I *shan't* excuse you. Take *that*. (*Gives him a violent 'oner'.*)

SMUG: Scowlygrowls you have struck me.

SCOW: I have.

(*As* SMUGGINS *turns he gives him a kick.*)

SMUG: Scowlygrowls you have kicked me.

SCOW: I admit it.

SMUG: Continue your present course of conduct and we shall fall out.

SCOW: Who cares. Come on! (*Flings himself into position.*)

SMUG: It's very wrong to fight.

SCOW: Come on you miserable little humbug.

SMUG: No, no, let us be friends. I like to live in harmony.

SCOW: I like to pass my whole life out of toon.

DUET – '*Proverbs*'. (*each interrupting the other*)
I rather think we'd bettah,
Indulge in a Duettah,
Come, something new can you suggest,
The oldest though are oft the best,
Would proverbs upside downy,
That's Christmassey and Clowney,
Haphazard do the trick,

'*oner*': severe blow.

Don't stop to choose and pick
For a pin a day cannot be caught with chaffing.
Or give a dog a bad bone, he will choke,
And shut the stable door,
When the cat's away – Oh lor!
For 'tis cruelty to kill a flea with laughing.

They say one fact is worth-a,
Here don't go any furth-a,
And whilst the grass grows make your hay,
The way the twig's inclined, I say!
Enough's as good as – t'other!
Too many cooks – Oh! bother!
Birds of a feather fly to – Bosh!
And cleanliness – Won't wash!
For a pin a day, etc.
(*At end of duet short dance and exit* SCOWLYGROWLS.)

SMUG: If it wasn't very wrong I should hate my brother prentice. But as it *is* wrong of course I love him and I prove I love him. I let him always open the door. I know he *likes* opening doors. I always waive my right to run errands because exercise is good for him. I always intercept his beer because beer's bad for a growing boy, and I've *done* growing. When he punches my head I say I *think* I've split it – because if I didn't qualify the assertion it would be telling a story, and I never tell stories. I'm such a *good* boy.

SONG
I'm such a good boy, I'm such a good boy,
With nice little books my time I employ,
I'm so very good, that I carol for joy,
I'm such a remarkable good little boy.

CHORUS
I'm a good little, dear little, sweet little boy,
And I never waste time upon toffy or toy.

I never tell stories and don't care for jam,
For such an exceedingly good boy I am,
I like bread and scrape and my tea very weak,
And words that are naughty I never will speak.
(*chorus*)

I never look cross when I'm ordered to bed,
I often declare that I'm much over fed;
When others in play, great amusement may find,
I sit in a corner improving my mind.
(*chorus*)

Some say I'm a sneak, others call me a prig.
For such appellations I don't care a fig.

> From study in vain me they try to decoy,
> I'm a serious, studious, Beast of a boy. (*At end of song exit.*)
> (*Hurry.* SCOWLYGROWLS *drags on* POLLY.)

POLLY: Oh! Peter, Peter, what are you about?

SCOW: To declare the parshon that devours me. *Your* parshon devours *you.*
Before the two parshons devour us both, and there's nothing *left of us* – let
us away, away, and be one – ah!

POLLY: *Left* of us indeed. It wouldn't be *right* of us.

SCOW: You love anothah! That 'nothah is a numbug – his name is Gullivah. He
dies, ah!

POLLY: What would you do?

SCOW: Him! To death, ah!

POLLY: If I wed *you* will you spare him?

SCOW: Yes.

POLLY: Then I won't!

SCOW: Mocked! Retticuled. Maiden would you madden me? (*Seizes her.*) I will
bear you off!

POLLY: No! No!

SCOW: Away, away! Come! Come where the ashpans quivvah! Come to the hold
hoak tree!

POLLY: Help! Help!

> (*Escapes from him.* GULLIVER *enters – knocks* SCOWLYGROWLS
> *down and rescues her.*)

GULL: Why I only left you whilst I went to the jeweller's. I've fetched you the
ring.

SCOW: (*rubbing himself*) Yes – and you fetched *me* the *knock.* But I'll be revenged.
I'll – be – (SMUGGINS *enters.*) – floored, and in the presence of that hateful
boy! Oh, this is bittah!

SMUG: Halloa! *He's* got it this time. If I wasn't so good, I should call out hoorour.

> FINALE

GULL: Should you venture with my Polly to go flirting,
                 I'll a drubbing give you which you won't rub out.

SCOWL: Oh, I'll be revenged for this here, you make certing.

SMUG: Oh, what is all this bobbery about.

POLLY: A chap like you to think of me, a maiden young and fair,
                 It's most owdacious in extreme,
                 All must admit it *air.*
                 One wonders how he dare.
                 Each in his proper station
                 Himself should always keep,

SCOWL: To utter spifflication
                 I'd like to send the heap.
                 (*Enter* CAPTAIN, PRESSGANG, PRENTICES, LASSES, *etc.*)
                 CHORUS

PRESSGANG: Three likely lads as ever we clapped eye on,

Hurry: technical term for music representing sudden activity in melodrama.

Your fortune lads the ocean you should try on.
No murmuring, his majesty wants sailors,
And though 'tis true that two of you are tailors,
The third's as smart a chap as ever chaff'd.
Seize 'em and bear 'em all aboard the craft.

ALL: Hence now away over foreign seas to rove.
Hence now away from friends and those we love
Away o'er the sea,
How ill we shall be.
The ocean deep,
Where lobsters sleep,
And the perriwink slumbers sound.
Where the big shark bares the whole of his gums,
Prepared for whatever across his way comes.
Where porpoises blow, and the octopus hides,
And all sorts of queer little fishes besides.

SCENE 2.   *'Tweendecks'. Melodramatic music. Enter mutinous* MATE – *he paces the deck.*

MATE: Once again has the junk been insufficiently briney. Once again has the grog
been so strong as to need extra water – the bread been crusty, the biscuits
served out in profusion, the tea too full of sugar. No one has been flogged for
a fortnight. The skipper permits us to sleep on our watches and he provides
us with extra tobacco and all the illustrated papers. How long – how long is
this hated tyranny to continue? My nature revolts at it, my soul rebels, my
gorge rises and my whole being grizzles! But to no purpose. I can find no
accomplice amongst the crew! Curs that they are! I cannot rise alone. A
mutiny of *one* would be rash. I must e'en bide my time, ah!

     SONG
I'm the awfullest wickedest party,
And I cheat when I play at ecarté.
At beggar my neighbour I swindle as well,
On *dry* land, as burglar I bear off the bell.
I go in for plunder and prigging,
I seldom go up in the rigging,
But rather I choose
To skulk in the caboose,
The grog of the mariners' swigging.
And that's where I get courage in tossing off the rum,
It often brings on tremens, that's called delirium.
What makes me meet all danger with bold defiant wink,
It's D.R.I.N.K. and that spells drink, drink, drink.

I'm the dreadfullest elderly sinner,

---

ecarté: card game for two people.   *caboose*: cabin used for cooking on ship's deck.
prigging: stealing.

Eat peas with my knife at my dinner.
I knock about folks who are smaller than me,
But I bolt when a chap who is bigger I see.
By most folks I'm abominated,
And by the rest I am hated,
That don't signify
A farthing to Hi.
I like to be blown up and rated,
For when down I get courage, etc., etc.

There, that has relieved *me*, though it may have depressed those who heard me. No mattah! I love to cause my fellow creatures annoyance, and to know that *they* are saddest when I sing as well as myself.

(*Enter* SCOWLYGROWLS.)

SCOW: (*aside*) I hear the accents of a congenial croaker. Something tells me I have met a man after my own heart. (*to him*) What cheer mess-mate?

MATE: Carse ye!

SCOW: Just so, allow me to reciprocate.

MATE: Do ye defy me?

SCOW: To the dath – a –

MATE: Ha! I have met my match. Now if I had only got my *gunpowder*.

SCOW: You would blow up the ship.

MATE: I would, ah.

SCOW: Ha! Good, ah. So would I.

MATE: You hate everybody?

SCOW: Like p-ison.

MATE: Are you game to help me scuttle the vessel, swim off with the millions of specie, make for a distant shore, change our names, thus defying detection, and lead a life of luxury amongst the dusky denizens of some uninhabited island?

SCOW: It has been the dream of my childhood – the ambition of my adolescence.

MATE: Your hand then.

SCOW: Take it – (*Gives* MATE *one.*)

MATE: This very night! at *once*.

SCOW: Sooner if possible.

MATE: Ha! Ha!

SCOW: Ha! Ha!

DUET (*sung very gloomily, with an air of depression*)
Oh, *who* would not be a mutineer
To sail on the pathless sea,
As free as the air, without ever a care,
That's the sort of a life for me.
Oh, who wouldn't be – there's loot in here,
For we're carrying off spe-ci-*e*.
And the Captain's got, of money a pot,

---

specie: coins.

And indulges in jewel-*ree*.
   Then hey for the mute,
   The merry, merry, mute,
      And hey, for his privateer;
   Which he buys with the tin
   That he's certain to win,
      Is the merry, merry, mutineer.
(*short melancholy dance*)
With pistols primed with lots of slugs,
No end of a snickersee.
With cutlass and knife, he's aware that his life
Is as safe as a life can be.
He laughs at thunder, lightning chaffs,
And roars *back* at the roaring sea.
And altogether, he despises the weather,
For a jolly mutineer is he.
   Then hey, etc., etc.
(*Dance and exeunt.*)

SCENE 3.   *Deck of the ship.* CAPTAIN *and sailors discovered. Sailors' chorus*
and dance.

CHORUS
If you want to give the girls a treat, I'll tell you what to do;
Take them down to Rosherville just for an hour or two,
But if they'd steam out past the Nore, object to such a thing,
They're certain to be far from well when the vessel begins to swing.
Swinging to and fro, it's awfully nice you know,
With your arm round the waist of the girl you love,
In a swing at a penny show – Oh!
Swinging to and fro, with ocean dark below;
Too deep to enquire, one doesn't admire,
The stormy winds that blow.

CAPT: Now then, luff you swabs! Luff! Belay there! Haul in your main top thingumygigs! Why don't you haul in your maintop thingumygigs? Nobody obeys
me. I shout out orders but they don't produce the slightest effect. And why
should they? Isn't the sea the life of the free? – Course it is. (*Shouts.*) So
here – *you*! Don't you bother about hauling in anything. I give everybody a
half-holiday and blow the expense. Ah! Here comes Gulliver.
   (*All hurray. Enter* GULLIVER.)

GULL: Captain you're a brick. You're a credit to your profession and your craft.
And your craft's a beauty. She skips over the sea like a little boy over his
lessons, and she's thoroughly *taut* which the little boy isn't.

CAPT: You do me proud.

GULL: Not a bit of it. But where's my friend Smuggins? Smuggins hasn't shown

---

tin: see note on p. 86.   *Rosherville . . . Nore*: Landmarks on Thames Estuary.
snickersnee: knife used as weapon.

since he's been on board. I fancy Smuggins like the youth in the ballad was
'never meant for the sea'.

(*Music.* SMUGGINS *enters pale and unsteady.*)

SMUG: Oh, I say. Where are we?

GULL: NNW by SSEE, fifty-two degrees below Zero and within half-an-hour's walk
of the Equator.

SMUG: You don't say so. I say. Can't we get out and go on by the bus? I'd rather.

GULL: Why, shiver my timbers!

SMUG: Yes, yes, *my* timbers *have* been shivering ever since I've been *aboard*. I
don't mean that as a joke – I wouldn't joke till I'm on land again for *any*
thing. Where are we bound?

GULL: Some port in Central Africa.

SMUG: Ha, I've tried African Port and I don't like it. I say can't we go back?

GULL: Of course we can.

SMUG: (*taking his arm*) Come on, then. How the vessel pitched about in the night.
I always *was* afraid of new bread, and I'd the indigestion at every *fresh roll*.
I never *could* manage a sea voyage. I tried to brave the ocean once as far as
Erith, but I had to give in. I – (*Staggers.*) – There's another of 'em. (*faintly*)
Where's the steward?

GULL: (*Slaps him on back.*) Bah!

SMUG: Yes, where's the *bar*? I think the least drop of – there's another of 'em.

GULL: Rubbish! You haven't found your sea legs yet?

SMUG: No, but if I lose my *land* legs and *don't* find my *sea* legs, where *am* I? Oh!
My – there's another of 'em. (*Staggers up.*)

GULL: Miserable pump! How different to the gallant Richard Carr – the young
sailor who sets us all an example in flying up the catlines, dancing the horn-
pipe, drinking his grog, and chaffing his mess-mates. Here he is, the young
scamp.

(*Music. Enter* POLLY *as* RICHARD CARR.)

POLLY: What cheer my heart? (*sailor's action*)

GULL: Aye, aye, your honour. (*ditto*)

POLLY: Gulliver?

GULL: Well.

POLLY: There's a chap aboard who means mischief.

GULL: I know there is. I've watched him.

POLLY: So have I. Scowlygrowls!

GULL: The same.

POLLY: He comes.

GULL: He do.

(*Enter* SCOWLYGROWLS.)

SCOW: Well, my noble commanders, how goes it?

GULL: First rate.

SCOW: Then we'll e'en indulge in a nautical ditty, (*aside*) whilst the mate prepares
to scuttle the vessel.

Erith: harbour near Dartford on Thames Estuary.

SONG
One sunny bright summer morning,
   Out in the Bay of Biscay,
Dangerous billows a scorning;
   'Cos there was none on that day;
All of a sudden we seed,
That of which we often read
But seldom see;
   Right on our lee,
Such a sea serpent at play,
As long as Nelson's monument.
That oceanic gent,
It's mouthpiece it was opened wide,
Old friends we saw inside.
Old friends who overboard had fell
Were in that oceanic swell.
We said tar, tar, and let them go,
And sung heave oh, heave oh!

One cool and clear afternoon we
Anchored in Botany Bay,
Singing a nautical toon, we
Sang in a reggeler way,
What should we see in the shade
But an allooring mermaid,
Combing her locks,
Like Mr Cox,
In Cox and Box, funny play!
A mighty winkle looked the belle
Denuded of its shell.
She winked at me, likewise the mate,
And nearly sealed our fate,
But we'd the strength of mind to shout
'You're lovely, but get out.'
We said tar, tar, and let her go,
And sang heave oh, heave oh!

(*aside*) By this time no doubt he has carried out his diabolical plan, and bored a hole in the side of the vessel. I am enveloped in a cork jacket, possess a *Cook's* ticket for all round the world, and a housemaid's for everywhere else, and can consequently defy the elements.
   (*Tremulous music. Enter* MATE.)
MATE: Though mild and meek,
   I'm forced to speak,
   We've sprung a leak,

Cox and Box: operatic adaptation by F. C. Burnand, with music by Sullivan (first performed in 1867), of John Maddison Morton's popular farce *Box and Cox* (first performed 1847).

	You mustn't shriek.
GULL:	'Twill be a squeak,
	The ship's of teak,
	With form unique,
	It's someone's pique,
	Combined with cheek.
POLLY:	Where are we, sneak?
MATE:	Near Mozambique.
SMUG:	The timbers creak,
	They can't be weak,
SCOW:	Our prospect's bleak,
	The biscuits seek,
	Of Frean and Peek!
(*chord*)	
ALL:	Ooooh!
	(*Rumble. All stagger.*)
ALL:	Now we shake with fear,
	Shipwreck's surely near,
	Horror! Horror pales each party's cheek.
	Down to depths below,
	All are bound to go,
	Food for hungry shark and porpoise sleek.
	Lifeboats do not here abound,
	If we'd only run aground,
	Somebody might reach the shore,
	Midst the raging billows roar. (*All repeat.*)
	(*shipwreck*)

ACT II

SCENE 1. *Palace at Lilliput. Enter* LORD CHAMBERLAIN *followed by two attendants.*

CHAM: I think that everything's prepared to please,
My royal master. On such days as these –
A royal birthday – all must do their best,
To show their loyalty and all the rest.
So let no frowns or angry looks appear,
On this the gladdest day of all the year.

1ST ATT: Lord Chamberlain your kind remarks we treasure.

2ND ATT: Pay us our wages and we'll grin with pleasure.

1ST ATT: At present laughter cannot well appear,
Not in our *eye*, when pay is in arr*ear*.

2ND ATT: Our prospects as to pay are rather murky,
They should tax double as they do in Turkey.

Frean and Peek: a well-known firm of biscuit manufacturers.

1ST ATT: What care we courtiers how these cads ground down are,
　　　　　So we, what's owing us, paid every brown are.
CHAM: Here comes his majesty, just for the while,
　　　　We'd better probably get up a smile.
1ST ATT: And as it's well to please the royal ear,
　　　　　We'll greet him with the customary cheer.
　　　　　(*Enter* KING *and* QUEEN.)
CHAM: Hooray!
KING:　Lord Chamberlain, you do us proud;
　　　　At all events you're loyal if not loud.
　　　　Our gracious majesties accept that cheer,
　　　　As the expression of our people here.
　　　　What says our Queen?
QUEEN: Your majesty's remarks
　　　　　Are simply scrumptious.
KING:　Let the numerous parks
　　　　Be open free to all. The Green Park, Hyde,
　　　　The Regent, Battersea and rest beside;
　　　　And let Trafalgar Square to all be free,
　　　　And the adjacent National Galler*ee*.
　　　　Mind the Thames Tunnel is an open way
　　　　To every person who may choose to pay.
　　　　Let all be mirth and cheerful, festive jollity,
　　　　And let the welkin ring with ritolollity.
　　　　But who comes here?
　　　　(*Enter* COMMANDER-IN-CHIEF.)
　　　　Ha! Ha! Field-Marshal say.
COMM: I've been insulted very much today,
　　　　Your majesty. That monster whom we caught
　　　　But yesterday – he ought to be – he ought!
KING:　Ought what?
QUEEN:　　　Ought who?
CHAMB:　　　　　Ought which?
COMM: Well he declares,
　　　　If Lilliput were taken unawares,
　　　　That England – Lilliput I mean – would be,
　　　　An easy victim to the enem*ee*,
2ND ATT: So please your majesty, I heard him say,
　　　　　Your majesty must raise the soldiers' pay;
　　　　　And make it pleasanter for the recruits,
　　　　　You'd find them then enlisting like 'old boots'.
1ST ATT: *I* understood 'like winking', and he added,
　　　　　The military chest was only padded;
　　　　　And wasn't muscle, whilst our ammunition,

---

brown: slang for copper coin.
So please your majesty . . . He do?: cut from version submitted to Lord Chamberlain.

Likewise our arms were not in a condition
To do much service should a foreign foe
Think of invading Lilliput you know.

KING: Who says that sort of thing indeed? He do?
Lord Chamberlain, we can't believe it true,
Still we can trust our royal ears – we must.

CHAM: They're *long* enough your majesty to trust.

KING: Shakesperian sentiment our system thrills,
And with emotion all the monarch fills!
Lilliput shan't – she never did of yore –
Lie at the proud foot of a conque-*ror*.
Henry the Fifth's remarks do we endorse;
Our Queen agrees with us –

QUEEN: My liege, of course,
Punish this prating giant.

KING: Yes, but how?
When fast asleep we bound him tight, but now
The monster is beyond our puny power.

COMM: Your majesty's aware within the hour
A grand review takes place. Why not permit
This monstrous man, who would in judgement sit
On our shortcomings, show us what's his skill
In military matters.

KING: Good – we will.
He shall the grand review himself conduct,
Since he us Lilliputians would instruct;
And should he make a mull as oft is done
When people go a soldiering for fun,
As an impostor all our troops shall riddle
The form gigantic of this individdle.

CHAM: Should he succeed?

COMM: (*aside*) I hope he won't – deuce take him!

KING: Head of the war department, then we make him;
Make him a peer – make him a peer most high too.

COMM: (*aside*) Make him ap-pear ridiculous I'll try to.
CONCERTED PIECE AND DANCE
Here in this land of famed Lilliput,
Every man a soldier must be;
Either on horseback or on fut.
As gallant rifleman or ar-til-ler-ree.
Fighting's our trade, each wields a blade,
No one of anyone here is afraid;

Lilliput . . . conqueror: cf. Shakespeare, *King John*, V.7.113.
England never did, nor never shall,
Lie at the proud foot of a conqueror.
mull: mess.

We're not partic-lar to a shade,
When we're in battle no more than parade.
Foes we defy, those who decry
Lilliput, let them look after their eye.

SCENE 2.   *Exterior of fortress at Lilliput. Grand review of Lilliputian troops.*
             CHORUS
             March, march, on without delay;
             March, march, boldly on our way.
             We our duty strictly do,
             And our exercise go through.
             March, march, firmly in a line;
             March, march, looking smart and fine.
             Ready on the foe to fall,
             Brave heroes all.

SCENE 3.   *Brobdingnagian cornfield. Enter* GULLIVER *and* POLLY *looking round in surprise.*
GULL: Escaped from Lilliput where all was teeny,
        Infinitesimal, minutely wheeny,
        Here we are thrown, upon a shore where all
        Appears most supernaturally tall;
        Massive, gigantic, overgrown, and large;
        Where every rowing boat looks like a barge.
        Perambulators big as omni*busse*s,
        Are wheeled about by elephantine 'nusses',
        The dogs and cats are big as cows and horses,
        The Isle of Brobdingnag then this of course is.
        Look at that cornfield – isn't it a funny 'un,
        The *corn* is big enough to be a *bunny-un*,
        But by the way for able-bodied tar,
        You haven't shown much courage, Richard Carr.
POLLY: I'll own my courage failed me on the raft.
GULL: And you cried out and everybody laughed –
        Because a tar don't *cry*.
POLLY: Well, I was frightened!
GULL: Likewise you screamed out loudly when it lightened,
        And then you asked if any one had got
        A smelling bottle – which of course they'd not.
        Why you might be a woman.
POLLY: Might I? – Pooh,
        I'm every bit as good a man as *you*.
        And all the lot of you I'll put to shame,
        Shiver my timbers! What's your little game?
GULL: That's better. For a time friend Richard Carr,
        'Specially when you called out for your 'Mar',
        We thought you were a gal in seaman's guise.

POLLY: Rubbish! I only meant to get a rise
        Out of the lot of you.
GULL: You did it well.
        Ha, here's young Smuggins and the other swell.
        (SMUGGINS *and* SCOWLYGROWLS *enter.*)
SMUG: Oh! I say, such a lark, what do you think?
        We went into a place to get a drink,
SCOW: Yes, a split soda with a dash of pale,
SMUG: Though as a rule my liquor's table ale;
        The very inno*cen*test that is brewed.
SCOW: Smuggins, don't interrupt me please, it's rude.
        We went into a public – hold your row!
SMUG: A *restaurant* – there are no *publics* now.
SCOW: Perhaps *you'll* tell the story.
SMUG: Oh, not *I*,
        I don't tell stories, I'm too good a *by*.
SCOW: Just so. And boys they took us both to be,
        Not only boys, but in our infan*cee*,
        'What' says the barmaid – she was, by the by,
        A neat young thing of over nine feet high –
        'What' says the barmaid, 'babies such as *you*
        Talk of split soda and of brandy too?
        If I knew where your relatives resided,
        I'd have you' – here her grammar failed – 'well hided'.
        They took us for a pair of little kids, sir;
        The smallest of kids – 'small sixes' – oh! they did, sir.
GULL: We've lighted on the Isle of Brobdingnag.
        Our only safety here consists in brag.
        We are Tom Thumbs in Brobdingnagian eyes,
        So let's be awfully cheeky for our size.
        CONCERTED PIECE
        In Brobdingnag the people all grow twenty-five feet high, sir;
        They use of flour fifty pounds to make a beefsteak pie, sir;
        They take to lubricate the crust a dozen pounds of suet;
        They feed their bullocks till they bust, and that's the way they do it.
        CHORUS
        Brob! Ding! Nag! It's a rummy, rummy sort of place.

        They sleep in beds like beds of Ware, *we* should be smothered in it;
        They take the most tremendous strides and walk five miles a minit.
        When'er they shout they make the welkin ring like any*thing*, sir.
        Though I *don't* know what welkin is, or why it's said to ring, sir.
        (*chorus*)

        The common folks have awful teeth, such pantomimic molars,
        They might belong to Russian bears, or to Icelandic Polars;

---

kids: gloves.

You say in horror 'what a nose', or 'oh! when will that mouth end?'
And every noble peer's as long as that there pier at Southend.
(*chorus*)

They're black, so every infant's an exaggerated Topsy,
Their beetles are like elephants afflicted with the dropsy,
Their sportive and eccentric flea a monster to appal is,
The smallest pill they ever take, the size of Albert Hall is.
(*chorus*)

Themselves and institutions are, upon a scale gigantic;
In parliament their repre*sen*-tative would look romantic,
He'd have to be of what one calls an overwhelming figger,
They wouldn't choose 'Parnell' you know, because he isn't 'Bigger'.
(*chorus*)

      (*At end* SCOWLYGROWLS *and* SMUGGINS *go up.*)

GULL: What say to wandering Richard Carr old chap, –
       Seeking adventure?

POLLY: Good, I'm up to trap,
       Pr'aps we shall come across pretty girls.

GULL: My Polly is the preciousest of pearls,
       The duckiest of diamonds, she's set,
       Within my heart.

POLLY: Another you may get,
       Who'll make you soon forget your Plymouth Polly.

GULL: Never!

POLLY: (*aside*) He loves me true! How awful jolly.

       (*Ballet music.* GULLIVER *expresses his affection.* POLLY – *aside –*
       her delight. This is short. Both exeunt. SCOWLYGROWLS *and*
       SMUGGINS *do a little ballet business of the same kind coming down*
       – they finish abruptly.)

SCOW: (*grasping* SMUGGINS*'s arm*)
       Smuggins, I smell a rat – d'you smell one too?

SMUG: No, Scowlygrowls, I can't say that I do.

SCOW: Why, haven't you observed this Richard Carr?
       He's not a sailor, he's no galliant tar,
       Can't smoke, can't drink, won't use bad language – Pooh!
       And then he only makes believe to chew.
       It's my belief my most respected pal,
       That that there individual's a *gal*!

SMUG: A what!

SCOW: A gal – a gal-lant gal I own,
       But still a gal – and one to *us* well known.
       It's wondrous *what* gals *will* do in their folly.

SMUG: Her name?

Topsy: character in *Uncle Tom's Cabin*. Slang for negro.
'*Parnell*' ... '*Bigger*': Charles Stuart Parnell, the Irish MP who led the movement for Home
Rule in Ireland. There had been much agitation in Ireland during 1879.

SCOW: There is a place named Galli-polli;
　　　 Ha! Ha! Gall*i*poli! D'ye twig?
SMUG: 　　　 Good gracious!
　　　 Of all the imperentest, most owdacious,
　　　 Females I ever – why I might have guessed
　　　 She was a *gal*, because when all the rest
　　　 When wrecked made for the *shore* – *she* once so coy,
　　　 Struck out and swam directly for the *buoy*.
SCOW: And when on land – I well remember can –
　　　 She said she 'hoped it was the Isle of *Man*'.
　　　 But that we know this yet we mustn't show.
　　　 We mustn't blow the gaff!
SMUG: 　　　 Oh, blow it, no!
　　　 Not that I know what such strange language means.
　　　 I'm much too good to –
SCOW: 　　　 Bosh! Behind the scenes –
　　　 I mean down yonder grove – with him we hate,
　　　 My Polly –
SMUG: Mine –
SCOW: 　　　 My destiny – my fate –
SMUG: *My* destiny – *my* fate –
　　　 Shut up – is walking
　　　 With Gulliver. *His* game we must be baulking,
　　　 I have a plan to settle *him* – anon
　　　 I'll tell it you – and when our rival's gone –
　　　 No doubt at first an overwhelming loss for her,
　　　 But she'll get over it, why then we'll toss for her.
　　　 DUET
SCOW: We'll toss, so heads I win or tails you lose,
　　　 She'll be mine, I opine, so prepare to lose.
SMUG: We'll toss, but that arrangement will not do for me,
　　　 Her I'll gain, I'll maintain in a brace of twos.
SCOW: You snob, you don't your station know or keep at all,
　　　 You relies on your size, insignificant.
SMUG: It's not because unfortunately I'm but small
　　　 Neath this vest – this fond heart
　　　 Don't for Polly pant.
BOTH: What happiness, oh, rare, 'twill be,
　　　 (When Mrs Scowlygrowls is she.)
　　　 (When Mrs Smuggins called is she.)
　　　 When married I shall settle down
　　　 (And take a crib in Camden Town.)
　　　 (And rent a cot in Kentish Town.)
　　　 I'll dance and sing the whole day long,
　　　 The polka and the gay doo-tong.

---

doo-tong: deux-temps – a very fast waltz.

I'll sing and dance the whole day through,
The doo-tong and the polka too.
(*At end of duet exit* SMUGGINS.)

SCOW: To thus disguise herself in male attire,
Ain't quite the sort of thing that I admire.
It's taken in poor Gulliver, he's not
A notion as to who's the pal he's got;
But whether Polly's plot will pay or no
Is pr'aps a question – and as matters go
Now-a-days 'Will it pay's' the thing
That influences folks – on which I'll *sing*.

SONG

We live in an unselfish age,
    So optimists declare;
When money is no object, and
    For 'dross' does no one care.
And yet it's odd a frequent phrase
    That greets us every day,
Is – when one names some enterprise,
    The question's – will it pay –
    Will it pay, etc.

We go to war and fight the blacks,
    We don't quite know for what,
In lands where now we get it cold,
    And sometimes get it hot.
We gloriously do our best,
    But as we end the fray,
One awkward question *will* arise,
    That question's 'does it pay'.
In Turkey soon of great reforms
    The Sultan's undertaker,
The Turks no longer mean to loaf
    Beneath an English Baker.
When everything's so honest grown
    Beneath his potent sway,
The bondholders no doubt will hint,
    'The question's will they pay'.

At Sheffield Waddy is returned,
    Let's hope he will fulfil
His promises to do his best –
    That *waddy-says* he *will*.
Meanwhile in many a virtuous spot

Waddy: S. D. Waddy was elected Liberal MP for Sheffield by a small majority at a by-election held in December 1879, after a seat had been rendered vacant by the death of Mr Roebuck, a Conservative.

        Constituencies say,
      In summing up their candidates,
        The question's *which'll* PAY.

SCOW: Whatever is successful folks respect.
        (*Enter hastily* GULLIVER, POLLY *and* SMUGGINS.)

GULL: Here, Scowlygrowls, it's lucky we were wrecked,
        That we were wreck'd co-rect you'll find to be,
        We've come across a fortune haven't we?

SMUG: We've only got to collar and escape.

SCOW: His-cape, and collar! What d'ye mean you ape?

GULL: Yo*u* ape superiority, but *we*
        Have something found worth many an ape-on*ee*.
        A Brobdingnagian Baby!

POLLY: Such a dear,
        Much bigger though than any of us here.

SMUG: Yes, through the keyhole, big as any winder,
        We saw the kid – we'll prig it – what's to hinder?

GULL: And having kidnapped the great napping kid,
        Sell it to some showman for the highest bid.

POLLY: Or better still, away to England bear it.

GULL: Show it ourselves – a fortune make and share it,
        For such a *rarity* would make a *rare 'it*.

SMUG: There's no one on the premises at all,
        And if the Brobdingnagian brat should bawl,
        Daffy's Elixir'll stop his infant chirrup.

SCOW: Just so – or Mrs Johnson's Soothing Syrup.
        I've often felt a showman's situation
        Was really my legitimate vocation.
        (*Shouts.*) Walk up and see the rarest of the rare!

GULL: Here! Here! The only baby in the fair!
        Measure two yards, the length of six fine boys,
        And weighs just sixteen stone – *havver-du*-POIS,
        Walk up, walk up, come bustle, bustle, bustle:
        Hobserve the yandsome hinfant's splendid muscle!

SMUG: When full grown it's supposed he'll reach the sky!

SCOW: The Brobdingnagian Baby! Hi! Hi! Hi!
        CONCERTED PIECE
        We'll take the Brobdingnagian Kid,
        And take an exhibition shop;
        We'll take the public, too, you'll see,
        And after that we'll take a drop.
        We'll charge high for admission
        To our swell exhibition,
        Nought under half-a-crown.
        The babby's sure to fetch the town;
        For anything that's frightful's bound to attract,
        The showman knows that is a simple fact.

SCENE 4.   *The nursery of Kitcheecatchee-get-out-of-the-way-oh! Pantomime*
music. SAMBO *runs on.*

SAMBO: What a pity I was born a dwarf. What was the use of my growing up
  when I didn't grow up no higher. Ha! Ha! Ha! Why was I like 'Grandfather's
  Clock' – Ha! Ha! Ha! – 'cos I *'stopped short'*. And here am I housekeeper,
  nurse, and head cook and bottle washer to old Kitcheecatchee-get-out-of-
  the-way-oh, and his beast of a baby. And the baby's twice as big as me.
  Whops *me*, the baby does. Why didn't *he* stop short, then I'd have whopped
  him.

    (*business – at end baby and dwarf sleep*)
    (*Enter* GULLIVER, POLLY, SMUGGINS *and* SCOWLYGROWLS –
    comic business, ladder, etc.)

GULL: The infant sleeps!
SMUG: So does its hideous nuss.
  To bear them off would need an omnibus;
  No cab could do it.
SCOW: How's it to be done?
  The two together must weigh twenty stun.
POLLY: Parcels delivery might –
GULL: Wouldn't take 'em,
  The best thing we can do at first's to wake 'em. (*music*)
    (*They wake them – business.*)

GULL: Ha! Ha! Don't scream!
POLLY: Don't speak!
SMUG: Don't sneeze!
SCOW: Don't wink!
  Of instant slaughter you are on the brink.
SMUG: Prepare to follow us, or meet your doom.
GULL: At the Egyptian Hall we'll take a room;
  Or at some public building of the sort.
SMUG: You shall show how you fight, indulge in sport,
  Cook your comestibles and gaily dance.
POLLY: We've ordered home the agent in advance.
SCOW: Your first performance will be over there,
  Under the patronage of the late Lord Mayor.
    CONCERTED PIECE. FINALE
  To England we'll go and take a show,
    And will exhib-it the crew;
  The people will crowd in great number, you know,
    To see a gigantic Zulu.
  For most people like what is savage and strange,
    Or anything come a long way;
  They don't care a jot if it's clever or not,

Egyptian Hall: venue for the exhibition of curiosities, located in Piccadilly.

> But a novelty's certain to pay.
> It couldn't help it if it was to try,
> If ugly it's attractive to the eye;
> And if we're told it's wrong, we're bound in crowds to throng,
> For we couldn't help it if we were to try.
> (*Hurry. Zulu parent appears – business to end of act.*)

ACT III

SCENE 1.   *Front street in Island of Comic Song. Enter* SCOWLYGROWLS.

SCOW: Where are we now? How strange the people seem,
The sort of coves about which parties dream
But precious seldom see. – The wind that blows
Bears with its airs of comic songs one knows.
The birds upon the trees so nice and rural,
Whistle ritolderol or tooral looral.
'Tippety Witchet' and 'Hot Codlins' float
Upon the breeze from neighbourhood remote.
Old comic ditties permeate the place,
Whilst snatches of *new* songs sometimes you trace.
All the inhabitants go on the same.
The poulterers all chant, 'The same old game',
'Not today Baker' is a frequent strain.
The butchers call out '*Meet* me once again'.
Then 'Tiddlywink the Barber' meets one's ear
From the hairdresser, Brewers' 'Bitter Beer',
Or else 'John Barleycorn', and such like things;
'Come back to Erring' the fishmonger sings,
Not comic in itself, but out of toon,
Remarkably – then 'Up in a balloon'
Proceeds from the one aeronaut they've got,
I *may* say that they *air-a-naughty* lot.
Whilst spiritualists shout 'Rap! Rap! Rap!'
The hatters revel in a 'Game of *nap*'.
The very chimney sweeps with songs approach 'ee,
Although they sing their ballads *sooty voce*.
It's just the queerest place I ever see.
      (*Enter* GULLIVER.)

GULL: I say, this island's somewhat of a spree;
Can't make it out – it isn't in the map.
What's come of Smuggins and the other chap?
      (*Enter* SMUGGINS *and* POLLY.)

SMUG: There's something in the air that's precious rum,

'*Tippety Witchet*' . . . '*Hot Codlins*': songs first made popular by the clown Grimaldi earlier in the century.

Have you observed it – there! 'Old Mother Gum!'
I hear it quite distinctly –
POLLY: Only fancy –
SMUG: It ain't –
SCOW: Now it's 'I wish I was with Nancy',
GULL: Which merges in 'Kafoozelum' – Hallo!
'Moses and Aaron'! Now it's 'Not for Joe'.
I say I don't like this.
SCOW: There – there! I'm blowed!
Dinna ye hear it – 'Keep in the middle of de road'.
The oddest vocal combinations throng.
                    (*Enter* CRIER.)
GULL: Where are we?
CRIER: On the Isle of Comic Song.
Don't interrupt me – for a proclamation
I am about announcing to the nation.
(*Rings bell.*) Oh yes! Oh yes! Oh yes!
GULL: Oh no!
CRIER: (*disconcerted*) Don't put me out.
Oh yes! Oh yes!
SCOW: It's very rude to shout.
CRIER: Really this interruption – do be quiet.
Oh yes! Oh yes!
SMUG: Here, don't kick up a riot,
Our ears have drums, and we don't want 'em split.
CRIER: But there's a gallery as well as pit;
The farthest boy upon the topmost row
What I'm proclaiming has a right to know.
And so, here goes again – (*Shouts.*) – Oh yes!
POLLY: (*Hits him on hat.*) All right!
CRIER: I'm not accustomed to this sort of slight.
This treatment is phenomenal – Per*haps*
You*'d* like to take my place, you cheeky chaps.
GULL: Certainly. We'll proclaim the stuff old feller,
You take his bell – I'll imitate his beller.
          CONCERTED PIECE.
          Listen to the proclamation,
          Which I utter to the nation;
          Sad's our monarch's situation,
          In this Isle of Comic Song,
          'Tis decreed by spiteful fairy,
          Very venomous and wary,
          That this King in a quandary,
          Should thus find himself ere long,
          If his lovely only daughter,
          Doesn't laugh, the which, she oughter.
          Oh yes! Oh yes!

Which means your ears we will distress,
Oh yes! Oh yes!

Though the fun we have been piling,
None have seen the Princess smiling,
Which has led to much reviling
From the monarch of these isles.
Every comic publication
Suited to her situation
Has but caused her lamentation,
E'en the works of Doctor Smiles.
He whose fun should cause her laughter,
Will become our *King* hereafter.
Oyez! Oyez!
(*music piano through following*)

GULL: I'll make the Princess laugh, I'll bet a penny.

SCOW: How?

SMUG: And by what means?
Let's hear – *are* there any?

GULL: I'll say that cabmen very seldom swear,
And bless you when you give the legal fare.

POLLY: I'll tell her in the elegantest rhyme
The underground trains keep their proper time.

SCOW: I'll tell her at this season of the year,
Folks in the workhouse all get extra beer.

SMUG: I'll say that presents always come prepaid,
And Christmas hampers never are delayed.

POLLY: I'll say policemen come when they're required.

GULL: I'll say the income tax is much admired.

SCOW: I'll say that mollified by champagne jelly,
Lord Beaconsfield has knighted Turnerelli.

SMUG: I'll say –

GULL: If to her face a smile you'd bring,
We'd better not *say* anything – but sing.
CONCERTED PIECE
Soon the Princess we will make to smile,
And fill with glee this comical isle.
The poor old monarch happy soon shall be,
We'll laughter wring from all as they shall see.
For our cunning,

Doctor Smiles: Dr Samuel Smiles (1812–1904), famous for his writings on moral subjects, including *Self-Help* (1859).
Lord Beaconsfield . . . Turnerelli: Edward Tracy Turnerelli, writer of ghost stories and works on Russia, believed that the prime minister Lord Beaconsfield (Disraeli) had slighted him by not publicly acknowledging the services he had rendered. To embarrass Disraeli further Turnerelli organised and collected money for a National Tribute to Disraeli, which Disraeli declined on the grounds that Turnerelli had been importuning for honours. Matters came to a head in 1879.

> Songs and punning,
> Shall prove stunning.
> Roars shall greet us,
> All shall treat us,
> To the island's very best.
> (*Repeat.*)   Soon the Princess, etc.
> (*At end exeunt.*)

SCENE 2.   *The Palace of Comic Song. March. Enter* GUARDS, COURTIERS, etc., *with* KING TOLDEROL.

KING: Stand all apart – I'm sad, would be alone,
> Though *small* I would indulge in a *full groan. (All laugh.)*
> That was a joke.
> They laugh, tis very well –
> Whenever Regalaye, or legal swell
> Indulges in a jest, however bad,
> Elderly and insufferably sad –
> In the reports we all read the day after
> The old 'Joe' was received with 'roars of laughter'.
> Sometimes one can't make out what raised the grin,
> Or quite distinguish where the laugh comes in;
> But there it is – and so though *you* mayn't smile,
> This royal personage it doesn't rile,
> For here I have a sycophantic crew,
> Who are well *paid* to do it – and they *do.*
> And though my jokes may not convulse the gallery,
> *Here* unappreciation means 'no salary'.
> What news?
OFFICER: Not none.
KING: Not none? And tempus fugit!
> That proclamation should have proved a huge hit.
> We sent the royal crier on his way,
> The boardmen, too, at eighteenpence a day,
> With handbills but our bills appear to me
> By no means taken up as they should be.
> Halloa, I say, you missed that – pay attention,
> Joke – 'Bill' and 'taken up' you heard me mention.
> It never *was* good – not in days of yore,
> But when your *King* makes it – I say no more. (*All laugh.*)
OFFICER: Unless you try a new one now and then
> I really cannot answer for my men.
> When you repeat them past a certain age
> I scarcely can control the army's rage.
> Do learn a few your majesty –

'*Joe*': stale joke, after Joe Miller, comedian, d. 1738.

KING: I must.
                  Get me the *Family Herald* – hem! on trust.
                  Its Random Readings are a gold mine – Stay!
                  Why does the luckless Princess stop away?
                  Luckless, indeed, for if ere the close of day
                  No one can make my pining daughter smile,
                  Or rather laugh, I lose my little isle,
                  Which wouldn't much distress me, though it *should*,
                  But what is worse, I lose my life – which *would*.
                  Go fetch her.

OFFICER: Yes, your majesty, but pray
                  Don't go on in your usual funny way –
                  It does depress her so. The doctor's task
                  You add to when conundrums you *will* ask;
                  And if again you pull a comic face,
                  They all declare that they'll give up the case.
                  They say you render useless all their drugs.

KING: And I am such a dab at pulling mugs.
                  I'll try and choke that brilliant wit and humour,
                  Which of my nature's simply the consumer,
                  But it will make me ill.

OFFICER: She'll soon be here. (*Exit.*)

KING: He's gone, and from his hateful presence clear
                  I'll make a joke. And if the army's *not*
                  Impressed, I shall disband it on the spot.
                  My reign will probably not last four hours.
                  (I'll spare them *rain* and its attendant *showers* –
                  They've had that pretty often.) Soldiers – men
                  When the great Wellington – you know him – *when*
                  He told his troops to 'go it', meant you know
                  To 'bonnet' – recollect the word – the foe;
                  Because, he said, the enemy's *there*, drat 'em,
                  Bonnet 'em – that's to say 'Up guards and *hat* 'em'.
                  That's all. (*All laugh.*)
                  That's fetched 'em. As for the Princess
                  At that she would have wept and spoilt her dress.
                         (*Enter* OFFICER *and* PRINCESS TRALALA.)
                         SONG

PRIN: No, alas! I cannot smile,
                  Though I try with might and main.
                  Serious I look the while
                  Songs are sung to me quite insane.
                  Dreadful wigs and fearful hats
                  Fail a smile to win.
                  Settled gloom's upon me, that's
                  Why, alas! I cannot grin.
                  Awful comiques, gruesomist parties,

Find unavailing all their droll art is.
All their riddles and their jigs,
All their irritating rigs,
Only prove to me depressing.
Each hid'yous chorus,
They sing before us,
Simply doth bore us,
And when they finish it seems a blessing.
They but anger
With their clangour
And their slang
About slap bang.
But they please not, simply rile,
And no they never make me smile,
Not ever smile.

KING: Will nothing make you smile? It's getting near
The time when I must abdicate, my dear.
The sad conditions upon which I reign
You've heard – but you shall hear them once again.
    SONG
Oh what a swindle, and oh what a sin,
That no one can raise the gleam of a grin.
A fairy who didn't receive wedding cake,
Declared I should die if nobody could make
My daughter smile e'er her twentieth year.
Alas, on her face never a smile doth appear,
To have a fine daughter who's never yet smiled,
You'll own is enough to make anyone wild.

Folks with big hats, and comical clothes;
Jokes that would make her convulsed you'd suppose.
The newest of riddles, the quaintest of songs,
Have only provoked 'get aways', 'go alongs'.
Clowns have absurdly exhibited feats,
Which most youthful folks would have looked on as treats.
She burst into tears when she ought to have smiled,
It's all up with her father – no wonder he's wild.

PRIN: Alas, alas, I feel for you most sadly,
And also feel I am behaving badly.
But what's a girl to do who can*not* grin?
Everything from me fails a smile to win,
Punch, Fun, and Judy weekly I peruse,
But all that's *red* won't dissipate the *blues*.
You've shown me every clown at every circus –
KING: There's nothing for your father but the *workus*.

Punch, Fun and Judy: humorous periodicals of the day.

(*Hurry. Enter* CRIER.)

CRIER: Your majesty, we've got a new sensation,
      Likely to cause the Princess cachination.

KING: What do I hear! (*to* OFFICER) Go, see to it.
           (*Exit* OFFICER.)
                I fear
      The new sensation must be something queer
      Indeed to raise a smile, much more a laugh,
      For this young bird's not to be caught with chaff,
      E'en if that chaff's most humorous and –

OFFICER: (*Enters.*) Sire,
      Four wandering English gentlemen desire
      To test their skill, believing that they can
      Make the Princess laugh heartily.

KING: Young man,
      Lose not a moment, introduce the four.
           (*Music. Enter* GULLIVER, SCOWLYGROWLS, SMUGGINS *and*
           POLLY. *They enter with the tumblers' trip and skip and finish by*
           standing in the stock attitude, with one leg up behind, and the
           action of teeth extracting.)

KING: You've heard of our position, it's a bore,
      But –

GULL: We were thrown upon your island here,
      And heard about you –

PRIN: (*aside*) What a little dear.
      How very differently he looks and speaks
      To *our* young men, who're all of them *comiques*;
      Wear hideous hats, and through the day long bore us
      With dreadful songs, all cockney rhyme and cruel chorus.
           (GULLIVER *makes up to* PRINCESS.)

POLLY: (*aside*) Already he's forgotten his poor Polly.

SCOW: (*Down with the* KING – *hits him.*) Don't be cast down old,
           old Cockywax, look jolly.

KING: Old Cockywax! Hem! Treat us with decorum.

SMUG: All right, depend on us old Cockalorum.
           (*Strikes him also.*)

KING: It strikes me, or I *should* say you *both* strike me.
      It's true you hurt me, but you seem to like me.

BOTH: Oh! We do – oh, yes. (*Shake hands violently.*)

SMUG: Fact is we have for you a great surprise,
      Which will bring pleasure to your daughter's eyes.

GULL: Perhaps a dance grotesquey and burlesquey,
      By you and Smuggins might come to the *resky*;
      Then Scowlygrowls *you* might attempt a ditty,

---

cachination: loud laughter.
'*Which will bring . . . Perhaps a dance*': see appendix for lines omitted here.

Something you know phenomenally witty.

SCOW: (*aside*) My serious efforts have been often chaffed,
At my songs sentimental folks have laughed,
Hoping to bring the tears into their eyes,
I haven't *done* it, but quite otherwise.
As that's the case (their taste of course was vile)
A tearful ballad may provoke a smile.

SMUG: (*to* POLLY) As you and I are called on for a hop,
Let's show them that they've come to the right shop.
(*Grotesque pas de deux – all stand aside.* SCOWLYGROWLS *and* GULLIVER *off.*)

PRIN: You haven't made me laugh a little bit,
For grace and elegance you'd score a hit.
But I am quite past smiling.

KING: Lost! Lost! Life's coffee's nothing now but chickory,
I'll cut my stick – hem! amputate my hickory.

OFFICER: Your majesty, a singist now would try,
To please our lachrymose Princess's eye.
He begs to state, although he *may* be wrong,
That his is not at all a comic song.
(SCOWLYGROWLS *enters and gives an imitation of the ultra-sentimental ballad singer – 'Just before the battle, mother'.*)

KING: Stop! Shut up! Seize him! Anything! Our daughter
Weeps so, her handkerchief's quite drenched with water,
And so do I – reddened's the royal beak.

CRIER: Hi! Way there for the *Champion Comique.*
SONG. GULLIVER

KING: Better than plaudits, better than encores,
She smiles! She grins! She laughs! By jove, she *roars!*
My life and kingdom saved! Joy lies before us.
Friends, nation, everybody join in chorus!
CONCERTED PIECE
Oh! what a swindle! and oh! what a sin!
That no one can raise the gleam of a grin;
A fairy, who didn't receive wedding cake,
Declared I should die if nobody could make
My daughter smile e'er her twentieth year;
Alas! on her face never smile doth appear.
To have a fine daughter who's never yet smiled,
We'll own is enough to make any one wild.

Folks with big hats and most comical clothes,
Jokes that would have made her convulsed, you'd suppose;
The newest of riddles, the quaintest of songs,

---

hickory: stick.
'*Just before the battle, mother*': popular sentimental ballad composed by G. F. Root.
SONG. GULLIVER: no song is printed in any version of the play.

Have only provoked 'get aways', 'go alongs'.
Clowns have absurdly exhibited feats
Which most youthful folks would have looked on as treats;
She burst into tears when she ought to have smiled –
It's all up with her father, no wonder he's wild.

ACT IV

SCENE.   *Amongst the Flying Islanders. A moonlight glade.* GRAND BALLET.

ACT V

SCENE 1.   *Another part of the island.*
              (*Enter* GULLIVER *and* PRINCESS.)
GULL: Yes, lovely Princess, everything I've told you is correct. I'm a bachelor, and
      a gay dog. I can't help it. Like the bee I have wandered from one feminine
      flower to another, sipping the sweets of flirtation, but never caring to settle
      down into the domestic hive.
PRIN: But they say reformed rakes make the best husbands.
GULL: Very likely. Can't say – I never *was* reformed.
PRIN: How clever you were to succeed in making me laugh.
GULL: Practice, all practice. You see I have been in the habit of making people
      laugh this ever so long. It's a way I've got.
PRIN: Now, having thrown off my melancholy, I feel as if I could go on laughing
      for ever.
GULL: Oh, bless us – don't do *that.*
PRIN: And you wouldn't care for me *then.*
GULL: You'll excuse me, I don't care for you *now.*
PRIN: But you must, it's one of the conditions.
GULL: Look here, Princess. I came to the rescue and by making you smile – I may
      go so far as to say by making you *guffau* –
PRIN: Oh! I didn't!
GULL: Oh, didn't you though! You screamed out as if you'd been tickled.
PRIN: So I was.
GULL: Very well – so far so good. I tickled you – admitted. By so doing I saved
      your dad's kingdom, to say nothing of his life. There was a sort of under-
      standing that the successful competitor was to marry your dad's daughter,
      but unfortunately I'm engaged elsewhere.
PRIN: And here pa and I come away with you and stopped here on our way on
      this flighty island, so that we should get married – spend the honeymoon in
      Laputa, and return to the Island of Comic Song, where you were to reign
      and –
GULL: And allow your dad an income as 'monarch retired from business'. Can't
      help it. I'm engaged to a young lady of Plymouth and to that young lady of
      Plymouth will be Lemuel Gulliver faithful.
PRIN: Then I'll go and find pa and get him to kill you. (*Exit.*)
GULL: Yes, there'll be no difficulty in finding him. There are plenty of public

houses in Laputa – and there are plenty of la-pewter pots in the public houses. In *one* of them the royal beak is inserted at this moment I'm certain. The way that respected but rollicking old sovereign has been wetting his regal and insatiable whistle lately would give Sir Wilfred Lawson the cold shivers with dismay. Talk about loose sovereigns, he's a *tight* one.

(*Enter* SCOWLYGROWLS *and* POLLY.)

SCOW: Hulloa, messmate, what cheer?

POLLY: This is a very unsettled climate isn't it? The island moves about like anything.

SCOW: Oh, there's nothing settled here. All the politicians are Radical Conservatives and the teetotallers are always drunk.

GULL: Yes, and there's nothing steady. Even the morals of the nation are shakey.

POLLY: And everybody's in a perpetual state of wobble.

SCOW: As soon as we can find that most reprehensible old monarch, King Tolderol, who would insist on joining us on our voyage and who, ashamed to indulge before his subjects, has made up for it by being in a chronic state of intoxication ever since we started, we'll start for home. I don't care a straw for foreign parts, and when I say I don't care a *straw* for foreign parts, perhaps you'll forgive me if I say – *Hay* for Old England!

TRIO. SCOWLYGROWLS, POLLY *and* GULLIVER
We'll sing of rapture and delight,
Irrel-levant, altho' 'tis quite.
But somewhere 'tis the proper thing,
Of rapture and delight to sing.
For music charms far more than cleverest words,
Or why should folks prefer to them the songs of birds.
(*Exeunt.*)

(*Enter* SMUGGINS *holding up* KING TOLDEROL *who is tipsy.*)

SMUG: Here, hold up your majesty.

KING: All right. I'm all right.

SMUG: Are you? You're all wrong.

KING: Look here, you two fellows; don't you hic – be insolent.

SMUG: Two fellows, I ain't two fellows.

KING: Don't you contradict *me*. I say, where are we?

SMUG: You'll be on your back in a minute.

KING: I didn't mean fizzy – fizzycally: but hic! but geo, hic! geo-graphically.

SMUG: Somewhere near the Equator.

KING: Ha, old friend of mine, I shall leave my card. I – I say, what's your name?

SMUG: Smuggins, if you please your majesty.

KING: Yes, you *do* please my majesty. I'll make you my prime minister.

SMUG: Oh, thank your majesty. I'd sooner be Chancellor of the Exchequer for choice.

KING: All right, Smuggins. Consider yourself Chancellor of the Excheckery. Have you – have you got half-a-crown handy?

SMUG: No, your majesty.

Sir Wilfred Lawson: an MP who campaigned for stricter licensing laws.

KING: Pretty Chancellor of the Excheckery *you* are. I dismiss you from office. I should certainly like a drop.

   (SMUGGINS *lets him fall with a bang.*)

SMUG: You've *got* it, your majesty.

KING: Smuggins, you and your friend are in a disgusting condition.

   (*Enter* PRINCESS *and* GULLIVER.)

PRIN: What do I see? Oh, pa! And before strangers, too!

KING: I'm – hic! all right, ain't I, Smuggins? 'Low me. The new Chancellor of the Excheq – cheq – check – hic! Good night, everybody. (*Settles himself.*)

GULL: 'Uneasy lies the head that wears a crown.'

SMUG: Yes, and wants to borrow *half* one.

   (*Enter* POLLY *and* SCOWLYGROWLS.)

SCOW: (*to* POLLY) What did I tell you? There they are together again.

POLLY: (*aside*) The monster! (*to* SCOWLYGROWLS) What's that to do with *me*?

SCOW: Oh, *I* don't know, if *you* don't. (*aside*) A nint, a palpable nint! (*to* KING) Come, old Thingumyjig; pull yourself together.

   (SMUGGINS *and* SCOWLYGROWLS *pull* KING *on his legs sharply.*)

PRIN: Pa, dear, this nice young man says he's engaged to a lady in Plymouth.

SCOW: (*to* POLLY) Gammon! Only his humbug!

POLLY: (*aside*) If he *is* false, I – (*to* SCOWLYGROWLS) Don't bother *me* about it.

SCOW: (*with extreme humility*) Oh no, suttinly *not*, suttinly not, miss. I mean, sir –

GULL: Yes, I'm engaged to pretty Poll of Plymouth.

KING: Plymouth, Plymouth! I'd like to go to Plymouth. Rather celebrated *gin* I believe in Plymouth.

GULL: Yes, I used to sing a song about her, bless her heart – didn't I Smuggins?

SMUG: (*very amiably*) Oh, yes, such a pretty song – so simple, suited *me*. Such a *good* tune! I do so like anything that's good. I can hear it now.

   CONCERTED PIECE
   I'm faithful to my Polly as my Poll would be aware,
   If only she was over here instead of over there.
   Oh, what a thing to faithful be to any girl you court,
   When it's generally said tars find a wife in every port.

ALL: For it's generally said a tar,
   It's said a tar, it's said a tar,
   It's generally said that tars wed wives in every port.
   But this young individual has never wavered yet,
   From Polly who's a jolly captivating little pet.
   For princesses in grand dresses Gulliver cares not a jot,
   For he'll marry Poll, and carry Poll to some secluded spot.

   (GULLIVER *and* PRINCESS, *and* SMUGGINS *and* KING *exeunt.*)

SCOW: (*Brings down* POLLY *melodramatically.*) Messmate, further evasion is *fruitless* – any more subterfudge is *bootless*, of no more value than a Yankee

---

Uneasy . . . crown: Shakespeare, *Henry IV Part 2*, III, 1, 31.

who is 'cuteless', no, nor of a German flute that is tootle-ess. Ha! Ha! Your
disguise is penetrated – your design discovered. You're found out Mary Calico, commonly called Polly by your familiars. You're no more an able-bodied
seaman than *I* am. You're a gal; a gal-lier gal never sailed in a gal-liant gal-ley.

POLLY: As you have discovered everything, further concealment were useless.

SCOW: *Were* useless? *Is* useless if you please.

POLLY: I'm as grammatical as *you* are. I say *were*.

SCOW: I say *is*, but no mattah? Confess you *are* a female.

POLLY: I are!

SCOW: Where's your grammar again? You mean *am*. Polly, in the inspired language
of the gifted and immortal Tennyson, 'what's your game?'

POLLY: If you ask my *favourite* game, I haven't made up my mind whether it's
grouse or *solitaire*.

SCOW: Evasive rejoinder! *Grouse* or solit-*hare*. 'Equivocation will undo you' –
hem! Shakespeare – more or less – Less for choice. Why are you here in this
disgy-ise?

POLLY: To keep my eye on Gulliver.

SCOW: Ha! Ha! 'Tis well. Your Gulliver is false! He loves another. He is smitten
with the Princess. Did you ever hear the ballad of 'Billy Taylor?'

            MUSIC. PIANO – '*Billy Taylor*'

POLLY: Of course, how he left his sweetheart –
            'Soon his true love follow-ed after'
            'Under the name of Richard Carr.'

SCOW: Richard Carr – Har! Har!! Har!!! That Carr not being a tramcar soon caught
him up, and –

POLLY: (*excited*) 'Soon she called for sword and pistol.'

SCOW: (*producing them – enormous pistol*)
            'Which did come at her command',
            'And she shot' – (*bang*)
                What's the matter?

POLLY: 'Her William Taylor'.

SCOW: Which, altering the name to Lemuel Gulliver, you'd better do at once.
There he is, meandering, philandering, spooning, caressing and canoodling
'With the young woman'.

POLLY: 'What was in his hand'.

SCOW: Right you are. Go it. It's a *hair* trigger. They call it a *hare* trigger because it
goes off *rabbitly*. Now then.

POLLY: But wouldn't it be a *fowl* blow.

SCOW: Never mind if it *is* fowl – *pull it*! One, two three!
           (*She pulls trigger – no effect – pause.*)

SCOW: Hem! Bang! (*a faint shriek heard*) That's settled him.

POLLY: But it didn't go off.

SCOW: Quite immaterial. So long as he's shot it don't signify.

POLLY: Oh, dear, I'm faint, I'm – (*Falls in* SCOWLYGROWL'*s arms.*)

'*Equivocation . . .*': Shakespeare, *Hamlet* V.1.149.

(SCOWLYGROWLS *drags her towards side in melodramatic jumps.*
Enter GULLIVER *and* PRINCESS.)

GUL: Here, I say, somebody's playing with firearms and been and shot Smuggins.

SCOW: Smuggins! My hated rival! Oh, rapture!

(*Enter* SMUGGINS *led in by* KING.)

KING: (*sober*) Here, I say, this is very awkward. A bullet's gone right through my
Chancellor of the Exchequer.

GULL: Yes, but I don't think it's touched any vital part.

SMUG: No it hasn't, but the *draught's* awful.

GULL: What do I see? Polly?

POLLY: Faithless one I've done with you.

(*Enter* SPIRIT OF CHRISTMAS CHEER.)

SPIRIT: Faithless! Not so! From *you* he ne'er did roam.

GULL: And who might *you* be miss, when you're at home.

SPIRIT: Don't let my sudden advent cause a shock,
But *some* one must wind up this Xmas clock,
This heterogeneous hodge podge of a play,
So that it may 'go on' from Boxing Day;
And who so fitting at this time of year,
As the embodiment of Christmas cheer.
Gulliver you are the embodiment
Of all that's faithful, and your excellent
Behaviour merits it is very clear,
The warm acknowledgement of Christmas cheer.
Good folks be happy, wicked folks be 'tother.

SMUG: I'm good.

SCOW: You!

SMUG: I refer you to my mother.

GULL: Polly, you hear her.

POLLY: Yes, and I regret
I ever raised my hand against my pet.
Forgive me.

SMUG: And forgive *me*,

KING: And also *me*.
I *did* exceed. Dear Tralala, you see.
We must return and find you out a spouse.

SCOW: But ere we make our grand concluding bows,
Our piece approaching now its final stage.
With a bright picture termed The Golden Age,
We ask of you at this our Christmas party,

GULL: To give our Gulliver a welcome hearty.
And if to find some faults you *may* have reason,
Ignore them at this charitable season.
CHORUS
At length the climax approaches,
For tempus fugit, you see,
And night on daytime encroaches,

So this the finale must be.
All plays, like all other small pleasures,
Must end eventual-lee;
So he who is sensible treasures
The present between you and me.
So before we disappear,
Greet us with a Christmas cheer.

GRAND TRANSFORMATION.

THE GOLDEN AGE.

Appendix I

THE PIER SCENE IN THE *LANCASHIRE LASS*

Act II, scene 2, of *The Lancashire Lass*, in which a boat steams on and disgorges its passengers on to a pier, then steams away, is what might be termed the 'sensation' scene in this particular play. Some of the effects required in the manuscript versions (LC and BB) are not printed in the published edition, but are nevertheless worth considering, since they throw light on how the scene was originally staged. In BB the following prompter's note occurs opposite the commencing lines of the scene:

> *the passing of the clouds over the gauze is done by magic lantern in 3rd groove . . . During the entire scene the theatre is very dark front and back.*

A stage direction in BB further requires:

> *Green limelight shining at the end of pier.*

When the boat enters later in the scene, LC contains the following directions:

> *The moonlight effect disappears; a small steamer crosses at back, quietly from left to right, and a boat moored at back of pier glides off. KATE is about to throw herself into the water when she hears the puffing of the steamboat.*

The following instructions are incorporated in the notes on scenery included in French's edition.

> *Pier-head and river in 5th grooves. On flat, Birkenhead, with lights of houses shown by perforations and lights behind. Canvas down for water; cloudy sky; limelight for moonlight; wharf left is built out on square piles; small house, eight feet high, four feet by five, left; no string piece; the corner spiles rise about four feet above pier level; ferryboat (see pictures of English steamboats in* Illustrated London News*) to be run on from right, smoke-pipe, black and white band round top, the edge serrated; a little blue fire to burn in it; paddle-wheel in box, not to work; water-coloured canvas hung around the side, falling from the supposed water-line; wheel for steersman; name* Egremont; *her length to be as much as can be disposed of off right; the stern is detached when she is backed off; gang-plank, with hand-rail, ready on pier; small boat, to hold two, on rollers, to be worked from right to centre; ship's stern, with sail hanging loose, as if drying from the spanker-gaff, in profile, right 4th groove, to run on as ferryboat is drawn off, and mask its bow when off.*

ALTERNATIVE (LC) ENDING TO *THE LANCA-SHIRE LASS*

ACT IV

SCENE 1. *The kitchen of an Italian wayside inn. Door right centre in front and door right. Long tables and forms, left. Round table, right. Chairs left centre, a little up. Discovered:* REDBURN, *his hair in foreign style, close cropped moustache, smoking.* SPICER *and he seated right. On stage some* ITALIAN PEASANTS *picturesquely dressed.* GIACOMO *and* ADELINA *bustling about. Lively music.*

GIA: You always attend to what your uncle says, my child, and you won't go wrong.

ADEL: So I do Uncle Giacomo.

GIA: 'So you do, Uncle!' Young girls nowadays think of nothing but dressing themselves instead of attending to the guests. When I was a lad, I never knew what it was to go to bed, until I was so tired, I could hardly stand; then up again in the morning, at day break, to work again. Work, work, work! That was the order of things in those days, my child. One suit of clothes in the year; plenty of beating and no holidays; *that* was the sort of thing to make a man of me.

ADEL: Yes, but you don't want to make a *man* of me, do you?
    (*The* ITALIANS *laugh.*)

GIA: Ah, you may laugh. A set of idle do-nothings wasting your time, (*aside*) and spending nothing.

ADEL: That's true – if they were like these fine *English* workmen, now –

GIA: I'll tell you what it is. You're much too fond of talking about these English workmen – especially their leader, Clayton; he's made a conquest, I'm afraid.

ADEL: Nonsense, Uncle. He's not the sort of man to care about *me*, I'm sure. He's in love already. *I* know –

GIA: Indeed. How do you know that?

ADEL: By his melancholy way even when his companions are mirthful. He never seems to enter into their conversation, but sits away by himself, looking oh! so melancholy. Not that he's unkind or proud to them, either.

GIA: No, that he isn't. A kinder, nobler fellow never breathed. Why, only last week, when one of his workmen hurt his leg, Clayton carried him home, dressed the wound himself, and sat up with him, though he must have been weary enough with his day's work already.

ADEL: Yes – and how brave he is. When that bad black-hearted fellow, Beppo, was molesting that poor woman on her way to [the piazza], the good young signor beat him well, and sent him off howling, more like a whipped dog than a great overgrown wretch, big enough to eat one.

GIA: Yes, and what control he has all those workmen under. They seem to mind *him*, though they're rough enough with everybody else, in all conscience.

ADEL: They'll be all in soon, Uncle.

GIA: Yes, and don't you let them be so familiar. It's not so pleasant to an uncle's feelings, to see a great hulking Englishman pull you on to his knee.

ADEL: Oh, they don't mean anything, and they're never rude, when their master's present. (*Turns up with* GIACOMO. PEASANTS *retire.*)

SPICER: Well, upon my word, old fellow, you're a wonder.

RED: The eighth wonder of the world, eh, Spicer? Well, I congratulate myself on meeting *you*. We were formed for each other. 'Sure such a pair was never seen, so justly formed to meet by nature'. Fond of poetry, Spicer?

SPICER: Oh, doosid fond of it.

RED: Yes. It's absurd among friends to conceal anything. You've told me *your* career, I've told you mine. Two very pretty romances in real life, they are. Of course, the charge against me broke down. The principal witness was not forthcoming and without his aid there was no case against me. It was a cursed close shave, I can tell you.

SPICER: Yes, you were well out of it.

RED: I glory in it. I may have been guilty – I may have been innocent – the law, with all its ramifications; with all its specialist means of information; all its detectives, and all the abracadabra and mumbo jumbo of Bow Street, is powerless to punish me. I take off my hat to the *lady* with the bandage and the pair of scales; apologise to Sergeant Donovan for the trouble I've occasioned him; salute the majesty of the law; and start for Wiesbaden, with all the pleasures in life. Ha, ha, ha!

    (*Enter* JOHNSON, *disguised as a German tourist; he sits with paper.*)

SPICER: Wiesbaden! Blissful word. Would I could return there!

RED: Ah, you've no self command. When you were accused of cheating at Ecarté, you lost your temper, as well as the stakes.

SPICER: *Well*, we can't all be as cool as you. I shall improve.

RED: I hope so. At present, you're more likely to do well by *honesty*; not that I'd advise you to *try* it, you'd find it so uncommonly difficult.

SPICER: Well that romantic part of your career, the accusation of murder against the countryman, who cut you out, and his escape; all that tells like a story in halfpenny numbers.

RED: My dear fellow, real life beats the *London Journal* into fits. Yes, he escaped, and he's safe enough, wherever he is. But the strangest part of the story is to come. Like a successful sensational novelist, I leave the most striking chapters for the end.

SPICER: I don't understand you.

RED: Since we joined together, we haven't done much to the good.

SPICER: Well, you broke the bank at Hombourg, and –

RED: Yes, I know; but that was one success amongst a hundred failures. We've been unlucky. We must make a grand *coup* to retrieve our position. I've found you useful. Your innocent appearance and gentlemanly manners are valuable stock-in-trade. You're a capital decoy duck, Spicer. But when we settle we must part.

SPICER: Settle!

RED: Yes. You wonder at the cause of my eccentric movements. The fact is, they're regulated by those of a certain family, whose footsteps I am following. I'm an old sportsman, and I'm 'marking down' the game, Spicer.

SPICER: The only game *I* can mark is billiards.

RED: You're a fool, my friend. I told you that *I* rejected the daughter of the man who rejected *me*.

SPICER: Yes!

RED: Time told me I'd been an ass. I see nothing for it but to settle. She'll come into her father's property. Old Danville's dying. They are travelling here in Italy, but he will never return to England. Death has his hand upon him, and I am following him – like a vulture.

SPICER: That was the reason then –

RED: Yes – that was why I left so suddenly. I was afraid of losing him. When he dies, as he will do, for I've taken care to consult his doctors in more than one place – when his daughter is left alone in a foreign land, with no one to turn to, but strangers, it will be a comfort and a joyful surprise to her, to see again the face of the man she loved. There is a time for all things, Spicer, and the first sad moments of her orphan state will be time for me to renew my affectionate attentions. A well-devised story of suffering, remorse and repentance; a little high-flown sentiment, combined with the fact that there is a friend to help and protect her; these must have their proper influence and her fortune's mine.

SPICER: You attempt high flights indeed. The attendant fall is too often unpleasantly deep, though.

RED: I cannot fall lower than I have done, man – like the confirmed drunkard, the thin white wine of rascality has no flavour for me. I must drink deeply the fiery brandy of a big villainy to feel the slightest pleasure in the draught.
    (*music*)

SPICER: But would you settle down and live respectably?

RED: Of course. Do you think that through these long years of knavery, I have never tried for the peace and quiet of an honest life? I carry it off with a laugh and a high hand, but the world little knows the wretchedness that underlies the thin veneer of joviality, hiding the real bitterness of a trickster's life. I seem to take existence pleasurably enough – I make money – no matter how, – but I make it – and so long as there's a pack of cards and a billiard table within reach, I can dine on my three courses and drink the choicest wines! But, I tell you, Spicer, there are moments when the mask falls off and I see only the hollow cheeks and the sunken eyes of the hideous reality. Then I feel how gladly I would change my lot with that of the honest labourer, who seeks his bed at night without the memory of evil deeds to mar his slumber, and who rises in the morning without a shilling in his pocket, but without the shadow of a crime upon his heart. (*after a pause*) Give me some brandy! (*Turns up. Gets brandy from* ADELINA.)

SPICER: (*in front*) Hem! Misanthropical and hipped! A dangerous confederate, one who has moments of remorse. Two minutes penitence might spoil all. There's one advantage about my milder scoundrelism – if I'm not such an unblushing scamp, hang it all I don't repent. One can always fall back on that, at any time.

RED: There, that's the only cure, I'm better now.

GIA: (*Rushes in.*) Adelina! Adelina!

ADEL: Yes, Uncle.

         (*music*)

GIA: Come here, my child, a carriage has broken down. Nobody's hurt, only a bit shaken, but the party are coming here to rest, 'til we can send them on. Come here, my child.

         (*Exeunt GIACOMO, ADELINA and ITALIANS. REDBURN and SPICER go to look off at door. JOHNSON goes to door. REDBURN moves for him to go out. They each bow politely.*)

RED: Ha, here they come. By jove, it's the Danvilles! They should have been at (. . . . . .) by this time. How shaky the old boy looks. Fate befriends me. Should he remain here, I may be saved further trouble. There is no mistaking that pallid hue. Doctor Dressler was right – a few more days and all is over. (*Comes and sits at table, back towards them.*)

SPICER: Doocid pretty girl, anyhow.

RED: Come away, and don't attract their attention.

SPICER: (*coming away reluctantly*) Hang it all, let a fellow look. They may brag of their olive complexions and long eye lashes out here, but give me the pink and white of a pretty English girl, before all your brown beauties of the South. (*Sits left of table.*)

GIA: (*without*) This way, this way. (*entering*) You will find everything comfortable – We are not very grand here, but we can – (*Enter DANVILLE leaning on MISS DANVILLE's arm.*) make you comfortable. As far as cookery goes, we will give in to no one, and you will find our wines excellent – indeed, it has often been observed, that as far as –

DAN: Tell this chattering fool to hold his tongue.

MISS D: If you will show us the private room you said you had vacant –

GIA: Certainly, by all means –

         (*Exeunt DANVILLE, MISS DANVILLE and GIACOMO bowing.*)

RED: (*writing*) Just a line – a mysterious line to pave the way for my appearance – something penitent and tender – I'll begin by calling myself the greatest villain on earth.

SPICER: Quite right. Nothing like stating the truth!

RED: Hem! (*Writes.*)

         (RUTH enters with SPOTTY. SPOTTY in livery as a smart tiger or groom; RUTH has a shawl and some wraps over her arm. Gives these to ADELINA, who shows her the way the DANVILLES have gone off. REDBURN doesn't see her. Exit RUTH. ADELINA turns to SPOTTY.)

SPOT: (*looking at her admiringly*) Ha, ha, ha, ha!

         (ADELINA laughs at him.)

SPOT: I say, you're a wicked one, *you* are.

ADEL: So are you.

SPOT: I believe you, awful! I say, though, ain't I glad our carriage broke down here, that's all.

ADEL: Why?

SPOT: Why? 'Cos I shouldn't have seen you, if it hadn't – Ha! Ha! (*Chucks her under chin.*)

ADEL: Ha, you're English, anyone can see.

SPOT: I should think so. You're fond of the English, ain't you?

ADEL: Oh, yes. All of them.

SPOT: No. I say. Come you know – not *all* of 'em?

ADEL: Oh, yes, *all* of them. Give me the English before any others.

SPOT: (*conceitedly*) Ha! Ha! Yes, we do *reyther* take the shine out of the pitiful foreigners.

ADEL: You forget – *you* are the foreigners *here*.

SPOT: Eh? Ah, so we are. I never thought of that. To think that I should live to be a foreigner, *anywhere*. Yes, my dear, I must compliment you on your taste; and you find us English gentlemen's gentlemen reyther superior to those poor ignorant 'curriers', as they call themselves. It's *reyther* a treat when we come here, ain't it?

ADEL: Oh, yes, *quite* a treat and that's why we like you so.

SPOT: (*conceitedly*) Like us English, eh? Ye-es, and a (*looking round, then putting his arm round her waist*) and may I make so bold, my dear, as to ask *why* you prefer us English to all other visitors?

ADEL: Because you're all such fools, and pay twice as much as anybody else.

SPOT: (*releasing her and rubbing his chin ruefully*) Oh!

ADEL: You think that by being rude and surly, you're maintaining your independence. So you *do*, but you always have to pay for it – to pay for it as you speak.

SPOT: How's that? (*nasally*)

ADEL: Through the nose! (*Goes off.*)

SPOT: (*with contempt*) Low-born *h*ignorance! But what can you expect from people as eats maccaroni with their fingers and washes themselves in a *h*egg cup. (*Exit.*)

RED: That'll do. Thoroughly respectful with a dash of mournful tenderness, and a touching earnest appeal for a moment's interview – (*row of* NAVVYS *outside*)
(*Enter* GIACOMO *and* ADELINA.)

GIA: Oh dear, oh dear, those fellows'll be the ruin of me!

RED: What's that landlord, an eruption of Vesuvius, or a revolution?

GIA: Worse, it's the nagivators, who are constructing the new railway. They're a rough lot, but I can't refuse them admission. I'll get rid of them as soon as I can.
(*Music. Enter the* NAVVYS, *laughing, shouting and singing. They come down and sit at long table.*)

BLACK BILL: Now Jackeymo, the regler!
(GIACOMO *and* ADELINA *come and place jugs and tin mugs for the* NAVVYS. BLACK BILL, *apparently a little drunk, catches* ADELINA *by the hand and drags her towards him. She disengages herself – he chucks her under the chin, she slaps his face soundly. He rises in a rage, but is pushed down by others.*)

NAVVYS: Sit down man. Quiet. What 'ee doing?

BLACK BILL: What does the wench mean by slapping I in the face then?

NAVVY: There – leave her alone. (BLACK BILL *sulks. Business of* NAVVYS
    handing him drinks, etc.)

GIA: There, there it's nothing much. Don't lose your tempers, my noble fellows.
    (*aside*) I wish they'd finished their railroad and been carried away by it.

BLACK BILL: (*rising*) What's that you say? Somebody ill, and we're to be quiet.
    I won't be quiet. (*Bangs table.*) I'll make as much noise as I like – I'm as good
    as anybody here. I'll shout or sing, if I like – who says I ain't to? (*pause*) No-
    body, then here goes –
        SONG

BLACK BILL: We're Navigators all –

ALL: Navigators – Navigators

BLACK BILL: We're Navigators all –
        With pike and spade, it is our trade
        To see the iron road well laid.
            'Cos why, 'Cos why.
        We're Navigators all.
            Navigators. Navigators.

ALL: Navigators all.
       We're navvy-navvy-navvy-navigators all.

BLACK BILL: We're navigators all.
            Navigators.
        We're Navigators all.
        With spade and pick, we do the trick
        And cut through rock through thin and thick.
            'Cos why, etc.

(*All hammer with their fists on table, making a row.*)

RED: (*to* SPICER) Fine specimens of the raw material, eh, Spicer? If we offend
    foreigners by the swells we send over, they can't complain of our 'cads', can
    they? Fine intellectual body of men, eh? Not at all savage and brutal.
    Famous contrast to the despised Italian with his knife and his nasty temper.

SPICER: It strikes me, nevertheless, that *we* should suffer in comparison. We don't
    break the Queen's English, and we don't break heads, but –

RED: We only break *banks*, don't we? Whilst those fellows raise 'em. (*throwing
    away cigar*) Don't let's argue about it.

BLACK BILL: Dam'me, we *will* have another song.

GIA: No – no – no –

BLACK BILL: I say we *will*. (*turning and rising*) Don't try and shut us up with
    your fine customers. Our money's as good as anybody else's, ain't it?

NAVVYS: Aye, aye, lad – Yes – lad.

BLACK BILL: Well, then, who's a-going to stop us? (*to* GIACOMO) *You* ain't –
    (*Looks to* REDBURN.) and – and *you* ain't, eh?

RED: (*with irritating superciliousness*) I beg your pardon. Did you address your
    remarks to me?

BLACK BILL: Why, ha, ha, ha – (*to* NAVVYS) I say, mates, here's a swell cove a
    actually beggin' *me* pardon – Ha! Ha!
        (NAVVYS *laugh.*)

SPICER: (*to* REDBURN) Don't irritate them – These fellows don't stand on trifles when they're half drunk.

RED: Leave *me* alone. I can take care of myself, never fear –

BLACK BILL: I was a saying, as you don't want to interfere with our *singing*, if we *chooses*?

RED: Certainly not, if you *call* it singing!
> (NAVVYS *laugh*.)

BLACK BILL: (*enraged*) What do you mean by that?

RED: Simply, that Italy being rather a musical country, I should advise you, as an Englishman, to confine your vocal efforts to something less national and, consequently, less noisy.

BLACK BILL: Why, you fine spoken, insolent upstart, I'll wring your dandyfied neck. (*approaching*)
> (NAVVYS *rise*. GIACOMO *in fright*)

RED: (*advancing*) What! Dare to life a finger to *me*, man, and I'll send a bullet through your ugly head before you can wink your eye.
> (*Music* – NAVVYS *murmur*.)

BLACK BILL: So, you're one of them sorts as carries fire arms, eh? Shouldn't wonder if you had a knife, too, from the look of you?

NAVVYS: Punch his head, Bill! Knock him over!

SPICER: What are you about, you set of vagabonds?

BLACK BILL: D'ye hear 'em?
> (*Enter at back, quietly*, NED. *He is dressed roughly and wears a beard*.)

NAVVYS: (*threateningly*) Aye! Aye!

BLACK BILL: Let's give 'em a ducking and teach 'em better manners.
> (*The* NAVVYS *rush at* REDBURN: NED *interposes and floors* BLACK BILL. NAVVYS *stand a little back*. BLACK BILL *picks himself up*.)

BLACK BILL: (*threateningly*) What do *you* mean by interfering?

NED: I had to thrash you once, friend Bill; don't force me to repeat the bitter dose. Lift your hand to me, and I'll break that bull head – (BLACK BILL *cowers and goes up with men, grumbling sotto voice*.) and now, sir, as a friend, let me advise you to avoid altercations with – (*Recognises* REDBURN. REDBURN *recognises him. They stand looking at each other*.)
> (*Picture. Music – loud. Close in*.)

SCENE 2. *Front chamber.*
> (*Enter* RUTH *hurriedly, followed by* SPOTTY.)

RUTH: I can scarcely believe my ears, Spotty. This is indeed a strange unlooked-for meeting.

SPOT: (*aside*) It ain't a meeting *yet*, but I've taken good care it *shall* be one. There's been some 'orrid mystery about it all, and I'll bring 'em face to face now I've got 'em (*Exit*.)

RUTH: That we should meet here – here in this foreign land, and amongst strangers. Oh, can it be Kind Heaven has in store for me the happiness I once dreamt of – that I shall now wake to find the vision a reality? Oh, no, no, that is too much to hope for – far, far too much.

        (*Enter* NED.)

NED: (*pausing awkwardly*) It *is* she! Ruth!

        (RUTH *turns with a hysterical exclamation but does not advance – they stand apart, their manner constrained and awkward.*)

RUTH: (*advancing a step*) Ned, *dear* Ned, do you not fear?

NED: Fear! I fear nothing. What have I to hope for, to care for? Is not life a blank to me, now? Has it not been so, since – since – but let me not recall the past – Ruth, you chose well and worthily, but you broke *my* heart, lass – I escaped a felon's doom only to meet my death in a foreign land. Ask those who have watched me – who it is that undertakes the wildest and apparently foolhardiest feats – who, in the pursuit of his calling, dares destruction to its face, and tempts the fate that, sooner or later, must meet his half mad recklessness? They will tell you, *I* am that man, Ruth. For, come when it may, it can but be a relief to one who trusted a lass whose heart was stone – a stone that crushed and broke him.

RUTH: You wrong me – cruelly wrong me. It was no stone; it was the wild beating throbbing heart of a trusting woman – a woman, dazzled, for a time, by a tempter's wiles, but one who turned to the true breast that beat with honest love for her. *Penitent*, oh, *how* penitent, to seek forgiveness for a wicked wrong. She seeks it now – now. Oh, Ned, by the love you bore me *then* do not let us part in anger. Say, but *one* word of forgiveness!

NED: (*bitterly*) Forgiveness! I have nothing to forgive. You chose your own path. May it be a happy one. May the memory of the man whose whole life your conduct drove to shame and degradation, never cross your bright and cheerful path. You see me, now, no blighted homeless wretch, as you heard of me in the Liverpool streets in byegone days – Look at me, I am not that saddened outcast you might have seen me had not that fearful night changed my own whole being – sobered me, and made another man of me. The life I lead now is fraught with danger, and *some* day the relief I seek *must* come – it's but a question of a little time, and then –

RUTH: (*seizing his hand*) Ned – Ned – you wrong me.

NED: (*turning fiercely*) Wrong you, woman? What was *my* return for your false conduct? What has been *your* return for the lie I told, to save you from contempt and shame? Urged by your imploring looks and hoping to save the girl I loved from public scorn, I struggled with my swelling heart; stifled the rising sobs that well nigh choked my utterance; and reading that, for which I would have given my life, *had* you written, and not the wicked, heartless faithless words upon the paper, I *saved* you, but I left the farm a broken man. But what cared *you*? You were free, free to marry one you *could* not love – free to marry Jellick – I trust you are happy, Ruth. I have it all, here, in a letter from him. He wrote to me under my assumed name, and told me his hopes would soon be realised, and asked my forgiveness – (*bitterly*) Oh, he has it – he has it –

RUTH: Spare your words. He is no more!

NED: Poor fellow. Well, there were many worse than he. Though the deed I was so thankful for secured his happiness after all.

RUTH: You do not know the truth. I admit my one wicked act of blindness, but I have atoned for that with misery enough. I was the humble instrument of your escape – You do not seem to believe me. (*clutching his arm*) Ned – dear Ned – you were accused of a great and fearful crime, and there was one who was prepared to swear he saw the deed. Nothing could have saved you, and in the wildness of my despair and dread for your life – I – I

NED: Ruth, Ruth – speak on, lass, speak on.

RUTH: I knew we could never be as we had once been – that, indeed, we should not, perchance, meet again – I thought you would never hear of the sacrifice I meant to make and when my tears, my supplications to your jailor – *all* failed; as a last resource, I promised I would be *his* wife – would he but set you free!

NED: Can I believe my ears? And it was to save my life – you – oh, fool – fool that I have been –

RUTH: Though you should never know it, it was some comfort in my wretchedness to think that I could save *your* life, Ned, even at the sacrifice of my own. The poor old friend loved me, but how could I *care* for him, save *as* a friend? But he was never to wed me, Ned, and a few days before we were to marry he died, almost suddenly, and I was free. But I would have married him and made him a true and patient wife, with one thought to lighten my sorrow – the thought I had saved *you*, although I had sold myself.

NED: Ruth, my noble-hearted lass, how have I wronged you. You ask *my* forgiveness – I beseech *yours*. How can I be sufficiently grateful for this meeting – and for the bright and welcome words that have dispersed the heavy clouds of doubt and anger, though they disclose a hopeless and a lonely future; though they tell me too distinctly what a priceless jewel I have lost.

RUTH: Nay – Ned – not *lost*. If I *am* the jewel that you think me – won't you – won't you set me in your heart?

NED: Aye, in my heart of hearts, my darling – my own brave and noble girl. (*They embrace.*)

                    (*Enter* SPOTTY, *after a pause.*)

SPOT: (*turning*) All right, I ain't a looking. Don't mind *me*. I'm case hardened, I am. But poor master's bad again, and is calling for *you*, Miss Ruth. It's strange he always wants you to be near him when he's ill, even more than Miss Fanny.

RUTH: (*disengaging herself*) Oh, I will go to him at once. (*turning to* NED) Oh, Ned, I'm so happy. I must go to poor Mr Danville. You won't leave us.
                    (*Exit* RUTH.)

NED: (*looking at her lovingly*) Spotty, women are too good for *this* world. (*Takes* SPOTTY's *hand.*) I feel no fear of apprehension, now; let them take me, and let *him* accuse me, if he *dare*. I'm sure of *her* love and with that knowledge at my heart, I'd brave a thousand witnesses, a thousand deaths. (*Exit* NED.)

SCENE 3.   *Best room in the inn. Large open window, on to balcony, going off left. Warm Italian landscape seen through window. Music.* REDBURN *discovered stealthily going from door to window.*

RED: It's my last stake and I'll play it boldly. Nothing venture, nothing win. Venture all and win a fortune. I've hunted down the game, and I'll still not miss bagging it without a struggle. That fellow, Clayton, here, too. Well, he's safe

from *me*. I've no wish to figure again in a Court of Justice. It's a sensation
that palls on repetition. (*Listens.*) Someone coming. I'll hide on yonder balcony – if I run too great a risk of discovery, it's not such a terrible drop to the
ground. I've risked my neck for less, ere this. (*Goes to balcony.*) I may hear
something, too. I was a bad eavesdropper once, but it's a habit that grows on
one – like snuff-taking. If I can but see her alone, I have sufficient confidence
in my own powers of pleading – to say nothing of the romantic nature of the
situation – to be sure of making an effect on the highly sensitive Fanny Danville. By jove, just in time. (*Exit hurriedly to balcony.*)

      (*Door opens and* DANVILLE *enters, leaning on* RUTH *and* FANNY.)

RUTH: Indeed, indeed, sir, you will be better soon. You know Dr Dressler said you
were needlessly alarmed.

DAN: (*Sits.*) No, child, no. In a little while I shall obtain the rest I have longed for –
prayed for. I shall leave all of you soon, and when I am gone, forget me,
Fanny, forget me.

MISS D: Oh papa, dear papa, don't speak thus. You are wild and fanciful tonight
and you will be better when you have slept.

DAN: Slept, slept! How can I sleep! Do I not lie awake with that hideous form –
that – oh, let me not think of it.

MISS D: Dear papa, be calm. The journey has wearied you.

DAN: Ruth, Ruth, I must speak with you alone – alone. Fanny, leave us. Leave us,
I say.

MISS D: Oh, papa!

DAN: Come here, my child. (MISS DANVILLE *goes to him and kneels at his feet.*)
Pardon me! (*smoothing her hair*) That brow is spotless. There's no lurking evil
in those eyes. Oh, may your future be a calm and peaceful one – unharassed
by bitter memories of the past. May your days be as peaceful as they are
innocent, and may you, when you hear your father's name reviled, remember
that, at least, he loved his child, my darling. There go – go for a little while.

      (MISS DANVILLE *goes off slowly, looking at her father.*)

DAN: (*after she has gone*) Here, here, Ruth, she has gone, has she not? She cannot
hear. Listen, I have but a short time to live – nay – do not attempt to buoy
me up with false hopes. I have a monitor here (*pressing his heart*) that bids
me speak to you at once, or it may be too late.

RUTH: (*aside*) What *can* he mean? Can this be delirium?

DAN: Delirium – would that it were. No – Ruth – it is an act of justice – of atone-
ment. It comes late, but it will serve my purpose and save the honour of an
innocent man. Come nearer – nearer – that young man – Clayton – escaped –
did he not? Got away – is free?

RUTH: Yes – he is here, in this very place. But if he is discovered –

DAN: No matter Ruth. He is innocent.

RUTH: But where is the proof?

DAN: (*rising*) I have it, girl.

RUTH: You?

DAN: He should never have suffered for another's crime. I would have disclosed all,
rather than that. But I could not meet my daughter's innocent glance, had
she known; but look, Ruth, [here] is a sealed paper. I confide it to *you*. Do

not open it till – till I am no more, and then do so and tell the story told by the really guilty one – the complete vindication of the man that was accused.

RUTH: I can scarcely credit what I hear. (*Takes sealed paper.* DANVILLE *staggers slightly; she places paper on table near open window, then goes quickly to* DANVILLE, *who sinks in chair.*)

DAN: It's nothing – a slight faintness. I am better now. Remember, Ruth, I confide that paper to your care, to be opened when I have left you.

(REDBURN *steals on a step or two from window, takes up sealed paper and retires.*)

RUTH: I promise you shall be obliged.

(*Enter* MISS DANVILLE *followed by* NED. NED *stops at door.*)

FANNY: Papa. I couldn't keep away any longer. Here is Mr Clayton, Ruth's old friend; he may be of assistance to you for –

DAN: Yes, yes, let me see him. Let me speak to him.

NED: (*advancing*) I am here, sir.

DAN: (*Looking at him, but sinks his eyes almost immediately and speaks in a constrained voice.*) You – you have known much trouble, young man?

NED: For the matter of that, sir, we've most of us had our share. Let's hope the clouds are breaking, and that there's sunshine left for all of us.

DAN: (*aside*) Though suspicion and danger hang over him, he speaks light-heartedly and seems happy, whilst *I* am crushed with an inward agony, yet no man points a scornful finger at me.

NED: You're what they call a hypochondriac, I'm afraid, sir. Change of scene and an easy mind should work a speedy cure.

DAN: (*taking his hand*) Give me your hand. When I am gone, say you will not malign my memory – promise me you will forgive me – for the sake of *my child*.

NED: (*aside*) Some strange wild fancy has taken possession of him. I will promise you, gladly, anything that lies in my power.

(REDBURN *comes in, unperceived, from window.*)

RUTH: I wish there was more air, the room is close, and – (*Turns. Sees* REDBURN. *Utters a smothered shriek and steps back, clasping with both hands* NED's *left arm. Picture; pause*)

RED: Pardon the unwelcome apparition. My visit was to Miss Danville. I am quite sorry to intrude upon so interesting a family group.

DAN: Your visit to my daughter, fellow? Fanny, what is this?

RED: Civil words, if you please.

NED: Robert Redburn, your presence here is an extra weight upon those already sufficiently afflicted. Leave the room. There's the door and there's the window. Which do you choose?

RED: My business is not with *you*. We are strangers now and you are free from molestation. I'm for plain dealing, Mr Danville. Business is business. I want Fanny's fortune. Don't fly into a passion. What I want, I mean to have – I'm ready to be bought off, but it must be at a heavy price.

DAN: (*to* NED, *who is about to advance*) Nay, nay, let me answer this madman. (*Advances.*) There is some strange mystery about you which I cannot and do not *care* to fathom. I have but one word for you, let it be a final one – *begone*!

RED: (*almost in his face*) Then – more than one word for *you*. The pier – the moonlight – the drunken face, and the rushing river. *Murder*!
> (DANVILLE *staggers back*, NED *catches him in his arms and places him in chair.* MISS DANVILLE *leans over and undoes his neck tie.*)

RUTH: Where is that letter? (*Turns to go to table.* REDBURN *clutches her by the arm.*)

RED: Don't be alarmed. It's been delivered.

RUTH: (*in horror*) Ah!

RED: Who dictates now?

DAN: Then on that fatal night, you saw –

RED: Never mind what I saw then. Your confession written in your hand – here – (*Shows letter.*)

DAN: Fiend, restore me that letter – (*Sinks in chair.*)

RED: And thwart the ends of justice, oh, *no*!

NED: Restore it or –

DAN: No – no – Oh, misery!

RED: Call up the people in the house and let them hear this magnanimous confession.

DAN: (*staggering towards him*) No – no – in mercy spare me – for the sake of my child – all will be over soon – wait but a little while, and –
> (GIACOMO, ADELINA, JOHNSON *and* ITALIAN PEASANTS *come on.*)

RED: Listen all – (*Reads.*) *The man accused of the murder of Johnson was innocent. In order to rid myself of a standing torment and perpetual threat of exposure, in a moment of madness and urged on by the promptings of my own agonised fear, lest he should reveal the past – I (Sees* JOHNSON *opposite, places his hand on his arm.*) Who are you?

JOHN: (*bowing and taking off his wig, spectacles, etc.*) Party by the name of Johnson! (*pause*)

DAN: Can the dead return to life? (*Rises.*)

JOHN: Not if they knows it. I was picked up by a boat belonging to a foreign craft. When I was recovered I was out at sea. But I'm back now. Not for revenge, Gregory, I'm a different being now. I only wants a cottage and a crust. You tried to get rid of me, but I don't bear malice. That night in the water washed the vengeance out o' me. (*pause*)

RED: (*aside*) Confusion! When I thought I had the game in my own hands. I'd better be off. Enough of this jugglery – Farewell to the lot of you. You shall be relieved of my presence. Ladies adieu! (*Bows.*) And now let drink and dissipation do their worst. I care not. I'll live my life out like a gentleman in spite of all. (*Exit.*)

DAN: Cling to me, Fanny, darling, cling to me. (*aside*) My crime is none the less for the lucky chance that saved me from the hideous deed men shudder at. Oh, that I may be spared to strive my utmost to repent the wrongs I have committed. (*a shout heard*) What's that?
> (*Enter* SPOTTY.)

SPOT: It's the navvys: they've got hold of Redburn as they've heard of his plots against Ned here. They're a going to duck him, I fancy.

NED: No, no.

JOHN: Leave 'em alone. They don't get much amusement here – (*Goes to balcony.*)
(*shout heard further off*)

NED: Ruth, the clouds are dispersing and the sunshine of a happy future glows radiantly through the vanishing mists. Rest here, my darling, after the storms and sorrows of the past three years, *here*, calm and happy on the breast of the man who has adored you from the first,
> my own true
> *Lancashire Lass.*

CURTAIN

Appendix III

THE ORDER OF SCENES IN *GULLIVER*

The order of scenes in the revised, unidentified edition of *The Gaiety Gulliver* is as follows:

Act 1, sc. 1	The port of Plymouth
Act 2, sc. 1	A cornfield in Brobdingnag
sc. 2	The nursery of Kitcheecatchee-get-out-of-the-way-oh in the kingdom of Brobdingnag
Act 3, sc. 1	'Tween decks
sc. 2	Deck of the vessel
Act 4	A moonlight glade in the Flying Island
	GRAND BALLET
Act 5, sc. 1	Street in the Island of Comic Song
sc. 2	The Palace of Comic Song
Act 6, sc. 1	A street in Lilliput
	Transformation dance
sc. 2	Citadel of Lilliput
	Grand review of the army of Lilliput
Act 7, sc. 1	The Orchid Grove
sc. 2	The Golden Age

A programme for February 1880 reveals a similar order, except for the following changes in acts 2-4.

Act 2	A cornfield in Brobdingnag
Act 3	A moonlight glade in the Flying Island
	GRAND BALLET
Act 4, sc. 1	'Tween decks
sc. 2	Deck of the vessel.

A programme for 29 December 1879 reveals an arrangement of scenes identical to that in the Aubert text.

Appendix IV

GULLIVER: ADDITIONAL TEXT

In act III, scene 2, the first method of trying to make the Princess laugh is to present her with a series of tableaux from previous Gaiety successes. Since these are cut from one of the published versions of *Gulliver* and since they would contribute little today, either in the reading or performing of the play, I have relegated the relevant passage to this appendix. H. J. Byron was writing burlesque exclusively for the Gaiety at this point and many of the burlesques referred to were his work, including *Little Don Caesar* (1876), *The Bohemian G'yurl* (1877), *Young Fra Diavolo* (1878), *Pretty Esmeralda and Captain Phoebus of Ours* (1879) and *Little Doctor Faust* (1877). The burlesque version of *Rob Roy*, first staged in November 1879, was still in the repertoire. By F. C. Burnand, it was entitled *Robbing Roy, or, Scotched and Kilt*.

SMUG: Fact is we have for you a great surprise,
        Which will bring pleasure to your daughter's eyes.
SCOW: Yes, it's an album. Perhaps you may have heard
        Talk of the Gaiety.
KING: I've heard the word –
        A theatre, if I rightly understand.
GULL: Precisely so – a playhouse in the Strand.
        Our album contains portraits of some parties
        Who've shown there.
POLLY: And a likeness every carte is.
        The notion's novel, and the Princess *may*,
        Smile at the reminiscence of some play
        Which during recent years has caused commotion.
        Fact is we're rather 'nuts' upon the notion.
GULL: The first instalment shown to the Princess:
        A small group from a Gaiety success
        And which we most sincerely hope will please her,
        Is a selected party from Don Caesar.
           (*picture*)
POLLY: The gipsy Maritana
GULL: And the Don;
        A reckless look his countenance upon.
        Thoughts of tomorrow ne'er *his* actions clog.
SCOW: Observe his majesty – he's 'such a dog!'
        (*Picture closes.*)

GULL: A figure, comical, but picturesque,
        From the succeeding (liter'lly) burlesque
        Upon our album pages next appears –
        He, hem! Count Smiff, my pretty little dears.
           (picture)
        The father of Arline, Bohemian Gyurl.
POLLY: Anxious his vocal banner to unfurl.
SMUG: Observe his constitutional chronic frown;
        They wouldn't let him sing, 'The heart bowed down'.
           (Picture closes.)
GULL: Young Fra Diavolo must not be missed
        With Giacomo and Beppo from the list.
        So in our small collection we've enrolled 'em,
        Hey, Presto! Whatshisname! Hoopla! Behold 'em.
           (picture)
        Behold the Fra, seductive and entrancing,
        And of a 'silly little thing' he *can* sing.
SMUG: Then Jackeymo might really be alive,
SCOW: Whilst Beppo says, 'I'll give you such a drive!'
           (Picture closes.)
GULL: The sound of castanets seems in the air.
        For Esmeralda if you please prepare,
        Or rather for that vagabond, Claude Frollo.
        And Quasimodo who is no Apollo;
        At least, not an Apollo Bel-videre,
        Though a bell ringer. Quick, the pair appear.
           (picture)
SMUG: Master and man, or rather slave and tyrin.
SCOW: I cannot see the least thing to admire in't.
POLLY: Would rather have seen Esmeralda much,
GULL: Or Phoebus with his *'Toothpick and his crutch'*.
           (Picture closes.)
GULL: A franco-German air floats on the breeze.
        Suggesting Gounod-Goethe, if you please.
        Of subjects, you'd imagine, you were choused,
        Without a group from 'little Doctor Faust'.
           (picture)
GULL: Behold the dashing youth who hearts doth rend,
        Likewise his 'guide philosopher and friend'.
POLLY: 'Oh, rare pale Margaret!'
SCOW: No – that's effete.
        The modern style's 'Lubberly Marguerite'.
           (Picture closes.)
GULL: Last, but not least, upon the recent list,
        A subject that is *Scotch* should not be *mist*.
        Nor Scot free be let off, so for our close,
        We'll take the kilt, – Hey, presto! Off she goes!

> (*picture*)
GULL: See, Francis Osbaldistone, smart and chubby,
SMUG: The Dougal Creature, picturesque, but grubby;
Given to fight, to steal, to howl, to ramble –
SCOW: The Gr-r-r-eat R-r-r-r-ob R-r-r-r-oy McGr-r-r-gor Campbell.
> (*Flourish – picture closes.*)
KING: You've tried in vain, the Princess still refuses
To smile, and so your king his kingdom loses.
GULL: Perhaps a dance grotesquey . . .

THE PLAYS OF H. J. BYRON

Richard of the Lion Heart, Strand Theatre, 23 November 1857.

The Lady of Lyons; or, Twopenny Pride and Pennytence, Strand Theatre, 1 February 1858.

Fra Diavolo Travestie; or, The Beauty and the Brigands, Strand Theatre, 5 April 1858.

The Bride of Abydos; or, The Prince, the Pirate and the Pearl, Strand Theatre, 31 May 1858.

The Maid and the Magpie; or, The Fatal Spoon, Strand Theatre, 11 October 1858.

Mazeppa, Olympic Theatre, 27 December 1858.

The Very Latest Edition of the Lady of Lyons, Strand Theatre, 11 July 1859.

The Babes in the Wood and the Good Little Fairy-Birds, Adelphi Theatre, 18 July 1859.

Jack the Giant Killer; or Harlequin, King Arthur and ye Knights of ye Round Table, Princess's Theatre, 26 December 1859.

The Nymph of the Lurleyburg; or, The Knight and the Naiads, Adelphi Theatre, 26 December 1859.

The Pilgrim of Love, Theatre Royal, Haymarket, 9 April 1860.

The Miller and His Men (with F. Talfourd), Strand Theatre, 9 April 1860.

The Garibaldi Excursionists, Princess's Theatre, 8 November 1860.

Blue Beard from a New Point of Hue, Adelphi Theatre, 26 December 1860.

Cinderella; or, The Lover, the Lackey and the Little Glass Slipper, Strand Theatre, 26 December 1860.

Robinson Crusoe; or, Harlequin Friday and the King of the Caribee Islands, Princess's Theatre, 26 December 1860. Music by W. Montgomery.

Aladdin; or, The Wonderful Scamp, Strand Theatre, 1 April 1861.

The Old Story, Strand Theatre, 29 April 1861.

Esmeralda; or, The 'Sensation' Goat!, Strand Theatre, 28 September 1861.

Miss Eily O'Connor, Drury Lane Theatre, 25 November 1861.

The Rival Othellos, Strand Theatre, 28 November 1861.

Puss in a New Pair of Boots, Strand Theatre, 26 December 1861. Music by F. Musgrave.

Whittington and his Cat; or, Harlequin, King Kollywobbol and the Genius of Good Humour, Princess's Theatre, 26 December 1861. Music by W. Montgomery.

The Rosebud of Stinging-nettle Farm; or, The Villainous Squire and the Virtuous Visitor, Crystal Palace, 21 July 1862; subsequently at Adelphi Theatre, 9 September 1863.

Goldenhair the Good, St James's Theatre, 26 December 1862.

Harlequin Beauty and the Beast; or, The Gnome Queen and the Good Fairy, Covent Garden Theatre, 26 December 1862.

George de Barnwell; or, Harlequin Folly in the Realms of Fancy, Adelphi Theatre, 26 December 1862.

Ivanhoe in accordance with the Spirit of the Times, Strand Theatre, 26 December 1862. Music by F. Musgrave.

Ali Baba; or, The Thirty-Nine Thieves, in accordance with the Author's Habit of Taking One off, Strand Theatre, 6 April 1863.

Beautiful Haidee; or, The Sea Nymph and the Sallee Rovers, Princess's Theatre, 6 April 1863.

Ill-treated Il Trovatore; or, The Mother, the Maiden and the Musician, Adelphi Theatre, 21 May 1863.

The Motto: 'I am all there', Strand Theatre, 16 July 1863.

Harlequin St George and the Dragon; or, The Seven Champions and the Beautiful Princess, Covent Garden Theatre, 26 December 1863.

Lady Belle Belle; or, Fortunio and his Seven Magic Men, Adelphi Theatre, 26 December 1863.

Orpheus and Eurydice; or, The Young Gentleman who Charmed the Rocks, Strand Theatre, 26 December 1863.

1863; or, The Sensations of the Past Season: with a Shameful Revelation of Lady Somebody's Secret, St James's Theatre, 26 December 1863.

Mazourka; or, The Stick, the Pole and the Tartar, Strand Theatre, 27 April 1863.

Timothy to the Rescue, Strand Theatre, 30 May 1864 (also published as *How to Tame your Mother-in-law*).

Lord Dundreary Married and Done for, Theatre Royal, Haymarket, 13 June 1864.

The 'Grin' Bushes; or, Missis Brown of the 'Missis'sippi, Strand Theatre, 26 December 1864.

The Lion and the Unicorn Were Fighting for the Crown, Her Majesty's Theatre, 26 December 1864.

Princess Springtime; or, The Envoy who stole the King's Daughter, Theatre Royal, Haymarket, 26 December 1864.

Pan; or, The Loves of Echo and Narcissus, Adelphi Theatre, 10 April 1865.

La! Somnambula!; or, The Supper, the Sleeper and the Merry Swiss Boy, Prince of Wales's Theatre, 15 April 1865.

War to the Knife, Prince of Wales's Theatre, 10 June 1865.

Lucia di Lammermoor; or, The Laird, the Lady and the Lover, Prince of Wales's Theatre, 25 September 1865.

Little Don Giovanni; or, Leperello and the Stone Statue, Prince of Wales's Theatre, 26 December 1865.

A Hundred Thousand Pounds, Prince of Wales's Theatre, 5 May 1866.

Der Freischutz; or, The Bill! the Belle!! and the Bullett!!!, Prince of Wales's Theatre, 10 October 1866.

Little Dick Whittington, Thrice Lord Mayor of London; or, Harlequin Hotpot, Poor Pussy and the Fairies of the Elfin Grot, Theatre Royal, Liverpool, 24 December 1866.

Harlequin Bluebeard, The Bad Bashaw and His Beautiful Bride; or, Selim, Shacabac, Sister Anne, and the Secret Chamber, Ampitheatre, Liverpool, 26 December 1866.

Pandora's Box; or, The Young Spark and the Old Flame, Princess's Theatre, 26 December 1866.

Robinson Crusoe; or, The Injun Bride and the Injured Wife (with W. S. Gilbert),
   Theatre Royal, Haymarket, 6 July 1867.
William Tell with a Vengeance; or, The Pet, the Patriot and the Pippin, Alexandra
   Theatre, Liverpool, 4 September 1867; Strand Theatre, 5 October 1867.
The Lancashire Lass; or, Tempted, Tried and True, Ampitheatre, Liverpool, 28
   October 1867; (with revised last act) Queen's Theatre, 24 July 1868.
Dearer than Life, Alexandra Theatre, Liverpool, 26 November 1867; Queen's
   Theatre, 8 January 1868.
The Wonderful Travels of Gulliver, Theatre Royal, Manchester, 21 December 1867.
Gulliver, Theatre Royal, Liverpool, 26 December 1867.
Blow for Blow, Holborn Theatre, 5 September 1868.
Lucrezia Borgia, M.D.; or, La Grande Doctresse, Holborn Theatre, 28 October
   1868.
Cyril's Success, Globe Theatre, 28 November 1868.
Not Such a Fool as He Looks, Theatre Royal, Manchester, 4 December 1868;
   Globe Theatre, 23 October 1869.
Robinson Crusoe; or, Friday and the Fairies, Covent Garden Theatre, 26 December
   1868.
Minnie; or, Leonard's Love, Globe Theatre, 29 March 1869.
The Corsican 'Brothers'; or, The Troublesome Twins, Globe Theatre, 17 May 1869.
Lost at Sea (with Dion Boucicault), Adelphi Theatre, 2 October 1869.
Uncle Dick's Darling, Gaiety Theatre, 13 December 1869.
Lord Bateman; or, The Proud Young Porter and the Fair Sophia, Globe Theatre
   27 December 1869.
The Yellow Dwarf; or, Harlequin Cupid and the King of the Gold Mines, Covent
   Garden Theatre, 27 December 1869.
The Prompter's Box: A Story of the Footlights and the Fireside, Adelphi Theatre,
   23 March 1870; As *Two Stars*, Strand Theatre, 5 October 1872.
Robert Macaire; or, The Roadside Inn turned inside out, Globe Theatre, 16 April
   1870.
The Enchanted Wood; or, The Three Transformed Princes, Adelphi Theatre, 4 May
   1870.
An English Gentleman; or, The Empty Pocket, Theatre Royal, Bristol, 8 November
   1870; Theatre Royal, Haymarket, 13 May 1871 (also known as *The Squire's
   Last Shilling*).
Wait and Hope, Gaiety Theatre, 1 March 1871.
Eurydice; or, Little Orpheus and his Lute, Strand Theatre, 24 April 1871 (revised
   'second edition' of *Orpheus and Eurydice*, 26 December 1863).
Daisy Farm, Olympic Theatre, 1 May 1871.
The Orange Tree and the Humble Bee; or, The Little Princess who Was Lost at Sea,
   Vaudeville Theatre, 13 May 1871.
Not if I Know it, Theatre Royal, Haymarket, 17 June 1871.
Giselle; or, The Sirens of the Lotus Lake, Olympic Theatre, 22 July 1871.
Partners for Life, Globe Theatre, 7 October 1871.
Camaralzaman and the Fair Badoura; or, The Bad D(j)inn and the Good Spirit,
   Vaudeville Theatre, 22 November 1871.
Blue Beard, Covent Garden Theatre, 26 December 1871.

Haunted Houses; or, Labyrinths of Life: A Story of London and the Bush, Princess's Theatre, 1 April 1872.
The Spur of the Moment, Globe Theatre, 4 May 1872.
Time's Triumph, Gaiety Theatre, Dublin, 19 August 1872; Charing Cross Theatre, 12 May 1873.
Good News, Gaiety Theatre, 31 August 1872.
The Lady of the Lane, Strand Theatre, 31 October 1872.
Mabel's Life; or, A Bitter Bargain, Adelphi Theatre, 2 November 1872.
Old Soldiers, Strand Theatre, 25 January 1873.
Fine Feathers, Globe Theatre, 26 April 1873.
Chained to the Oar, Prince of Wales's Theatre, Liverpool, 16 June 1873; Gaiety Theatre, 31 May 1883.
La Fille de Mme Angot, Philarmonic Theatre, Islington, 4 October 1873.
Sour Grapes, Olympic Theatre, 4 October 1873.
Don Juan, Alhambra Palace, 22 December 1873.
Guy Fawkes, Gaiety Theatre, 14 January 1874.
An American Lady, Criterion Theatre, 21 March 1874.
The Thumbscrew, Holborn Theatre, 4 April 1874.
Normandy Pippins, Criterion Theatre, 18 April 1874.
The Pretty Perfumeress, Alhambra Palace, 18 May 1874. Music by J. Offenbach.
The Demon's Bride, Alhambra Palace, 7 September 1874. Music by G. Jacobi.
Old Sailors, Strand Theatre, 19 October 1874.
Oil and Vinegar; or, A Matrimonial Moral, Gaiety Theatre, 4 November 1874.
Our Boys, Vaudeville Theatre, 16 January 1875.
Weak Woman, Strand Theatre, 6 May 1875.
Married in Haste, Theatre Royal, Haymarket, 2 October 1875.
Tottles, Gaiety Theatre, 22 December 1875.
Wrinkles: A Tale of Time, Prince of Wales's Theatre, 13 April 1876.
£20 a Year, all found, Folly Theatre, 17 April 1876.
Little Don Caesar de Bazan, Gaiety Theatre, 26 August 1876.
The Bull by the Horns, Gaiety Theatre, 26 August 1876.
Widow and Wife, Theatre Royal, Bristol, 11 September 1876.
Old Chums, Opera Comique, 16 December 1876.
Pampered Menials, Opera Comique, 26 December 1876.
The Bohemian G'yurl and the Unapproachable Pole, Opera Comique, 31 January 1877.
Guinea Gold; or, Lights and Shadows of London Life, Princess's Theatre, 10 September 1877.
Little Doctor Faust, Gaiety Theatre, 13 October 1877.
A Fool and His Money, Globe Theatre, 17 January 1878.
Ali Baba and the Forty Thieves, Gaiety Theatre, 13 February 1878. With W. S. Gilbert, F. C. Burnand and R. Reece (final scene by H. J. Byron).
Il Somnambulo and Lively Little Alessio, Gaiety Theatre, 6 April 1878.
The Crushed Tragedian, Theatre Royal, Haymarket, 11 May 1878 (revised version of *The Prompter's Box*).
A Hornet's Nest, Theatre Royal, Haymarket, 17 June 1878.
Conscience Money, Theatre Royal, Haymarket, 16 September 1878.

Uncle, Gaiety Theatre, Dublin, 4 November 1878; Gaiety Theatre, 1 February 1879.

Young Fra Diavolo; the Terror of Terracina, Gaiety Theatre, 18 November 1878.

Jack the Giant Killer, Gaiety Theatre, 21 December 1878 (revised version of pantomime written for Princess's Theatre, 26 December 1859).

Pretty Esmeralda and Captain Phoebus of Ours, Gaiety Theatre, 2 April 1879.

The Girls, Vaudeville Theatre, 19 April 1879 (submitted to Lord Chamberlain as
  Pelican Lodge, 1875).

Handsome Hernani; or, The Fatal Penny Whistle, Gaiety Theatre, 30 August 1879.

Courtship; or, The Three Caskets, Court Theatre, 16 October 1879.

The Gaiety Gulliver, Gaiety Theatre, 26 December 1879.

The Upper Crust, Folly Theatre, 31 March 1880.

Il Trovatore; or, Larks with a Libretto, Olympic Theatre, 26 April 1880.

Without a Home, Theatre Royal, Cardiff, 24 May 1880.

Bow Bells, Royalty Theatre, 4 October 1880.

The Light Fantastic, Folly Theatre, 20 November 1880.

Michael Strogoff, Adelphi Theatre, 14 March 1881.

Punch, Vaudeville Theatre, 26 May 1881.

New Brooms, Gaiety Theatre, Dublin, 18 July 1881.

Pluto; or, Little Orpheus and his Lute, Royalty Theatre, 26 December 1881
  (revised edition of *Orpheus and Eurydice*, 26 December 1863).

Fourteen Days, Criterion Theatre, 4 March 1882.

Auntie, Toole's Theatre, 13 March 1882.

The Villainous Squire and the Village Rose, Toole's Theatre, 5 June 1882 (revised
  version of *The Rosebud of Stinging-nettle Farm*, 1862).

Frolique, Strand Theatre, 18 November 1882. With H. B. Farnie (from French
  vaudeville *Charlot*).

Open House, Vaudeville Theatre, 16 April 1885.

The Shuttlecock, Toole's Theatre, 16 May 1885. Completed by J. A. Sterry.

The following plays are ascribed to H. J. Byron in Fench's acting editions of his
plays, but no published editions, records of performance or submission of manu-
scripts to the Lord Chamberlain can be traced:

My Wife and I

Our Seaside Lodgings

Sensation Fork

That Dear Old Darling

Valentine and Orson (part author)

SELECT BIBLIOGRAPHY

Editions

Aladdin, ed. and adapted Gyles Brandreth, London: Davis-Poynter, 1971
Cinderella, ed. and adapted Gyles Brandreth, London: Davis-Poynter, 1971
Robinson Crusoe in *English Plays of the Nineteenth Century, V: Pantomimes, Extravaganzas and Burlesques*, ed. Michael R. Booth, Oxford University Press, 1976

There are no full-length studies of H. J. Byron. Recent assessments of H. J. Byron's work can be found in the following books:
Booth, Michael R., *English Plays of the Nineteenth Century*: vol. II *Dramas 1850–1900*; vol III *Comedies*; vol. V *Pantomimes, Extravaganzas and Burlesques*, Oxford, 1969–76
Leech, Clifford and Craik, T. W., eds., *The Revels History of Drama in English: Volume VI 1750–1880*, London, 1975
Nicoll, Allardyce, *A History of English Drama 1660–1900: Volume V Late Nineteenth Century Drama 1850–1900*, Cambridge, 1959
Rowell, George, *Theatre in the Age of Irving*, Oxford, 1981
    The Victorian Theatre 1792–1914, 2nd edition, Cambridge, 1978

The following books provide useful references to H. J. Byron's work:
Archer, William, *English Dramatists of Today*, London, 1882
    The Old Drama and the New, London, 1923
Baker, H. Barton, *A History of the London Stage*, London, 1903
Bancroft, Squire and Marie, *Mr and Mrs Bancroft On and Off the Stage. Written by Themselves*, London, 1888
    The Bancrofts. Recollections of Sixty Years, London, 1909
Clinton-Baddeley, V. C., *Some Pantomime Pedigrees*, London, 1963.
Cooke, Dutton, *Nights at the Play*, London, 1883
Fitzgerald, Percy, *Principles of Comedy and Dramatic Effect*, London, 1870
Granville-Barker, Harley, 'Exit Planché – Enter Gilbert' in *The Eighteen-Sixties: Essays by Fellows of the Royal Society of Literature* (ed. John Drinkwater), Cambridge, 1932
    ed., *The Eighteen-Seventies: Essays by Fellows of the Royal Society of Literature*, Cambridge, 1929
Hatton, Joseph, ed., *Reminiscences of J. L. Toole*, London, 1889
Hibbert, H. G., *A Playgoer's Memories*, London, 1920
Hollingshead, John, *Gaiety Chronicles*, London, 1898
Knight, Joseph, *Theatrical Notes*, London, 1893
Mander, Raymond and Mitchenson. Joe, *Pantomime*, London, 1973
Meisel, Martin, *Shaw and the Nineteenth Century Theatre*, Princeton, New Jersey, 1963

Pascoe, Charles E., *Our Actors and Actresses: The Dramatic List*, London, 1880
Pemberton, T. E., *Edward Askew Sothern: A Memoir*, London, 1889
   Sir Charles Wyndham, London, 1904
Reynolds, Ernest, *Early Victorian Drama 1830–1870*, Cambridge, 1936